The Partisans of Europe

The Partisans of Europe

In the Second World War

KENNETH MACKSEY

STEIN AND DAY/*Publishers*/NEW YORK

The photographs on pages 95, 96, 97, 98 (top), 99, 100, 101, 102 (top), 104 (bottom), and 105 are printed here by courtesy of the Imperial War Museum, London; those on pages 102 (bottom) and 103 by courtesy of the Polish Library, London; that on page 104 (top) by courtesy of P. A. Interpress Photos, Poland; and that on page 98 (bottom) by courtesy of C.T.K.

First published in 1975
Copyright © 1975 by Kenneth Macksey
Library of Congress Catalog No. 74-78526
Designed by Ed Kaplin
Printed in the United States of America
Stein and Day/Publishers/Scarborough House, Briarcliff Manor, N.Y. 10510
ISBN 0-8128-1724-9

CONTENTS

LIST OF ILLUSTRATIONS

————————————

between pages 95 and 105

Oil storage tanks in the Lofoten Islands burn, 1941
German infantry in action
Russian infantry in 1941
A Russian partisan band
Germans searching for partisans in Russia
Tito
Heydrich's car after the attack
Russian partisans planning a raid
Another Russian partisan band
The aftermath of a railway demolition job
A heavily armed British SAS jeep party
A Lysander mission behind the Italian front, 1945
U.S. Flying Fortresses delivering supplies to the French Resistance
Members of the FFI
Bor-Komorowski
At the Warsaw barricades, 1944
Polish youths armed with petrol bombs
German troops during the Warsaw uprising
Zervas's Greek guerrillas
A British sniper in Athens
Captured guerrillas in Athens

LIST OF MAPS

LIST OF ABBREVIATIONS
USED IN THE TEXT

BCRA   Bureau Central de Renseignements et d'Action: French
        intelligence and operational branch in London
CLN   Committee of National Liberation: Italian all-party
        coordinating organization for resistance
CLNAI   Committee of National Liberation for Upper Italy
CNR   Conseil National de la Résistance: coordinating organ-
        ization at national level in France
CVL   Corps of Volunteers for Liberty: Italian organization of
        unified command
DMN   Délégué militaire national: French operational com-
        mander at national level
DMR   Délégué militaire region: French operational commander
        at departmental level
DMZ   Délégué militaire de zone: French operational commander
        placed over DMRs. There was one in the south and one
        in the north of France.
EAM   Popular Front Party: Greek Communist Party
EDES   National Democratic Union: Greek Republican Party
EKKA   National and Social Liberation: Greek Republican-aligned
        party
ELAS   People's Liberation Army: military wing of the Greek
        Communist Party
EMFFI   Etat-Major des Forces Françaises de l'Intérieur: French
        joint command organization in London and France
FFI   Forces Françaises de l'Intérieur: French Resistance
        organization
FNC   Franc-tireurs et Partisans: military wing of the French
        Communist Party
GS(R)   General Staff (Research) Branch of the British War Office
IRA   Irish Republican Army
LDV   Local Defense Volunteers: British anti-invasion militia
LRDG   Long Range Desert Group: British desert reconnaissance
        and raiding force
Milorg Secret Army of Norway

9

NKGB ⎫
NKVD ⎭ Branches of the Russian Security Organization

NSB   National Socialist Movement: Dutch right-wing, Nazi-aligned party

NSDAP   National Socialist German Workers Party: German Nazi, right-wing party

OG   Operational Group: U.S. raiding force

ORA   Secret Army originating in Vichy, France

OSS   Office of Strategic Services of the U.S.

OSVO   Falcon: Czech Sokol Organization of Resistance

PIAT   Projector Infantry Antitank: light British antitank weapon

ROA   Russian Army of Liberation: Vlasov's anti-Stalin army under German sponsorship

SA   Sturm Abteilung: German paramilitary wing of the NSDAP

SAS   Special Air Service: British deep raiding force

SBS   Special Boat Service: British canoe-raiding force

SD   Sicherheitsdienst: German security agency

SHAEF   Supreme Headquarters Allied Expeditionary Forces

SOE   Special Operations Executive: British organization for raising resistance in enemy-held territories

SS   Schutz Staffeln: élite element of the German NSDAP

WA   Military wing of the Dutch NSB

INTRODUCTION

Within the past three decades partisans have come to occupy an important, at times almost dominant, part in the resolution of political and diplomatic problems. Along with nearly every radical, religious, or nationalistic confrontation are to be found either the threat or actuality of guerrilla warfare, be it in the form of local assassinations and bomb attacks or much more widespread action by organized bands. The process is, of course, as old as history but it is only since the Second World War that it has come to be recognized as a worthwhile method of waging war. Before 1939 there were only scattered outbreaks of indecisive partisan warfare, most of them in the East; the war introduced it on a large scale to Europe, and propaganda turned it into a heroic cult so far as the anti-Axis forces were concerned. It is largely upon the experience of European partisans in the Second World War that modern practice is based.

On the German side we have Hitler's words: "I want to fight the terror of sabotage and attacks . . . with exactly the same weapons . . . if some of our strong points are attacked by terrorists . . . then those terrorists will be hunted, surrounded and wiped out in fighting; and I do not want military courts, which only create martyrs." And on the Russian side those of General Ponamarenko, their wartime chief of the Partisan Forces: "Many thousands of supremely loyal fighters and organizers arose from the ranks of the people and devoted themselves to the one great task: the annihilation of the criminal army of invaders by every means accessible to the people." Restraint was rejected by both partisans and their foes.

At the trial of the German war criminals at Nuremberg in 1946, both the prosecution and the defense squeezed whatever advantage they could from quoting breaches of international law committed by the other side. In fact, both were well aware that the law was ineffective. As General Alfred Jodl, chief of the German Armed Forces (OKW) Operations Staff, was to say in his evidence, "I knew that never yet in this world has there been a war in which infractions of International Law did not occur." He summed up the dilemma of those in the higher echelons of command who grappled with clandestine warfare. "I should like to conclude by saying that because there were no regulations governing air warfare, deplorable confusions in terminology arose, for instance, between rebellion and legal warfare, between *franc-tireur*, bandit and scout, spy and scout, demolition crews and saboteurs. At any time, with the help of aircraft, a rebellion could be changed into a legal war, and a legal war, on the other hand, could be reduced to the state of rebellion."

For those of us in arms who, with powerful mechanized armies, moved to conquer Germany during the closing months of the Second World War, the appearance of the partisan forces—men and women distinguished by arm bands, a strange miscellany of weapons, and an air of nationalistic pride—was yet another reminder that it was not we alone, the khaki-clad soldiers, who had made the invasion a reality. I myself heard the saga of resistance and found so confused a story difficult to comprehend at the time. Some of us even began to question the partisans' credibility. How could these bands prevail against the proven professionals of the German Army whom we, in all our might, found so hard to defeat?

Yet one knew that these people had risked everything in their efforts to eject the enemy from their homeland, and as time went on, and the tale of the guerrilla armies began to appear in print, a legend began to take shape, a kaleidoscope of tales of adventure, brutality, and horror linked with the excesses of Nazism and antipartisan forces. Only much later did it become plain that idealism was not the only force impelling the partisans to action. For in the aftermath of the fighting came to be revealed the pressures which compelled partisans to take up arms—the demands of party political loyalties, the impulse to salve national pride in the shadow of defeat, the urges of personal ambition and gain, the fear of coercion and terror, the thought that to be excluded from the role of resistance work was to risk ostracism, imprisonment, and perhaps execution.

While historians are compelled to admit to the inevitability of war as a method of settling major political issues, as compassionate beings they yearn for a reduction in levels of violence. They may wish to show that the most profitable wars are those using limited resources, governed by constrictive rules and recognizing ancient battlefield and siege conventions which reduce the destruction of life and property. Partisan or guerrilla combat, particularly within the setting of total war, has always been the antithesis of a philosophy of limitation, and this was clearly foreseen by those senior statesmen who instigated it in the Second World War. There is ample scope for argument about the theories of partisan warfare. In the years since the war my normal duties as a regular army officer with a bent for history have led me to study guerrillas and formulate a skeptical if respectful opinion of their powers. In my opinion there is a need to examine the achievements and failures of partisans in the days of their rise to prominence in order to gain a better understanding of their present role and of their future. This I have tried to do in this book.

My thanks are due to those who have helped in my search for material—expartisans and antipartisans among the serious students of war who have guided and encouraged me—in particular Major F. Cardozo, Lieutenant-Colonel R.H.A. Cockburn, D.C. Davidson, Esq., R. Drepper, Esq., Professor M.R.D. Foot (who most kindly read my first draft), Major-General Sir Colin Gubbins, Professor W. Hahlweg, the Kramer family, Dr. K. Peball, H.H.A. Thackthwaite, Esq., General W. Warlimont, and G. Whitehead, Esq. To L'Amicale Action I am indebted for their immense hospitality and for the benefit of the reminiscences of their veterans of the French Resistance. The directors and staffs of libraries of the British Imperial War Museum and Ministry of Defence and of the U.S. National Archives provided me with a mass of documents, plus their characteristic, friendly cooperation.

Finally I owe thanks to Michael Haine, who drew the maps, Helga Ashworth and Peter Kitchen, who, respectively, translated documents from the German and French, John Carpenter, who dotted the i's and crossed the t's, Margaret Dunn, who typed the entire work, and, as usual, my wife, who listened to readings, criticized, and read proofs.

The Partisans of Europe

CHAPTER ONE

A Slow, Gradual Fire

From the earliest times man's struggle for survival assumed the character of partisan warfare. The Oxford Dictionary states that a partisan is: "a member of a party of light or irregular troop employed in scouring the country, surprising the enemy outposts and foraging parties and the like—a member of a volunteer force, a guerrilla." And if there is some slight contradiction when the dictionary further defines guerrilla warfare as "an irregular war carried on by small bodies of men acting independently"—overlooking the times in history when separate partisan forces have grown into armies—there is, by implication, an important modification of the original definition: that partisans forsake their primary character once they come into line with regular forces. Thus they remain partisans only so long as they are operating behind the enemy lines or as rebels within a recognized state: by Lenin's definition, agents who aggravate a political crisis by terrorism.

The Hague Conference of 1907, Article IV, on the Laws and Customs of War on Land attempted to define the status of legitimate belligerents and included in them guerrillas, militia, and volunteer troops provided they (a) were properly commanded, (b) wore a fixed emblem recognizable at a distance, (c) carried arms openly, and (d) conducted their operations in accordance with the laws and customs of war. An exception was made in the case of spontaneous uprisings upon the approach of an enemy: then it was deemed necessary only to comply with the last two conditions. Spontaneity was virtually undefined, but these were the basic rules governing partisan warfare when war broke out, in August 1914, between the Central Powers—Germany and the Austro-Hungarian Empire—and the Allies, comprising, at first, Serbia, Belgium, France, Russia and Great Britain.

Germany was among the nations which most heartily welcomed the Hague Rules, because, with everything staked on swift, orthodox campaigns by a regular army, it was in her best interests to frame rules which would eliminate the danger of long-drawn-out battles among a hostile populace. Germany wanted to fight an aggressive war of limited scope on terms of advantage to herself regulated by the rules of war she had helped establish. Nevertheless her troops who invaded Belgium in August 1914 were filled with fears of a repetition of the guerrilla warfare against *franc-tireurs* in the Franco-Prussian war of 1870. In fact there were hardly any genuine *franc-tireurs* active in Belgium but innumerable patrols or parties which had fallen behind in the abrupt retreat of the Belgian Army to Antwerp. These were immediately accorded the status of *franc-tireur* if they failed to surrender. Swift repression followed—within the rules of war, but frequently carried to extremes. There were reprisals, hostages taken and shot— probably some five thousand people paid with their lives. But from repression emerged something that is inseparable from partisan warfare—a campaign of hate.

It is generally held that the First World War was notable for its lack of guerrilla warfare. Some Germans actually claimed that their failure to control guerrillas in the Second World War stemmed from ignorance of the art due to lack of practice, but history belies this claim just as it rejects any suggestion that the Germans are poor guerrilla fighters.

There were several quite large outbreaks, however. In the early stages light armored car patrols operating in the German flank and rear during their advance to the Marne were described by their innovator, Winston Churchill, as "motorized guerrillas." The action by small demolition parties in Rumania in 1916, under the command of a British Member of Parliament, John Norton-Griffiths, in almost wiping out the Ploesti oilfields and destroying the grain stocks caused damage estimated at over fifty-six million pounds. The German commander on the spot freely admitted that the calamity far exceeded in magnitude any defeat in the field. In East Africa, throughout the war, a small German Army under Paul von Lettow-Vorbeck raided far and wide and caused a most annoying distraction. But in a theater far removed from locations of strategic importance, it was indecisive.

The most celebrated outbreak of guerrilla warfare was that initiated by about five hundred Arab rebels under the Grand Sherif Hussein in 1916 against the Turks in Arabia. Yet it would not have lasted had not the Allies helped the Arabs with gold, men and munitions—and an organizer, T.E. Lawrence. Lawrence was the man who harnessed a new technology to the Arabs' inherent methods of desert raiding and was their liaison officer with the regular armies fighting the Turks in Palestine. In effect the Arab irregulars grew into something more than a guerrilla force. In the latter stages of the war they formed a highly mobile flank-guard to the British Army in Palestine as well as the arm of emergent Arab nationalism.

The essence of Lawrence's methods was orthodox in its unorthodoxy—the quick rush for the kill after an ambush; the stealthy planting of demolition charges to break a railway line, wreck a train, or bring down a viaduct; the use of armored cars as a means to give protection when the operation was against a heavily guarded target. The ultimate inclination was to engage in set-piece battles as his partisan forces became stiffened by a strong regular, well-armed element, while they themselves became more "regular" in their outlook and tactics. Yet the essential bestiality of guerrilla warfare was only just below the surface, as the butchery of civilians at Tafas by Turkish soldiers, enraged by the work of Arab irregulars, showed. Lawrence has recorded his horror at the sight of men, women, and children who had been shot and bayonetted in the burning village, and recalled the vengeance wreaked upon the Turks responsible: "We killed and killed, even blowing in the heads of the fallen." Lawrence's achievements could hardly have gone unnoticed, even if press publicity had been less dramatic. The Germans certainly had no excuse for ignoring them, since their troops—the Asian Korps—were more than once an Arab target; their overall commander, Liman von Sanders, was made as much aware of Arab impact as anyone else—an impact his book explained to his countrymen after the war.

It was the Russian Revolution in 1917 which gave the strongest impulse to partisan warfare in its modern guise, although the contagious disease of political murder, bank robbery and blackmail had long been attendant upon the rebellious movements in that country. Secret police forces grappled with underground movements: repression had been spread throughout Europe and other parts of the world as the philosophies of Marx and Engels became better known.

The start of the Revolution in 1917 found the Russian Army at its nadir and the nation exhausted and disillusioned. Political strife went unchecked because the traditional bulwarks of order had fallen into disarray. The birth of a plethora of miniature armies, both within and outside the regular forces, and the traumatic changes in the central government, from monarchy to republicanism and then to Bolshevism, undermined the rule of law. Every imaginable type of anarchical group could thrive among the warring elements of Bolshevik Reds and Tsarist Whites; there were dissident Poles setting up their new homeland; Czechs fighting their way to Vladivostok; Germans advancing into the Ukraine; and British, French, Americans and Japanese intervening in an attempt to reestablish prerevolutionary government in opposition to the Germans. In the midst of this confusion even regular forces began to assume the function of guerrillas.

The clear recognition of opposing forces (which, in any case, frequently changed sides as circumstances altered) was a difficult matter even when command was stable and arms were openly carried, which was rarely the case. Uniforms and administrative procedures were heterogeneous to say the least. David Footman describes an anti-Bolshevik group which, in 1918, became the cadre for a White Army: "Uniform was motley; the men wore what they had and sewed a white strip on their caps to distinguish them from the Reds. Most detachments had a machine-gun or two, and some of the larger ones a field gun, but arms, and especially ammunition, were short. Transport and supply were primitive. As a rule . . . when the firing died down, the men's families would come up to the line and bring them food. After an engagement any Red prisoners taken were tried by an improvised court martial and if found to be Cossacks were usually executed." Drozdovsky, a White commander, referred to the Reds as "wild, depraved hooligans" for whom there was one law—"an eye for an eye." But the composition of *his* force at this time—667 officers, 370 soldiers, 14 doctors, chaplains and military clerks, and 12 nursing sisters—was hardly representative of the Russian people though its quality was high as a cadre for expansion into a regularized army.

The revolution sprang to life at the urging of a handful of determined radicals, not all of whom by any means fitted Pisarev's definition of the greatest fanatics as "children or adolescents." Lenin and Trotsky were practical men whose notion of revolution was founded upon professionalism. Lenin attacked terrorism as inefficacious and regarded the revolution as a military act before it became economic. But while Lenin, in 1917, urged the arming of the poor and the formation of a proletarian militia with "a comradely discipline practiced with enthusiasm," the more businesslike Trotsky, given the task of strengthening the Red Army, saw in the proliferation of small private armies a sourse of weakness that had to be eliminated. He considered that private armies would perpetuate an anarchy such as Bolshevism rejected in its task of unifying the Russian Soviet. The creation, in April 1917, of military commissars, a large number of them Jews, and many of them satisfying Pisarev's definition, was intended to bind the army into the evolving Soviet system. They were to ensure that the various military establishments did not become "foci of conspiracy or instruments against workers and peasants." They were to become the main instruments of Trotsky's rationalization in 1918, which was founded upon the liquidation of partisanship, the intensification of political work and the strengthening of recruiting.

Success at arms was a superb recruiting sergeant. Each local victory garnered its influx of new adherents to the cause, regardless of political standpoint. Failure and defeat simply put the process into reverse. Nevertheless strong leadership, even in adversity, could work miracles, and its outstanding exponent in maintaining the strength and morale of a large force over a protracted period was the Ukrainian anarchist Nestor Makhno. From the summer of 1918 until 1921 he led the people of his village, Gulyai-Polye, and then a large body of Southern Ukrainians, in an aggressive defense designed, primarily, to maintain local autonomy in the face of invading Germans, Ukrainians, Cossacks, Whites and Reds. Anybody willing to fight alongside Makhno was an ally so long as he recognized the inviolability of Makhnoism. Nobody was safe who demonstrated a challenge to Makhno's authority—an authority based on his brilliant intuitive leadership (he had had no formal military training) and total sharing of everyday perils with the people. Yet Makhno was no bandit—as at least one writer has derisively called him. He was an outstanding commander who, in the Russia of 1919, could call on a private army of four infantry brigades, a cavalry brigade, a field-artillery detachment and a special five-hundred-machine-gun unit—a force numbering in all fifteen thousand men.

Mostly Ukrainians, they were a remorseless crew—variegated in dress, boastful, ruthless and frequently drunk—prepared to take on the world, in order of priority, Whites, Reds and then the Europeans. Discipline stemmed from Makhno, who hired and shot the leaders who failed him. Looting was the bane of the force and never suppressed. The maintenance of equipment was also bad. But, for all this, the army fought with a remarkable cohesion, improvising tactics of mobility allied to a quite staggering rate of advance by horse and cart—Footman says at twice the speed of regular troops. Villages were bases, ambush the basis of tactical method; and this strategy was commendably maintained until 1921, in a country quite unsuitable for guerrilla warfare—where communications were comparatively well developed, few forests grew in which to hide and no uninhabited spaces existed into which to disappear.

In due course the end had to come when the Cheka and the Red Army closed in as the revolution consolidated itself. In great battles towards the end of 1920 Makhno did well to win fight after fight, but they were Pyrrhic victories. The Red Army, freed from its commitments in Poland, constantly produced replacements while the Makh-noites shriveled. In a bitter winter all the hard-bought heavy equipment was lost. The end came in August when he and a few survivors escaped into Rumania.

If the essential political prerequisite of a successful armed rebellion is the promotion of governmental instability, its prime military requirements are sound leadership, financial backing and supply—above all, arms supply. Popular support has also to be forthcoming, but this, as often as not, is the product of the rebels' labors as they demonstrate their effectiveness and prove they are a strong, indelible element. In Germany at the end of the First World War, where the disappointment of defeat (coupled with staggering losses and acute famine) utterly undermined faith in the monarchy, sound political leadership was at a premium. Violence and coercion predominated and were encouraged by the revolutionary representatives of Bolshevik Russia. A nation which, for generations, had lived under a strong authoritarian regime now lay in a state of shock and anarchy at the mercy of militant factions whose powers of oratory far exceeded their ability to govern. Suddenly the overture to guerrilla warfare was played. There were four hundred political murders between 1919 and 1922. Armed mobs became the fickle servants of wavering central and provincial governments while the Army, itself undermined by revolution, could only march home leaving its leaders to struggle for their old influence as a prop to firm government.

For five years after 1918, individual political parties vied for power, putting more trust in their private, armed bands than in votes won at the ballot box. But it was the epitome of traditional German reliance on propriety that their guerrilla bands were properly attired: a recognizable uniform was *de rigueur,* an arm band the lowest acceptable form of identification. The ill-armed and badly led Spartakists of Rosa Luxemburg fought and lost in the streets of the principal cities to the improvised but well clad and armed army of the Socialist (SPD) government—the Freikorps. This Freikorps, devised probably by the future chancellor, Kurt von Schleicher, was the most formidable of all the German guerrilla-style armies. Led by war heroes and recruited from a generation that had been educated by war, its units amounted to anything from a storm troop to a division—the total corps, at its peak, amounting to some two hundred thousand strong. Brought into existence as an expedient while the army recovered, they received Reichswehr approval while fighting Germany's battles on the Eastern front, covering the return of the army from Russia and holding back predatory westward moves by the newly created Polish state under Pilsudski. But their most important task was the suppression of internal rebellion to gain time for the reestablishment of a government of the center and a reviving Reichswehr.

The antiguerrilla war in Germany was fought with all the excess of its Russian counterpart: in a wave of hatred, stirred by evidence of Russian massacres, the death toll rose to thousands. Freikorps executed Reds without mercy; after the fighting at Dachau in 1919 the Reds killed five hostages for every man they had lost. Putsch followed putsch in a seesaw struggle for power. Armed bands grew stronger as the violence increased, though simultaneously the discarded weapons of four years of war were being hidden in substantial caches against the day when the terms of the Treaty of Versailles would restrict the German Army to one hundred thousand men. As fast as the government proscribed one private army, another took its place—and usually with Reichswehr consent. The disbandment of the Freikorps in 1920 merely transferred its stauncher members to the Reichswehr and its more reprehensible types to paramilitary exservicemen's organizations such as the Stahlhelm or any of a number of secret societies—including the shadow army known as the Black Reichswehr—another of Schleicher's creations. One prominent member of the Freikorps, Ernst Röhm, joined the Nazi Party (NSDAP), which Adolf Hitler formed in January 1921 out of the enfeebled Deutsche Arbeiter Partei. Röhm was the archetypical guerrilla, a master at forming clandestine gangs, the controller of the illicit arms caches—and the man who put muscle into Hitler's uniformed private army, the Sturm Abteilung (SA), after it was formed.

Yet just as Trotsky had deemed it essential to eliminate partisans so too did General Hans von Seeckt when, as the new chief of staff, he imposed his will upon the new Reichswehr and the government itself. Gradually he curbed the private armies and, in successive confrontations between 1920 and 1923, put down by force of arms each uprising. Rough gangs—even those of Röhm's SA quality—had no chance against a properly disciplined body.

Nevertheless the SA, which first paraded in uniform in Munich in August 1922, was never wholly suppressed, simply discouraged. Though it failed during the Munich November beer hall putsch, because of poor organization, ineffective discipline and low morale, it was saved, as was the Nazi Party, by Hitler's prolonged speech of mitigation from the dock during the post putsch trial—saved because its militancy suggested something dear to Germany's aspirations of renewed power. "One day the hour is coming when these untrained bands will become battalions, when the battalions will become regiments and the regiments become divisions," declared Hitler. The SA believed Hitler even though, in 1925, he was to repudiate any suggestion that it should be incorporated in the Reichswehr "as a trained reserve . . . impregnated with Nazi idealogy"—to quote Wheeler-Bennett. Nevertheless the SA was eventually to act as a first cadre for the established forces and, from within, was to foster the SS—an organization that eventually supplanted the regular forces. The Schutz Staffeln (SS) had been formed in 1922 as Hitler's personal bodyguard but was reformed as Protection Squads in 1925. It provided the dynamic of Nazi insurgency, separate from, yet subordinate to, the SA. In 1929 it was no more than two hundred strong, but it waxed fiercely in the period of Schleicher's greatest influence and, as violence in Germany arose once more, came under the command of Heinrich Himmler, a fervid nationalist and a bureaucrat who gave boundless loyalty to Hitler.

In the political conflict which overspilled onto the streets until the Nazis came to power in 1933, the SS outdid the SA in dedication to combat—demonstrating the essential differences in quality between a well and a poorly disciplined body. Sometimes alongside and sometimes against the Communists, the SA and SS fought for influence in every German city. This amounted to a continuous campaign of intimidation in which firearms were used several times. Wheeler-Bennett quotes 42 deaths from political violence in 1929, 50 in 1930 and over 100 in the first half of 1931, with 15 deaths and over 1,200 casualties in April and May alone. Stahlhelms and the organized supporters of the ruling SPD—the Reichsbanner—awaited the signal to throw off their guise of passive resisters to take up arms from the hidden dumps against the Nazis and Communists. With the police overstretched, criminals took the opportunity to operate with impunity. It was often impossible to differentiate between robbery for party funds and for personal gain. Yet each strong-arm squad was a participant in a guerrilla warfare in which the Nazi supporters were the best trained, supported by an outstandingly astute propaganda department, under Josef Goebbels.

A crucial factor in Hitler's winning of the political campaign was the terror and disruption caused by his uniformed shock troops. In their primary role they were urban guerrillas, striking swiftly at opponents and then withdrawing to the cover of their homes; simultaneously they were antiguerrillas who infiltrated the established peacekeeping organizations in order to be at hand to combat every counterguerrilla attempt of their opponents. They coerced the unions and stifled the press. Better than any other party they were able to fix a firm grip upon the civil power before Hitler became chancellor in January 1933. After that they could revert wholly to the role of an antiguerrilla force, applying pressure against each dissident element in turn until, within a few months, the entire nation was subverted into a police state. Governed from the center and administered, at first, by the existing police and judiciary it was soon watched over by something new—Hermann Goering's Secret State Police, the Gestapo. Then it became the turn of the old police chiefs and judiciary to be replaced by SS and SA men until it was Röhm himself, Schleicher, and one thousand old guard Nazis who were liquidated by the SS in June 1934. This marked the end of SA power and made the SS, linked with the Sicherheitsdienst and the Gestapo under Himmler, the central operatives of antiguerrilla warfare in Germany—and in any other country German hegemony was to encompass. Himmler was later to define the SS code in a speech at Posen. "One basic principle must be the absolute rule for the SS man. We must be honest, decent, loyal and comradely to members of our own blood and to nobody else. What happens to a Russian, to a Czech does not interest me in the slightest."

A Germany which voted only forty per cent Nazi in 1933 was by no means antiauthoritarian in its outlook. The unemployed were first to join the Nazis and the people as a whole gave their support to Hitler and his partisans because they were persuaded that he alone could free the nation from the fractionalization of a democratic system plagued by a score or more of aggressive political parties, not one of which looked fit to rule. If Germany had rebelled in 1918 because her people had suffered enough under the monarchist regime she rebelled again in 1933 because she was more than tired of vacillation. But there were old ambitions which moved many Germans towards the Second World War. As a young middle-class girl, Melita Maschmann, put it: "I was obsessed by the vision of a Greater German Empire. . . . My mother expected from her children the same unquestioned obedience as she required of the maids or of my father's chauffeur. This attitude drove me to a rebelliousness which went beyond the purely personal rebellions of adolescence and was directed against the bourgeois values which my parents represented." She became an ardent Nazi. She might just as easily have become a Communist.

If the Nazi guerrillas seemed of importance in helping the overthrow of a German government, guerrillas were at the very root of the revolution against the British in Ireland in the early 1920s. The few Irishmen who actually took part in the incident of Easter 1916 did so partly because they thought the solution to their problems had been too long shelved and that force alone was the answer, and because German assistance was expected. But there had been no popular support for the Easter Rebels until inept British governmental action generated it. The secret and dilatory nature of the courts martial which made martyrs of the fifteen rebels who were executed, and the detention without trial of two thousand more, created a partisan movement where none worthy of the name had existed previously.

The Irish Republican Army of 1920 was a model of the nationalistic kind. A ruthless, dedicated minority adopted a policy of intimidation of any who opposed the cause. This meant that they were able to acquire early support from waverers as well as deter those who were against them; it, therefore, provided them, too, with the most productive sources of information and a tactical advantage over the British in the crucial battle between the intelligence and propaganda organizations. By recruiting from Irishmen who had served in the British Army, the IRA inherited a ready-made supply of proficient shots (marksmanship is often at a premium in a guerrilla force) and explosives experts. Though at first it operated in a variety of uniforms, these were soon discarded in favor of plain civilian dress.

Whether or not the British government cared to recognize its political opponents as a properly constituted government, its campaign of repression against the IRA bred violence on every side. As the British Army and the Royal Irish Constabulary became overstretched, the need for a special antiguerrilla force became apparent. The British created the Black and Tans and the Auxiliaries—English, Scottish and Welsh exsoldiers recruited into the RIC, fully armed but taught only the rudiments of law and the peacekeeping methods of police. The Black and Tans were looking for a fight and got one.

In return for each "murdered" Loyalist, they, the antiguerrillas, felt bound to retaliate in kind, and did so, what is more, with the tacit approval of the British Prime Minister, David Lloyd George, on the understanding that it was perfectly all right to shoot two Sinn Feiners for every Loyalist—a low rate of exchange by Communist German standards. A policy of blatant suppression stood far less chance of success in 1920 than it had in 1916. The British were no longer shielded by wartime censorship, but under close observation by the world's press. Though the Chief of the Imperial General Staff, General Sir Henry Wilson, described it as "suicidal," the Secretary for War, Winston Churchill, had some hope that "rough handling" might succeed.

The struggle intensified, becoming more mobile and better directed by their brilliant and mercurial leader, Michael Collins. Negotiations dragged on between the British government and the Irish nationalists. In the summer of 1921 they had reached an impasse at a time when the British soldiers felt they were getting on top of the IRA, when the Irish feared outright civil war if they intensified the fighting, and as the British government became aware that, unless they ended it quickly, there was a danger of American participation—on the Sinn Fein side. The final treaty partitioning Ireland was agreed on after the Irish delegates had been threatened by the British with all-out war.

In Ireland what was made to appear as a victory for partisans represented, in fact, a political compromise, though a turning point in the evolution of this type of struggle. The illusion of a military victory by a small irregular army was enough to give encouragement to every aspiring nationalist with rebellious ambitions. An internal guerrilla civil war was to be waged in Southern Ireland as the British withdrew. Collins was to be assassinated.

The British too were doomed for the succeeding decades to fight a succession of guerrilla wars—even if one excludes wars on the empire's periphery, which some prefer to classify as "colonial." The task of policing Palestine in the 1930s, in an effort to pacify Jews and Arabs, arose from an opportunist, ambiguous political arrangement concluded during the First World War, which provoked the Arabs to the point of rebellion.

Almost invariably, in those interwar years, popular support of a kind was an essential element in waging a successful guerrilla campaign. Mussolini's armed Fascist gangs who marched, thirty thousand strong, on Rome in 1922, were as well supported in this way as were Hitler's SA. It could be claimed that the prolonged resistance by the Spanish government from 1936 to 1939, against General Franco's unified and well-armed Fascists, stemmed from the inbuilt rebellious determination of the polyglot Republican armies, which hated the oppression represented by Fascism. But let it not be forgotten that Franco, no matter what he later became, started the Civil War as an antiguerrilla action. His first aim was quickly to take over the country and restore unified government. When this failed to the accompaniment of horrible slaughter by both sides, he adjusted his strategy, as any good soldier should, to a more limited war of slow attrition. "Do not oblige me to win at top speed," he wrote to his helpmate Mussolini, "for this would mean killing more Spaniards, destroying a greater part of the national wealth, and, in consequence, would make the foundations of my government ever more unsteady."

George Orwell, in his *Homage to Catalonia,* brilliantly describes the *ad hoc* nature of the Republican force, the youths and children clad in a weird assortment of garments that barely resembled uniforms, the archaic arms and haphazard ammunition supply, the utter inefficiency of the commissariat. He catches the feeling of enthusiasm within the anti-Fascist forces, whose quite extraordinary variety of separate organizations thwarted any hope of unity until a formal, Popular Army was formed, under Russian guidance, in 1937, ostensibly absorbing the original groups which had been distinguished by what Orwell calls "a plague of initials"—the PSUC, POUM, FAI, CNT, UGT and many more besides. It was also part of Orwell's complaint that, as the Popular Army was formed, the armed women who had first taken their place in the firing line, were derided and converted into camp followers. Maybe this was a turning point in itself.

In practice the Spanish Republican Army survived for as long as it did after 1936 because the guerrilla element was suppressed and replaced by a regular Popular Army. Enthusiastic but volatile guerrillas were no more effective in this major war than in any other. They might cause temporary embarrassment by committing sabotage along the lines of communication or by assassination. On the other hand they were a standing threat to internal security and future Spanish stability no matter which side won—and so they naturally became targets for suppression by regular forces.

None of this would have counted for much had not the Spanish Civil War taken place on the eve of the Second World War. Valuable lessons might have been learned had the attention of the military prophets been less firmly fixed upon operations by mechanized, orthodox armies and air forces and more upon the activities of irregulars. But as the armies of Europe moved towards their hour of greatest destiny, firmly convinced that wars were intended to be decided by regular forces, it was symbolic that the philosophers of war failed to point seriously to an irregular alternative.

Clausewitz, whose monumental work, *On War,* is said to have conditioned all important military thought in the nineteenth century, held strong views upon guerrilla warfare, even if he allocated far less space to the subject than to philosophy and orthodox warfare. This imbalance may in itself have been responsible for the comparative lack of interest in partisan forces during the First World War, as well as the overwhelming attention paid to conventional forces between the two world wars. In the atmosphere of tension between great nations, and the state of widespread rearmament with the most powerful weapons —tried and untried—which dominated the 1930s, nobody bothered much to consider irregular affairs in Europe—though in China Mao

Tse-tung was busy formulating his thoughts and General von Seeckt was acting as adviser to General Chiang Kai-shek in his successful antiguerrilla operations against Mao.

Highly penetrating though Clausewitz was in his understanding of partisan action—as well he might have been, in view of his association with the underground movement which operated in Germany during the days of Napoleonic domination—he remained a skeptic. "Militia and armed civilians should not be employed against the main force of the enemy," he wrote; ". . . they should not try to crack the kernel, but only nibble along the shell and the edges." "However brave a nation may be . . . it is an undeniable fact that a people's war cannot be kept up in an atmosphere too full of danger." But most significantly, in view of what was to come after 1939, "the more an enemy extends himself, the greater the effect of an armed populace. Like a slow, gradual fire, it destroys the bases of the enemy force."

The validity of Clausewitz's dictum was never seriously tested in the First World War, while the situation in Revolutionary Russia was so confused that, even today, we are uncertain what really happened. Throughout the 1930s and 1940s, therefore, interest in partisans was lacking, because, apart from one or two isolated examples, evidence of their concrete achievement was absent. In any case, they were political dynamite; the creation of partisan bands had invariably sounded the overture to rebellion, and so no government which valued stability dared to give publicity to the efficacy of guerrillas. German experiences with the Freikorps and, in Russia, against multifarious irregular bands were sufficient to dissuade them from advocating guerrillas as a primary way of making war.

Stories of the Arab revolt and the Irish Rebellion were told in abundance, and the lessons from these campaigns undoubtedly influenced the two most important military philosophers of the day—J.F.C. Fuller and B.H. Liddell Hart. At first, as serving soldiers, they were made cognizant from firsthand reports of the true scope and nature of the different partisan wars being waged in various parts of the British Empire. In their early writings they concentrated almost entirely upon the general modernization of the British Army—its mechanization and the reform of its infantry. In *The Future of Infantry*, published in 1933, Liddell Hart suggested that the infantry soldier "should profit by the lessons of irregular warfare, so that he may develop the rusefulness and groundcraft of the guerrilla fighter" but this was by no means an appeal by a convinced advocate of partisans. In fact, he merely reiterated the "motorized guerrilla" concept that was being proposed by Fuller. And after Liddell Hart had eulogized Lawrence in his 1934 book (in which he described Lawrence as a Great Captain, closer attuned to the demands of modern war than any general of the First World War) he became skeptical of guerrilla warfare's prospects. In 1935 he wrote, "The only chance for the ill-equipped nowadays lies in guerrilla warfare tactics. A people thus handicapped would be wise to adopt them from the outset. It is far more difficult to change to guerrilla tactics after a shattering reverse. . . . Aircraft and mechanised forces greatly diminish the prospect. . . ." Even in 1933 he had written, apropos the Arab revolt, "What the Arabs did yesterday, the air force may do tomorrow." This was politically more realistic than the 1935 proposition, for it is a bold government which, in peacetime, plans war on the assumption of defeat—as planning for guerrilla warfare implies. It is better to look for strong allies. The overemphasis on air power, however, was crucial—and peculiar to Western European philosophy.

Fuller was a slightly more convinced protagonist of the guerrilla —chiefly the motorized type—than Liddell Hart. He was also first of those to publish concrete proposals as to how they should operate. In his *Lectures on FSR II* of 1931, he wrote, "It is inconceivable, now that civilized countries are looking forward to the day when 'one man, one car' will become a possibility in peacetime, that this enormous mass of cars is not to be made use of in war." Later he expanded the subject in the highly provocative 1932 *Lectures on FSR III,* in which he envisaged the creation of a "guerrilla swarm," which he compared to the light cavalry of Alexander the Great. Fuller may have been impressed by motor guerrillas in Ireland, but the lines of his proposals more closely resembled Lawrence's 1918 operations. Thus his projection of the future is of an orthodox battlefield infested by "a veritable army, a fast-moving swarm which will not only search the area of advance, picket bridges and tactical points, block roads etc., but will fight off the enemy swarm, and so clear the area of advance. Should the enemy reinforce his army of motor-guerrillas with tanks, then his opponent will have to do likewise; but, generally speaking, I consider the tank will be too valuable a weapon for guerrilla warfare." Fuller also foresaw aircraft communication stations moving within the swarm, passing information. But it is clear he paid little attention to genuine guerrillas as participants in internal warfare, and as an instrument of political and strategic decision. These so-called unorthodox functions he reserved for aircraft and mechanized armies, though they, in fact, were merely orthodox instruments of formal war.

Most percipient of all the European writers was General Max

Hoffmann, one-time German commander on the Eastern Front, whose *Sketches* were published in 1930. Hoffmann envisaged a new type of prolonged warfare, prompted by Moscow-inspired Communists, which would push the colonial powers out of their overseas possessions, cause disruption and consequently deprive them of markets. National revolutionary wars could not be put down by main force, as the battle constantly flared up again. So, "If troops remain constantly in a state of alert, without being able to see an end to it, then their morale will be broken, and they will become victims of propaganda . . . that would be a battle without end in which England's resources would be exhausted." He added: "The more the European Powers fight peripheral combats kindled by Moscow, instead of marching against Moscow, the more they are playing Moscow's game." Read with hindsight, how penetrating those words seem today. But in 1930, they were studied hardly at all by professionals.

Possibly the most acute treatise on the techniques of partisan warfare was assembled, though unpublished, by T.E. Lawrence—unpublished in itself, that is, though the underlying philosophy could be read in *Seven Pillars of Wisdom*. From Lawrence came a lucid definition of partisan bands: "A thing intangible, invulnerable, without front or back, drifting about like a gas. Armies were like plants, immobile, firm-rooted, nourished through long stems to the head. We might be vapour, blowing where we wished, our kingdom lay in each mind." But there was much practical advice too, for those who would take it—the fundamental pronouncement that a guerrilla army "must have a friendly population, not actively friendly, but sympathetic to the point of not betraying rebel movements to the enemy. Rebellions can be made by two per cent active in a striking force, and ninety-eight per cent passively sympathetic." Yet again, perhaps because, as Lawrence wrote, "Guerrilla warfare is far more intellectual than a bayonet charge," orthodox soldiers paid little attention.

In Germany there was Hitler and *Mein Kampf*. But, to many minds, *Mein Kampf* lacked common sense, and was read as much out of curiosity as conviction. More to the point were Hitler's public utterances, such as when under pressure during his trial after the Munich putsch, he explained, "We never thought to carry through a revolt against the Army; it was with it that we believed we should succeed." This was a realistic understanding of the true worth of partisan forces which had become blurred by the time he wrote, in *Mein Kampf*, "The SA must not be either a military organization or a secret society . . . its training must not be organized from the military standpoint but from that of what is most practical for Party purposes." So the Germans translated Liddell Hart's *Future of Infantry* for study by the élite Waffen SS, who were to become the principal German antiguerrilla arm.

Not that the Germans rejected the raising of clandestine operations behind the enemy lines. Their Intelligence and Counter-Espionage Service—the Abwehr—had been given teeth as well as ears and eyes by that remarkable intellectual, Captain Canaris, after he took charge in 1934. Canaris, in fact, disliked violence and abhorred Himmler's methods almost as much as he detested those of the Bolsheviks. Nevertheless Abwehr Section II under Colonel Lahousen was responsible for sabotage and special duties that included anything from seizing a bridge in the enemy rear, by *coup de main*, to assassinating one of the enemy's leading figures. Captain von Hippel, of this section, had served with Lettow-Vorbeck in East Africa and he fostered a special "Abwehr Platoon" to operate small parties behind the enemy lines; to prepare, for example, secret and illegal airfields behind the Czech fortifications, ready to receive airborne troops and to seize vital industrial targets ahead of the Wehrmacht wherever it advanced. A number of Abwehr Kampftruppen were formed in 1939 and grouped in the Ebbinghaus Battle Group, which was nothing short of a band of guerrillas armed with grenades and light automatic weapons. They were to spearhead the invasion of Poland disguised as coal miners; in October 1939 they were developed into "Special Duty Training and Construction Company No. 800"; and in January 1940 expanded into the battalion that seized the Maastricht bridges during the invasion of Holland in May. Later that same year it was to increase still further into the Brandenburg Training Regiment. These, in essence, were commandos who specialized in deep raiding rather than a prolonged sojourn in the enemy rear or the raising of partisan bands. The basis of their tactics, however, was the old-fashioned *ruse de guerre*. Thus was created the German "Fifth Column"—a very different sort of formal military organization from the civilian rebels who worked for General Franco in Madrid at the start of the Spanish Civil War in 1936. The Abwehr, in actuality, raised a scientific underground force backed by the latest explosive and communication techniques, and also a sophisticated antiguerrilla force that vied with the Gestapo in clandestine operations.

In France, they studied Lyautey as the master of antiguerrilla warfare. He was the man who coined the "oil stain" analogy of guerrilla war ("it will advance not by columns, nor by mighty blows, but as a patch of oil spreads") in a colonial setting. In Britain imaginative soldiers of Wavell's caliber corresponded with Lawrence and practiced antiguerrilla warfare in Palestine—at the same time, catching the interest of future practitioners such as Orde Wingate and Bernard Fergusson. There were statesmen, too, who took note—the Russian ex-partisan Josef Stalin, for instance, who, in the early 1930s, seems to have contemplated the reestablishment of a guerrilla force, probably as a counter to the Red Army as it increased in political power. Indeed the greatest forcing house for guerrilla warfare undoubtedly was to be found in Russia. To Moscow came revolutionaries of every nation, to study their art in a university dedicated to rebellion, sponsored by the Comintern. Throughout the 1930s a cadre of unified activists was being trained to spread the gospel of international Communism. If, at a later stage, a remarkable similarity in the raising of diversified rebellions is detected, it must be to the Comintern that we look for its impetus and homogeneity.

In essence the relative stagnation in philosophical writing about guerrilla warfare in the interwar years reflected the limited successes which had been achieved by partisan forces. Practice had demonstrated that when regular and special antiguerrilla forces worked under firm governmental control and enjoyed popular support, there was failure—at best stalemate—in store for guerrillas.

Naturally there were the fictional outpourings of authors seeking to project the trends of the day into the future, to shock people out of complacency, and they often drew closer to the truth than the professionals. The Russian Revolution induced a plethora of books concerned with the mass uprising of workers—all geared to the current fear of spreading Bolshevism. But this trend of the 1920s gave way to prophecies in the 1930s of a more conventional kind—the exploitation of scientific knowledge surrounding the kind of technological war which remained unfathomed in 1918—gas war, air war and so on—the halfway house to science fiction. I.F. Clarke in his *Voices Prophesying War* has pointed out that in this period "the center of anxiety has shifted within the tale of the war-to-come. All the pre-1914 unquestioned certainties of the self-righteous nations have vanished." The professionals—Fuller, Hoffmann, Lyautey and the others—were largely ignored in the tempestuous days of rearmament. Yet the old wisdom of Clausewitz held good. The embers of the fire which had been lit in the First World War, and doused in its aftermath, still lay glowing. It only needed a strong breeze of desperation to rekindle the flame and establish that terrible, slow, gradual fire which Clausewitz feared and Hoffmann anticipated.

In 1938 the British Foreign Office set up a new section (EH) to study ways of influencing German public opinion and yet another (D) to see if disaffected Communists and Jews could be persuaded in time of war to injure the German war effort. Then in April 1938, the War Office created GS(R) composed of a Royal Engineer, Major J.C.F. Holland, and one typist to do research into future guerrilla warfare and write Field Service Regulations on the subject. Holland, soon to be joined by Major C. Gubbins, was a confirmed advocate of guerrilla warfare: he had suffered from it in Ireland—as had Gubbins. In quick time they wrote three pamphlets—*The Art of Guerilla Warfare, Partisan Leaders' Handbook* and *How to Use High Explosives*—and in the summer ran short courses for potential saboteurs, civilian explorers, mountaineers and businessmen. They drew closer to the heart of coming war when Gubbins visited Warsaw and came back with designs of time fuses and incendiary devices which, later, were to be of universal application. Gubbins also secretly toured the Danube valley (considering destroying, once more, the Ploesti oilfields and, in addition, blocking the river at the Iron Gates) and Baltic countries. He searched, too, for allies in a future guerrilla war. But on August 25 he was off to Warsaw again, this time to become chief of staff to the British Military Mission. Two days earlier Molotov and von Ribbentrop had signed the Russo-German nonaggression pact, which gave Germany a free hand for the invasion of Poland.

CHAPTER TWO

Set Europe on Fire

For Hitler the invasion of Poland came as the culmination of more than a decade's uninterrupted success—a period in which, by main force, he had completely subjugated the German people, driven underground or eliminated all party political opposition (including that of the Communist Party), absorbed Austria, the Sudetenland and Memel and, in addition, seized Czechoslovakia, which was the first non-German territory to fall into his hands. So swift and ruthless had been the German expansion that nowhere did any internal dissent arise. Even in Czechoslovakia, whose post-1918 independence had been achieved by strife and tough negotiation, no defiant shots were fired. There, as in the rest of Europe, where it had been earnestly hoped that Hitler would be satisfied by the gift of the Sudetenland in October 1938, the sudden invasion of March 1939, breaking the rules of international law, caught the Czechs defenseless. Nothing had been done to form resistance groups, no arms caches lay hidden—the entire army, with all its equipment, was dissolved.

As members of a sophisticated nation with the highest standard of living among the newly created states of the Versailles Treaty, the Czechs traditionally rejected outright rebellion. Their struggle for independence amid the old Austro-Hungarian Empire had been conspiratorial rather than violent, unlike that of the Poles, who were inveterate belligerents. Initially stunned, the Czechs were slow to oppose the Germans and had difficulty in gathering the substance of resistance. Part of the country was given to Hungary. The rest was dismembered either by Germanization or by being placed under German control as protectorates. The outcome was the same, for the processes which controlled the German people were now extended to the Czechs by Himmler's omnipotent organizations—but in greater severity. Thus the Czech people became "extras" in a rehearsal of Nazi legislation, the first foreign country to experience the calculated devaluation of the currency, replacement of the judiciary by outsiders or local Nazis, direction of labor, registration and rounding up of Jews—above all a remorseless reduction in the quality of everyday life. In resentment the people reacted in the only ways possible. First they called upon their own ingenuity for survival amid the new conditions and from this developed primary resistance in the form of evasion of regulations.

Passive resistance in a police state is one thing, but secret warfare quite another. A secret army demands strict organization of the "two per cent" dedicated instigators Lawrence had specified. First at work on this aspect were Czech Army officers who formed the nucleus of a group called "Defense of the Nation." They were later joined by two political groups of amateur status, and the OSVO—the Falcon Organization of Resistance—based upon the nationwide Sokol (Falcon) gymnastics organization. In their early days these groups were able to communicate not only internally but also in relative freedom with the outside world. Mostly the frontiers remained open to couriers (often sponsored by the nascent British political subversive sections) who could carry messages to and from Dr. Benes and those of the old Czech government who had fled the country. In due course two secret radio transmitters were established—one political and the other military—to maintain a quicker (if insecure) two-way flow of information and instruction. In so far as the Anglo-French were concerned, at this stage, it was information they mostly needed—a scenario of evolving political trends depicting the growth of opposition centers: the concept of active resistance was divorced from their minds except as a sideshow if war came. But the Czech committee in London was always eager to ferment a militant unified resistance movement within their country, one that would embarrass the Germans and simultaneously enhance their people's sense of purpose and morale. A little progress was made, though more noticeably because the Russo-German nonaggression pact of August 1939 was accepted as good enough reason for their party to desist from anti-German activity while the other parties lacked solidarity. Hence the Czech resistance movement, split from the outset, was quite unable to mount any serious form of sabotage or guerrilla warfare. In Poland it was different.

To all outward appearances the German Army's subjugation of the Poles in seventeen hectic days of battle confirmed Hitlerian domination by demonstrating the hard knuckle backing his earlier threats of force. To Hitler himself the victory was intoxicating. As Camus writes, "As long as he was successful he chose to believe he was inspired." Now, by prearrangement, as Russian armies occupied the eastern half of

Poland, Hitler could turn his full strength against the foes in the West while Dr. Hans Frank established the German police state in Poland, employing Himmler's men with enthusiastic brutality.

For months on end Germans had provoked Poles in the Free City of Danzig. There had been clashes, and casualties had been incurred by both sides while the German propaganda department poured vilification upon the Poles. At the end of August the Poles found arms and explosives in the hands of the German-domiciled *Volksdeutsch,* and the London *Times* noted that, on the frontier, there was lawlessness which amounted to guerrilla warfare. After the invasion had begun some of the *Volksdeutsch* took up arms. At Bromberg the sniping was particularly heavy and the Poles retaliated in full measure, reaching a climax on September 3 when a great many people were slain, not only by local fighting, but by bombing, too. German propaganda, for obvious reasons, exaggerated the number killed to sixty thousand; a much lower German estimate puts it at six thousand. Six or sixty thousand, the result was an escalation of German detestation of everything Polish, and ample excuse to intensify their persecution of the Poles.

Poland, in the autumn of 1939, provided a fertile breeding ground for partisan warfare. Scattered throughout the land lay an abandoned mass of war material while, in the Carpathian Mountains, among the forests (one fifth of the country's total acreage) and in great cities like Warsaw, Kraków and Lublin, there were a myriad hiding places awaiting the arms caches being eagerly formed by a people with a traditional bent for subversive warfare. The larger portion of the army entered the German and Russian prisoner-of-war cages, among it the best trained men. Of the officers in Russian hands few would ever be seen again. Formal resistance may have ended in the first week of October but it was revived almost immediately by sporadic acts of sabotage undertaken by stubborn soldiers who, in desperation, refused to admit defeat. Lawrence's two per cent rule never much hindered the Poles, even if, in the early days, there were misgivings among the population as a whole concerning the wisdom of overt action. The Poles steadfastly refused to provide the Germans with collaborators —and the Germans, wholeheartedly despising the Poles, declined to countenance even a puppet government, relegating their new subjects to the status of slave laborers. To quote Hans Frank, the governor: "Mincemeat could be made of them."

In the last days of September during the siege of Warsaw, the foundation of a Secret Army was laid, but this, like its political counterpart, was divided in both hierarchy and policy. There were those for whom the future struggle was against "Two Enemies." The Russians they looked on with as much hatred as the Germans. But there were others who realistically understood that, though the Germans might be defeated and in defeat yield back part of Poland's autonomy, the Russians were too big to overcome; for them some sort of compromise was admissible. Eventually, under the guidance of General Sikorsky, the moderate soldier-statesman who had taken charge of the émigré government in the West, the policy of "One Enemy" was adopted and a single secret army—later known as the Home Army—formed to combat the Germans.

The original scheme envisaged one organization in the Soviet sector and another in the German, but this suffered a setback when, in March, General Tokarzewski, who had been sent to control the eastern group, was arrested by the Russians. This left General Rowecki in command in Warsaw, soon to be joined by General Komorowski with responsibilities for southwestern Poland, based on Kraków. It was Rowecki, forty-five years of age, energetic and free from the political attachments of his seniors, who most clearly visualized the future and laid practical plans; and it was he who foresaw the time when Russia might be at war with Germany and defeat her. He wrote, "It would be madness to attempt any action against such an army marching into Poland. . . . Our role would then be to keep the apparatus in hiding, carrying on the conspiracy, waiting for the moment when the Soviet side and system begin to crack." The apparatus he built was as realistic as his thinking, composed as it was of "provincial, area, sector and outpost commands, with staffs, special diversionary-action platoons, and combat platoons. . . . The platoon, about fifty men, was to be the basic organizational and tactical unit. The reserve included all undisbanded military organizations whose membership comprehended military tactics and operational procedures."

First among the European nations to organize a genuine guerrilla army, Poland also led the way in discovering the hazards. Throughout the winter of 1940 when the foundations were being laid and undermined by both Germans and Russians, the difficulty of communicating along tenuous and insecure tentacles inevitably hindered progress. There were no external radio contacts, although a courier service, operated by the émigré government and by the London Section GS(R) (now called MIR) managed to pass messages through the neutral countries that bordered Poland. It was a slow and risky business because bulky documents, easily discovered, might put information into German hands that would lead to raids, arrests and the disruption of the secret army command system. Only later would microfilm be used. The Poles, though by tradition furtive, were also careless; lapses in security were a persistent cause of breakdown.

Nor were the Germans the only foe. East of the Brest-Litovsk demarcation line the Russian police state was hard at work—the NKVD infiltrating every layer of society. Here, too, resistance took root slowly despite Russian efforts to cloak their suppression in the guise of democratic participation. At a general election of the Supreme Council of the Polish Socialist Republic Comrade Stalin and his followers received more than ninety-nine per cent of the vote because the vote was compulsory and the candidates only of the Communist Party.

Though only trivial direct aid could be given by Poland's allies in the West it comforted the Poles that they were in contact and their cries heard—and that their Anglo-French allies were committed to war with the Germans. In any case arms were not as yet highest in their list of requirements. It was morale which had to be boosted and for this the faintest act of resistance was good. Daily the pressures mounted as the Germans deliberately ignored the Hague Conventions, trampling on the statutory rights of people in an occupied country. A vast compulsory reshuffle of population was begun by Himmler, acting upon Hitler's orders. In one way this migration tended to disrupt the Secret Army, as Poles were moved out of Western Poland to make way for German settlers; in another, it assisted its formation by actually concentrating the most embittered groups in the area of Frank's government-general. Poland was to be the testing ground for the most extreme measures inherent in Hitler's New Order, providing practice for the SS Einsatzgruppen (special Action Squads) in their task of clearing the ground for colonists, squashing resistance and liquidating racially unwanted peoples such as the Jews and gypsies. It therefore also became the zone where the seeds of partisan warfare were soonest sown, earliest germinated and quickest reaped. A flourishing underground press ensured that news of growing repression was widely spread.

Admittedly only an embryonic, ill-trained fighting force had been brought into existence by the spring of 1940, but its efforts at railway and industrial sabotage could be no more than an irritant that rebounded against it when German countermeasures gained in severity. Sikorski brought this to an end when France was knocked out of the war in May, and it looked as if Britain, too, was doomed. On June 18 he ordered all armed action to cease and on the 20th sabotage, too, as senseless and provocative. The wisdom of Clausewitz held good; the foe was as yet insufficiently dispersed and weakened to allow active guerrillas to survive. Small partisan uprisings have to be closely coordinated with major operations. But partisan bands thrive on continuity and action, and Sikorski's standstill order meant the opposite of that. In June 1940 the Secret Army was 75,000; a year later 54,000. In October 1940 there were 2,190 platoons: in March 1941 only 1,466.

One can sympathize with the Poles. The German seizure of Denmark and the best part of Norway in April had been a disappointment to them, but the overrunning of Holland and Belgium, catastrophically followed by the collapse of France, was a traumatic disaster. No longer could they hope for a quick solution of their problems. Now they knew the partisan struggle had to become a slow war of attrition, much more carefully prepared and with scant assistance from outside. Soon, too, as Hitler's influence spread, external access through neutral countries would be severely curtailed just when contact by air became almost impossible. Allied aircraft were forced to fly to Poland from Britain at the extreme range of their endurance and could only hope to make the journey in the longer winter nights.

If the French débâcle quelled Polish hopes of a quick solution, the prospects for an extension of partisan warfare within Europe as a whole were, in theory, immensely stimulated. The Germans, by capturing the entire Atlantic seaboard from North Cape to Biarritz and occupying Norway, Denmark, Holland, Belgium and part of France, had enormously widened the arc and area of their defenses and, because of the need to police vast new territories, greatly extended themselves. Much would depend upon German treatment of the conquered people, still more upon the attitude of the people themselves and, to a rather lesser extent, upon what the British, locked up in their island and themselves facing invasion, would do.

The Germans' occupation policy was, in fact, as varied as the countries they had seized. It depended upon the whim of Hitler, the respect in which he held each nationality, and the caliber of men he sent as governors. It also rested upon the armed forces—the Wehrmacht, whose jurisdiction was paramount in areas of military operational importance (such as the coastal regions and airfields), and the SS, whose activities overlapped Wehrmacht responsibilities, but which was supreme in the zones of specific Nazi civil government.

Denmark (her people, in Hitler's view, were akin to Germans), though first to be conquered, was never, technically, at war with Germany. She was allowed to retain her monarchical government along with a veneer of independence under the "benevolent" direction of Dr. Werner Best—who, by comparison with other SS overlords, was indeed a liberal.

Norway fought back but, when defeated, sent King Haakon and

his government to Britain to continue the struggle from there. This left the way clear for Vidkun Quisling, the leader of the small and uninfluential National Union Party (Nazi type), to form an alternative government. But within a week he demonstrated his ineffectiveness as it became apparent that the Norwegians resented Quisling even more than they resented the Germans. According to normal German practice, the military government of Norway, like any other occupied country, should have been under General Nikolaus von Falkenhorst, commander of XXI Corps, which had carried out the invasion. And, indeed, ten days after it started Hitler gave Falkenhorst full powers for rapid pacification of the country, along with a recommendation for severity. At the same time he appointed one of the Nazi party hacks, Joseph Terboven, as Reich Commissioner, an appointment almost immediately confirmed as giving Terboven full authority over the civil sector—an authority he intended to exercise with all the ingrained, dictatorial arrogance of a hard-line Nazi. But in June he held his hand while the last of the Allies were cleared from northern Norway and he tried hard to woo the people by peaceful persuasion. So long as this went on and the initial shock of invasion persisted, the populace stayed quiet. There was no attempt at resistance by other than the regular forces, who fought on until they were evacuated on June 8.

Shock was, of course, the true deterrent to immediate opposition against each German incursion into Western Europe in 1940. Holland, conquered in four days' intensive aerial and ground attack aimed, except for the bombing of Rotterdam, at specific military objectives, had nothing to offer by way of partisan warfare. She did not even possess an intelligence network. With her queen and government evacuated to Britain there was nothing to go on fighting for, and so the Reich Commissioner, Dr. Arthur Seyss-Inquart, took over what virtually amounted to a political vacuum and mainly found himself vying for power with the German military governor. Yet he stated an intention to rule the country with respect for Dutch wishes while attempting to form an alliance with the Dutch Union, an authoritarian group quickly formed by Dutchmen to act as a bridge between Nazi ideology and Dutch liberalism. But while the Germans regarded the Dutch, like the Danes and Norwegians, as racially acceptable, their purpose was total exploitation.

Gradually that summer, in response to Hitler's long-term aim of annexation, the screw was tightened; instinctively the people reacted. If at first the Dutch Union and the National Socialist Movement (NSB), under Engineer Mussert, gained new members, this was countered by the flood of recruits into the opposition parties of religious and

Communist orientation—though the latter, like Communists every-where, held back from opposition to the Germans out of respect for the Russo-German pact. Friction occurred at intervals. Dutchmen pub-licly celebrated Prince Bernhard's birthday on June 29 (he was a German by birth after all); the Germans arrested the Dutch Army's Commander-in-Chief, General Winkelman, who led the way to the Royal Palace to sign the birthday book. Isolated and petty sabotage, begun by a few hotheads, was swiftly crushed. In September, after an NSB member was shot dead, Hitler exerted additional pressure on Mussert to create a Dutch SS out of the NSB, under Himmler's overall control, but the Socialists in the Dutch Union retaliated and bom-barded marching NSB men with tiles and anything else to hand. At the same time routine Nazi methods of replacement of officials by their own minions, including ambitious young Dutchmen with Nazi lean-ings, went on behind the scenes. The Communist Party was sup-pressed. Long before a viable partisan movement could be formed within a highly civilized country which was environmentally totally unsuitable for guerrilla warfare, the antiguerrilla forces had clamped down. Nevertheless effective movements were formed—first the Order Service, with the object of maintaining order if the Germans collapsed, but later more aggressive groups in addition to the "LO," which helped people "on the run."

It was much the same in Belgium, except that there the king surrendered to the Germans and went into voluntary captivity while members of the government shifted purposefully to Britain. Support for the German military government came only from a few extremist Flemish Nationalists and some Walloons—these would later form the nucleus of the Belgian SS. But the majority of the populace, regardless of racial differences, cast their memories back to the previous war and concluded that the stern measures of the military governor were as bad as—potentially worse than—anything they had known before. This time there was early, empirical resistance urged on at the outset by broadcasts from the BBC in London. By Armistice Day 1940 public demonstrations were taking place—and the Germans were tackling them and thereby accelerating the whirlpool of hatred.

In France, however, it was altogether different. Though the Dutch and Belgians might blame their defeat on lack of military preparation rather than poor fighting spirit, the French could not. Their forces had enjoyed ample time in which to make ready during the months of "phoney war" and had boasted openly about their martial prowess. The French in June 1940 were suffering from something worse than shock; they were in despair, hunting for scapegoats (of whom the

British stood high on the list), divided by an arbitrary partition into two political zones, and quite uncertain of their future as a power. Their will to fight had largely evaporated and so it was hardly to be hoped that they could continue the struggle from North Africa or in their own country by guerrilla warfare. Partisan warfare as a means to carry the fight to the enemy might become British Cabinet business on May 25, as the result of a proposal by the British Chiefs of Staff, but when Churchill suggested it to the French on June 13 to strengthen their government's morale, it was only as a last hope. If France remained in the struggle, he said "with her fine Navy, her great Empire, her Army still able to carry on guerrilla warfare on a gigantic scale ... then the whole edifice of Nazidom would topple over." But the French Premier, Paul Reynaud, replied that he could see "no light at the end of the tunnel." Beaten in council, he handed over to Marshal Pétain and that orthodox soldier made the immediate overtures for peace with the Germans that eventually led to the partition of France, the seizure of Alsace and Lorraine by Germany, the creation of the Pétain-governed Vichy zone of central and southern France, and the domination of the north and the entire western coastline by Germany's military government as they prepared for an invasion of England.

Smoothly on the heels of the conquering German Army arrived the Security Forces—the military Abwehr, followed by Himmler's henchmen. They found a country in disarray, one that lacked both the will and organization to raise effective resistance. Indeed, there was a much higher chance of collaboration on the part of Frenchmen than by the other subjugated nationalities; when the Germans broke the country into three geographical segments the political elements fragmented, each fragment becoming engaged upon aggrandizement—with German assistance if it was shown to be advantageous in the short run. Vichyites vied with Royalists, Fascists, Communists and the host of political parties which comprised the French political structure. To these had to be added the newcomers—men who offered allegiance to Brigadier-General Charles de Gaulle in Britain, the small, self-styled Free French who, alone, made outward signs of continuing the struggle as opposed to merely covert threats mouthed by the parties remaining in France. To Pétain, de Gaulle and his followers were outlaws; it has to be admitted, too, that they were the second best choice of Churchill and the British government, who would have preferred the legal French government as an ally. A schismatic France could well be of greater assistance to the Germans than to the British.

Within weeks, in fact, French sentiment was veering strongly towards the Germans. It has been suggested, by some Frenchmen, that many people were strongly in approval of the excellent bearing and behavior of the well-equipped Wehrmacht as it took up its post in their midst: in this host they recognized virtues they had longed for and found lacking in their own armed forces. It was certainly true that Frenchmen were almost immediately forced to concentrate on the art of existence in an environment of compulsion that was wholly foreign to their previous way of life. France, a sophisticated nation that welcomes authoritarian rule more readily than is sometimes admitted—or healthy—was unequal to, as well as unprepared for, extreme manifestations of partisan warfare in 1940. She had surrendered her sense of self-preservation and pride. For some time to come she would be rudderless. Comparison by Frenchmen of the initial, more gentle German methods with rugged British countermeasures bore well in the German favor. It was not so much the minor and irregular bombing raids by the RAF which influenced them, nor the knowledge that Britain harbored the Free French, nor that a few despairing patriots were already engaged in sabotage of a trivial nature. Mistrust was far deeper seated, harking back by generations to memories of past conflicts, carefully nurtured by German propaganda, which played on every possible Anglophobic chord. Then in July the British sank or damaged French warships at Oran and Dakar, killing over a thousand French sailors in the process. The French were never allowed to forget this, even if they had wished to do so, or if there had been an indisputable case in favor of an act which, in fact, was contentious. Nobody would now change the minds of the majority of Frenchmen who rated the British as an enemy who, having attacked their fleet, would not in future stop at acquiring her empire—as events in Central Africa soon suggested might be the case. Nobody could change their minds—unless it was the Germans themselves, and the French had yet to learn that Adolf Hitler regarded the Gallic race as an inferior species. Yet even had they known this in 1940, it remains doubtful if their liberal instincts would have comprehended the full extent of the German menace.

Although German rule produced varying effects in different countries, there existed a certain uniformity of attitude throughout Western Europe, though in the east Poland descended into a special hell of its own. Everywhere the Wehrmacht was busy collecting the vanquished's equipment—an orderly process since so complete was defeat that only scattered attempts were made to hide weapons. Inevitably they also stood guard against guerrillas, not only as a result of previous experience as an army of occupation, but mainly because it is the duty of every soldier and military unit to provide for its own protection.

Nevertheless, although the Wehrmacht took a firm line in its dealings with each local, Western populace, it also behaved with rigid correctness and, far more often than not, with humanity. Better than anybody else the senior officers (because they were past masters of invasion) understood how their men's morale might sink during a prolonged sojourn if the populations became hostile. At first there was tranquility in mutual bewilderment, followed by degrees of collaboration outside official contact—rarely blatantly but frequently in private and often after dark between German soldiers (whose normal desire for company and love could not entirely be satisfied by periodic leaves in Germany) and ladies whose menfolk had been transferred to German prison camps. Frenchmen recognized that the Germans earnestly desired to be liked—and some approved of that motive and dreamed of a united Europe.

Resistance evolved to a fairly standard pattern dependent upon the degree of provocation on the Germans' part. Nowhere was it destructive or important throughout 1940—or even in 1941—and hardly ever did the ethics of control intrude heavily upon German conscience. They expected to rule by force and, in the crunch, would break international law to suit the occasion—though, for reasons of sense and economy, the breach usually was delayed for as long as possible. The commonest German move was the rapid erosion of civil liberties and the imposition of innumerable new laws to baffle and suffocate the people's initiative. The introduction of strict food rationing was at once provocative because it coincided with massive purchases on the open market by Germans who took advantage of a deliberately inflated rate of currency exchange. From induced shortages would come widespread malnutrition. Then would follow a black market in goods of short supply with its scrambled underhand dealings and an implied erosion of morals. These introduced subtle distractions in the minds of the populace, quite the opposite of the shock arrest of apparently innocent citizens, above all the Jews, that was instantly disturbing as well as sinister.

Resistance of a minor kind was endemic. Most valuable to the lonely British was the almost immediate and spontaneous improvisation of escape channels for soldiers left behind in the retreat to the coast, and then the growth of a traffic in airmen who had been shot down behind the lines. This trickle of highly trained men was to grow into a stream of immense value. But more important still was the establishment of contacts and, above all, a widespread information service to provide intelligence of the enemy's order of battle, his intentions, targets for aerial bombardment and the development of secret weapons along with the building of new industrial premises. The gathering of useful intelligence is more than a matter of welcoming each single new item of interest; the art lies in extensive coverage of the whole spectrum of enemy activity, in confirmation and in evaluation. The search for information can make such demands on resources that it becomes prohibitive as well as time-consuming. Therefore a proliferation of voluntary local intelligence sources is to be welcomed—and none better than those in closest contact with the enemy which provide a regular, if unspectacular, flow of reports. Whatever else the irregular forces achieved in the Second World War, their gathering of intelligence was of the highest importance to the Allies. Without intelligence even the clandestine forces were blind.

In June 1940 the British government was torn two ways in its efforts to sustain the war. In one direction it tried to keep France in the fight, in the other it sought ways to maintain the initiative if France fell, and prepared to meet an invasion. When France surrendered, however, defense of the United Kingdom became paramount and complex, the principal consideration being how best to defeat an assault from the sea or by parachute landings. In addition, internal sabotage mounted by the IRA might well have been a serious threat had the IRA not staged an abortive campaign of sabotage in Britain two years previously and as a result seen its principal operators jailed. In 1940 the Abwehr tried to parachute an agent into Southern Ireland to join the IRA staff and establish a radio link with Berlin. But the agent landed in the north by mistake, lost his radio and, a shaken man, arrived at last at his destination, where he found the IRA split by internal dissensions (so like all guerrillas) and not in the least prepared to take orders from Germany.

So the British prepared internal cells of resistance (the Auxiliary Force [1]) to act as anti-German guerrillas should the invasion come and succeed, and interned a few well-known, extrovert local Fascists along with anybody else with dissident views. But the British defensive period was shorter-lived than the invasion threat itself and at no time wholly diverted attention from the essential strategic need to attack the new German Empire. As has been shown, Churchill was already interested in the guerrilla idea and thus ready to support proposals aimed at creating a War Office directorate of irregular activities. Moreover he also appreciated that the launching of a full-scale military

[1] Conceived purely as a short-term expedient in time of invasion, it was never, according to its front commander, Colin Gubbins, intended as the cadre for protracted resistance. That was dismissed as impracticable, despite Churchill's idea of "taking one with you."

campaign on the Continent was years hence. The British Army was virtually disarmed and, in any case, no match for the German Army. To regain the initiative Churchill could only use the weapons then in existence and in the summer of 1940 that meant peripheral and indirect naval action, plus direct attacks from RAF Bomber Command. Bombers, however, were practically incapable of aiming sustained or accurate blows, although at least they could strike deep within enemy territory. There was another alternative, the newly formed "Striking Companies," proposed for maritime raiding by Lieutenant-Colonel Dudley Clarke in a paper written on June 5, but these could only make an impression on Europe's periphery. In due course they would be called "Commandos," part of the special raiding forces which Churchill called for in a minute of June 6, along with proposals for landing tanks on enemy beaches, a system of espionage and intelligence, and parachute troops.

Raiding from the sea and air came to dominate military thought and a Directorate of Combined Operations was set up on June 15 to develop the gambit of amphibious warfare. But subversion was outside Combined Operations' scope: that came under the separate heading of political warfare and was sponsored a few days later by the Foreign Secretary, Lord Halifax, the Colonial Office, the newly formed Ministry of Economic Warfare, under Hugh Dalton, and the War Office Directorate of Military Intelligence. Dalton was the firebrand among the sponsors, eager to throw spanners into the Nazi machine. He demanded "movements in enemy-occupied territory comparable to the Sinn Fein . . . or—one might as well admit it—the organisations which the Nazis themselves have developed . . . ," and visualised them indulging in "industrial and military sabotage, labour agitation and strikes, continuous propaganda, terrorist acts against traitors and German leaders, boycotts and riots." Not only did he demonstrate his grasp, as a practicing socialist with a reputation among his contemporaries for intrigue, of partisan warfare, but he projected his ideas on a grand scale. The new organization should become, as he entitled a paper written in August, "The Fourth Arm." Trotsky might not have approved, but there is no evidence to suggest that political opposition to the creation of a British resistance movement ever took shape in fear of an ungovernable internal threat—not in 1940 anyway.

On July 16—and it is worth noting that, in a period when several vital decisions were taken in a matter of hours if not days, this one took a fortnight—Churchill decided to launch what was later to be known as the Special Operations Executive (SOE) and place it, most secretly, under Dalton as part of his Ministry. It would absorb MIR and the other subversive sections and operate worldwide. A former prime minister, Neville Chamberlain, wrote the terms of reference: "A new organisation . . . to co-ordinate all action by way of subversion and sabotage, against the enemy overseas." He provided for staff and intercommunication with the Foreign Office, Service Ministries, Ministry of Information and any other departments which would necessarily come into contact with SOE. Of vital importance, in the light of the danger of departmental overlapping, was a proviso added to the general aim of SOE's irregular offensive: it "should be in step with the general strategic conduct of the war." This needed to be said because the sort of men most likely to be involved were bound to be arch-enthusiasts with scant respect, in some cases, for bureaucracy and higher authority. Were it otherwise the scheme might not have worked at all.

Churchill, for all his initial enthusiasm, seems also to have harbored serious doubts. Much later, in another connection, he was to warn, "Anything for the battle, but the politics will have to be sorted out later on." He had already experienced the effects of partisan warfare upon postwar politics and knew, firsthand, the hatred it aroused. In any case he was romantically chivalrous by instinct; even in war the underhand was repugnant to him. Furthermore, he had been disturbed by the unsatisfactory outcome of the first cross-Channel raids. Near Boulogne, on June 5, three officers had landed on reconnaissance in German-held territory from a trawler and had returned one short, rowing hard, thirteen hours later. On June 23, 120 men from a Striking Company went ashore from four RAF launches, brushed with the enemy and returned, scarred, but little wiser for the experience. A raid of equal dimensions was next attempted against Guernsey on July 14, and this too went sadly awry. One boatload made, in error, for Sark, two broke down and another struck a rock. The Germans were unmolested and can scarcely have detected what was afoot. These raids underlined the deplorable unreadiness of Britain for war of almost any kind, let alone specialized operations which demanded the highest state of training. Ironically the failure of the first commando raids rebounded on SOE before it had even been formed. Churchill was quick to call them "a silly fiasco" because "the idea of working all these coasts up against us by pin-prick raids and fulsome communiqués is one to be avoided." This was a line which failed to recommend itself to the military minds, of course. They presented the landings as traditional replicas of the time-honored art of "trench raiding," which had gone on nonstop throughout the First World War. That they overlooked the political implications of a routine military act was characteristic. Churchill realized the effect on the local populace and, in due course, supported the émigré governments whose aim it also was to preserve their infant resistance movements and save the people from needless suffering. During five years in office, Churchill was occasionally to give SOE vital support, but there were limits to the excesses he would condone. He objected to a suggestion that SOE should become involved in an Albanian scheme to poison Italian troops. Dalton took the view that this was the local custom and comparable to Western practice in withholding food by blockade, asking, "Is there any moral difference?" Churchill had replied, "It is the difference between treachery and war."

Nevertheless in the first flush of enthusiasm as SOE was forming, it was Churchill, the man who had been close witness to the effects of Sinn Fein and who nursed a horror of Bolshevik methods, who said to Dalton, as he took up his task, "And now set Europe ablaze."

But striking matches in the rain is never easy.

CHAPTER THREE

The Intolerance Level

How does one stimulate fiery aggression in populations suffering from shock, apathy and hostility to one's own cause? It was Britain's task to solve this problem in 1940 and the years to follow in her efforts to raise partisan warfare in Europe. Inertia, of course, was neither uniform nor wholly widespread for, as we have seen, the Czechs and, above all, the Poles were inclined to offer violence out of sheer desperation and rebellious intolerance. In Holland, too, there were signs of the will to exchange blows, for the Dutch never lost faith in a British victory. But the French were largely convinced that it was the Germans who would win, and this was crucial because France occupied the central political and strategic position in occupied Western Europe. If the French, with cities, mountains and forests which were only partially suitable for guerrilla warfare, stood aside from the fight, a weighty influence was neutralized; and when their Vichy government rejected the likelihood of a British victory and officially prohibited resistance it became much more difficult for patriots to influence the population. In any case, it was difficult to enlist passive support for agents and sabotage gangs, because they disturbed equanimity and threatened local well-being. A shot in the night could provoke a week of harrying by the Germans.

So SOE's task of establishing "a suitable climate of opinion" for resistance and then putting in "a nucleus of trained men who would be able to assist as a fifth column in the liberation of the country" was dependent upon convincing the populace of Britain's ultimate victory and upon provoking the Germans into angering the people with indiscreet countermeasures. But SOE was in a dilemma. To begin with there were virtually no recognized credible agents living within the occupied countries (except, of course, in Poland and Czechoslovakia). So the first parties, sent in by air or sea, had often to land "blind," gambling on a friendly reception (perhaps from one of the escape organizations) or, at worst, the opportunity to "set up shop" undisturbed. To make matters more difficult they were inhibited by the reticence of their political masters at home. SOE functioned through national Sections (France in fact was to have three, one called RF being responsible for de Gaulle's Free French, another, F, helping the remaining Frenchmen who were simply anti-German and a third, EU/P, dealing with Polish minorities in France—mostly coal miners in the north). SOE had hoped to operate with a comparatively free hand, its sponsors rather ingenuously believing that international politics could be excluded in line with government policy of giving assistance regardless of local internal politics. This was naive. Each émigré government had, perforce, a finger in its section's pie and applied pressure through the British government in what it judged to be the best interests of its peoples. In 1940 and early 1941 they were unanimously in agreement with Churchill in his insistence that trivial provocations would do irreparable—perhaps fatal—harm if, by inducing savage reprisals, the first shoots of resistance were damaged.

So SOE was forced to adopt a policy of gradual expansion in the operational sphere, though this in no way dampened Dalton's sweeping plans for the future. Linked to the concept of a "Fourth Arm" that would be equal in status to the other three services, his staff drew up formidable demands for manpower, equipment, air and sea support as well as a claim to political independence. Here, in fact, was the embryo of a European Commission; though it was dedicated to war, it attempted to unify the nations.

M.R.D. Foot, in one of the most lively official histories, *SOE in France,* says of SOE's inception: "For over a year . . . much of the energy of the high command of SOE was sapped away from the body's proper object . . . by bureaucrats' squabbles and intrigues about the future of political warfare." Dalton pleaded in his August paper for cooperation from all three fighting services, but SOE's list of demands so staggered the individual services that they reacted adversely and went on guard against a seemingly greedy newcomer. SOE asked for quantities of equipment and aircraft out of all proportion to what was then, and for many years would be, available, let alone what could be delivered without bringing every other activity to a halt. It was true that the Royal Navy could provide some transport, since it had available small ships for coastal raids related to the anti-invasion task. However, agents who landed from the sea inevitably entered the most intensely guarded sector of Hitler's Europe and would, therefore, start work "on the run." Easily the best method of infiltrating agents was by air, but aircraft were in shortest supply of all in a war that appeared to be dominated by the air weapon. In any case senior airmen, recognizing the opportunity to prove the validity of winning a war by bombing alone, resisted every attempt to divert their efforts—not only to SOE but also by way of direct support to the Navy and the Army. Air-Chief Marshal Portal, the RAF's greatest chief of air staff, denigrated SOE's schemes. "It is anybody's guess. My bombing offensive is not a gamble. Its dividend is certain; it is a gilt-edged investment. I cannot divert aircraft from a certainty to a gamble which may be a goldmine or may be completely worthless." Postwar analysis was to lower the gilt-edged price a little: only in the aftermath were the defects of strategic bombing to be revealed. In 1940 the air weapon offered a great panacea. Nevertheless the striking of an accurate balance of cost effectiveness between the air and the subversive weapons was—and is to this day—central to the debate surrounding both of these unorthodox methods. Enough to say that, in August 1940, SOE had the use of just two three-seater Lysanders, supplemented in September by a couple of Whitley bombers; and, a year later, still only one Lysander, eight Whitleys, a Maryland and a couple of the big Halifaxes. These were the aircraft in which the pioneer agents went forth to set Europe ablaze—and at the end of each "moon period" of intensive flying the aircrews were exhausted by too many missions.

In August the sort of rebelliousness which had already fitfully appeared in Holland had spread tentatively throughout Western Europe. The German military authorities took routine measures to curb it—imposing curfews and laying down rules for the taking of hostages against keeping the peace. SOE had nothing to do with these disturbances, since it had yet to receive an official directive from the Chiefs of Staff. Nevertheless SOE had tried to initiate exploratory missions. A radio party had been sea-landed in Norway, two or three had approached France by sea and turned back, while the first attempt at dropping a French agent by parachute on November 14 failed for the fundamental reason that the agent declined to jump. De Gaulle's Free French were doing rather more than SOE and by the end of July 1940 had established contacts in France. But the Free French suffered from self-induced difficulties. They were renegades in the eyes of those few of their countrymen who knew of them, and certainly regarded as such by the police whose antiguerrilla activity sometimes rivaled that of the Germans. They were also distrusted by most Frenchmen after their attempt to take Dakar in September, and by the British who suspected that they had blown the Dakar gaff to the Germans.[1]

---

[1] A suspicion which, it is now known, was utterly groundless—though typical enough in time of war.

The first genuine attempt at sabotage of a specific target was a combined British and Free French affair. The RAF asked SOE if it could ambush the pilots of Kampfgeschwader 100 at Vannes as they traveled by bus to the airfield. This unit contained the first Pathfinders, specialist crews who navigated to the target by beam-radio and lit fires as a guide to the rest of the bomber force over England. Gubbins planned the mission but, for want of ready-trained operatives, had to call on the Free French, who happened to possess some trained parachutists. Even so it was not until March 15, 1941, that a party of five set out in a Whitley to be dropped safely near the target. Only then was it discovered that the pilots no longer traveled by bus but went instead by car. So the French dispersed, making by different routes (that took in Paris and Bordeaux) for the coast where, after several scrapes, they were picked up by a submarine. The primary mission had been a failure, yet the impromptu reconnaissance had been of immense value by providing information about conditions in France. For example, it was found that, as yet, rail travel was absolutely uncontrolled; a clearer knowledge of rationing and new regulations was also gained, information which was vital to those who followed. Furthermore Bergé, the leader, took this opportunity to visit his fiancée's father and obtain permission to marry her back in London!

The mission revealed something more—orthodox military repugnance of SOE's intended methods. When Portal and Air-Marshal Harris heard that the ambush was to be laid by plainclothesmen they objected on the ground that this was the sort of operation with which the RAF would not wish to be associated. It was a matter of ethics, the difference between dropping a spy and encouraging assassins. It threatened, too, the survival of ordinary airmen shot down in combat. In law it was wrong, giving the Germans justification for taking reprisals against civilians.

Even had the Germans been aware of the Vannes operation, they could not ignore events in Holland. There, in February, the Defense Troop (WA) of the Dutch SS had begun openly to oppress the Jews, forbidding hotels to serve them and dragging them off in public. At once a few young Jews formed Action Groups and fought the WA when, on February 11, contrary to orders it entered the Jewish quarter. A member of the WA was killed and more were beaten up. In rapid succession other incidents followed; these included an attack on German police, which caused the Germans themselves to intervene on February 19. With brisk efficiency, they arrested 425 young Jews—and confidently expected the trouble to abate. Instead, there was escalation. Contrary to its previous policy, but undoubtedly in an effort to extend its prestige, the Communist Party called a series of wildcat strikes which culminated in the demand for a one-day protest strike on the 25th—a call publicized on thousands of leaflets, which also asked the people to give shelter to Jews. The strike was wildly successful, and spread beyond Amsterdam. Accustomed only to the servility of their own populace, but remembering the events of the 1920s, the Germans reacted violently, moving in police and soldiers who indulged freely in the use of firearms, killing a number of civilians. A curfew was imposed, and the streets cleared, but still the strike went on, provoking Himmler to order a state of emergency, and the arrest and deportation of 1,000 strikers. More people were killed, and then, as suddenly as it began, the strike collapsed.

The Dutch insurrection followed the Dalton prescription, but had nothing to do with SOE. It was highly significant, however—the first overt display of resistance by a large section of western populace and a warning of the danger inherent in flaunting the arrest of Jews. It also indicated the Communists' potential in raising rebellion. But it demonstrated, too, the ease with which, by the use of immediate uninhibited force, a handful of Germans could suppress the masses. Never again would the Dutch rise in flagrant opposition. Nor would the deportation of Jews stop—quite the contrary, it would increase, though more stealthily. Nevertheless Dutch temper had been demonstrated, and an undercurrent of feeble resistance given direction, even though it was recognized that, while there could be no compromise with the Germans, petty activity in partisan warfare did not pay.

In Norway, on March 4, the Germans experienced yet another type of uprising, this time externally inspired by British commandos, when they raided the Lofoten Islands, to destroy the local fish-oil factories and stocks. A small German garrison was captured, and the Norwegian inhabitants thrown into a state of ill-considered celebration, despite the destruction of their source of livelihood. But the celebrations ended once the British departed to leave the people to face the inevitable wave of repression. In London the Norwegian government was seriously upset by the raid for, to them, its short-term advantages were completely outweighed by long-term damage to their budding secret army. "Milorg"—the secret army HQ under General Ruge—made strong protests, raising a serious mistrust of SOE. SOE agents, for their part, were instructed to avoid contact with Milorg. It took a year's careful diplomatic negotiation to restore a working liaison between the Norwegian government and SOE, a year in which SOE tried to provoke Milorg into action and Milorg strove to stay passive while remaining the master of its own destiny, under command of the Norwegian government in London.

The position of partisan groups was indeed most delicate. Everybody realized that, in the absence of initial resistance, the prospects of building dynamic forces in the future were remote and that, therefore, the spirit of the people might decline. On the other hand there was a point at which overt attacks had to be withheld for fear of provoking such harsh retaliation that morale and organization might be utterly destroyed. To juggle the point of balance between discretion and indiscretion would always be crucial to the success or failure of nascent partisan forces. Judgment was made difficult by the distance between London, where impulses started on thin information, and indigenous groups in close touch with the actualities of German opposition. Misunderstandings between the two terminals were also aggravated by the uncertainties of radio communication. To prevent the Germans from fixing a radio station's position by Direction Finding (DF), transmissions had to be kept short and sent, of course, in code or cipher. Messages thus had to be short and were liable to arrive distorted. A perfect ratio between the escalation of violence and the demands of survival was impossible. The British felt compelled to sponsor operations that went beyond the level of social tolerance in the occupied countries, hoping that, in so doing, they would covertly place the onus for overt terror upon the Germans. But instinctively the local partisans refrained from committing suicide.

There was a dreadful irony about Britain's situation of 1940. At her moment of greatest weakness, when she most needed allies, there were, on the other side of the Channel, several million passive individuals a proportion of whom sympathized with her cause and, above all, desired liberation. If only they would stir up a ripple of unrest the Germans might be driven to expend disproportionate resources in keeping the peace within the base from which the invasion of Britain was meant to be launched. It might just shift the initiative the British way. Despite Churchill's reservations, Dalton and the army tried to move too fast for the politicians and for the embryo resistance movements, as in Norway. The millions held back, partly because there seemed little sense in making trouble on behalf of a nation which was patently losing and partly because organization and arms were lacking. Usually the various nationalities "policed" themselves and so the Germans needed but a few thousand men of their own on call to deal with exceptional outbreaks such as occurred in Holland. The Occupation in no way overstretched Germany and, indeed, from the economic point of view, redoubled her strength. The lesson was obvious: partisans are not much use to the losing side unless they are prepared to make enormous sacrifices. Nobody in Western Europe was ready for sacrifices in 1940, when it was better to wait and see if unification under Germany might produce long-term benefits—as a unified Europe might well do of itself.

In Poland, however, the future prospects were clearly intolerable. The reallocation of frontiers having been dictated and the Poles brought under strict control on November 2, 1939, Hans Frank issued a decree instituting Jewish ghettoes in the major cities. Before the war Poland contained three million Jews—a population about that of Norway. Now they were to be herded into walled-off enclosures chiefly in Warsaw, Kraków, Vilna and Bialystok, there to manufacture for the Germans while awaiting the Final Solution—which, as time passed, was to mean extermination at Treblinka and in similar camps. The Jewish ordeal in the Warsaw Ghetto is summarized by this account of working conditions: "In murky rooms, in dark caves, they sat on stools and benches" making clothes and all manner of goods. The workers who made brushes cut the bristles by hand and bent the wires by hand. "The fingers of the women and children were always bleeding. Their eyes were heavy-lidded with fatigue and their shoulders bowed." The food ration fell below starvation level. Discipline was administered with the utmost severity by Jewish police in the first place, backed up by a handful of Germans if necessary. When, at last, Europeans began to recognize and understand the meaning of this sort of thing, in terms of the future of humanity and the development of German policy, it was the sharpest of all spurs to resistance. But in the early years it went largely undetected and so nothing was done by outsiders and little enough by Polish Jews and the Poles themselves.

What became known in 1942 as the Polish Home Army had received a serious setback due to the June 1940 moratorium on its activities. The Polish population adopted a passive, wait-and-see attitude because they were far more fearful of offending the Germans by minor acts of hostility than of an unimaginable holocaust. Moreover, although the Jews, in addition to the Poles, had created resistance groups, all were virtually defenseless. Though the caches laid down in 1939 had partly been used up, local arms manufacture had begun in secret—in cellars and German-sponsored factories; but this was on only the most tenuous scale, liable to interruption and quite inadequate to sustain a prolonged fight. A Russian mission flown to Poland in January 1942 to form a workers' party based on Communist cells and to accelerate operations against the Germans achieved little. From the

British nothing except a few key parties could be expected: their most precious contributions were radio sets and expert weapon instructors ready for the day when the weapons would perhaps arrive. The more agents that were sent, the fewer the supply containers. Also the more subversive activity there was, the greater became German counter-measures by raids which discovered arms almost as fast as they were produced.

Flights to Poland took so long that they could only be undertaken by an occasional Whitley aircraft sortie in winter. At extreme range they were repeatedly interrupted by foul weather and subject to such great navigational difficulties that accurate location of the correct dropping zone was always a matter of chance. Once an agent was delivered he probably stayed unless, in dire emergency, he could be extracted by a hazardous journey through some neutral country. France and Belgium could be reached by the little Lysander aircraft which would land and take off from small fields, but this was absolutely impossible for the clumsy long-range bomber types in Poland. The first SOE flight to Poland took place on February 15, 1941—and was the last until November—although there were progressively more in the next three years. Even in later days teams sometimes took off four or five times before it was at last possible to land them. Many, including the first, dropped in the wrong place, lost their equipment and actually came down in Germany and had to walk to safety. But as time went by and communications between England and the Home Army improved, the planning of flights became more efficient, aided by radio reception of weather reports from Poland and a recognized marking system of dropping zones. None of these systems could be activated until the first pathfinders had been sent in "blind." There were more friends than enemies at the other end, provided they avoided German or Russian centers of occupation, but chance took care of the majority. Out of the forty-eight parachutists who went in before May 1942, forty-six survived the first few hours on Polish soil, a proportion which remained much the same as time went by and German air defense improved.

The first SOE agents [2] did not take part in Polish partisan warfare. It was their task to restrain the Poles until some as yet undefined moment arrived. But in the field of intelligence they were of immediate importance particularly when, in the spring of 1941, signs became

[2] Although SOE sponsored agents and "vetted" flights to Poland, those agents came under control of the Polish authorities once they set foot on Polish soil and were supplied with Polish, not SOE, codes. Nearly all were of Polish nationality, though several were of British extraction recruited from the commercial community.

manifest of a redeployment of German military resources into western Poland on a scale far in excess of police requirements. It matched what had already taken place in southeastern Europe, as the Germans entered Hungary, Rumania and Bulgaria in preparation for the absorption of Yugoslavia and Greece. Information from these countries, however, had quickly been acquired in Britain because neutral observers could move about freely. From Germany itself, of course, accurate news was extremely sparse, even though the Americans had missions resident in the country and were willing to transmit what they saw. Poland was isolated, however, and the secret radio network in its infancy. Hence confirmation of hints that the German concentration was against Russia, and not simply the Balkans, was slow to appear and, but for the work of Polish agents, might never have arrived at all. For the Polish Home Army itself, these reports were of paramount local importance too. Soon, it seemed, they would acquire a new, if suspect, ally—and on their doorstep.

Yet, as the war advanced to another climax, partisan warfare lay fast in the doldrums. Life went on within close limits of tolerance.

CHAPTER FOUR

With Nothing to Lose

Until Hitler launched his invasion against Yugoslavia and Greece on April 6, 1941, German success had a steady beat, the assimilation of its victims following a regular pattern. By now his leaders had become accustomed to the subservience of conquered peoples. Yugoslavia, a disunited consortium of six independently minded provinces, seemed scarcely the nation likely to raise homogeneous resistance, while Greece, exhausted by five months' overstrained mountain warfare against the inept Italian invasion, was approaching the end of her tether. In overflowing confidence Hitler behaved increasingly with undisguised depravity.

The instructions to invade the West in 1940 had been tempered by a degree of humanitarian caution. But in 1941 the Wehrmacht was told "to attack Yugoslavia in a concentric way as soon as possible, to destroy her armed forces and to dissolve the national territory," while the Luftwaffe was "to destroy the capital Belgrade in attack by waves." Such violence reflected Hitler's contempt for the nations of Eastern Europe but ignored their spiritual differences with the West. Western political and racial factions were inured by generations of liberal association to mild and relatively unrebellious government; Serbs, Croats, Slovenes, Montenegrins and Macedonians remained prone to settle their disagreements by sudden resort to violence, while the Greeks maintained a healthy distaste for dictatorial government sharpened by a decade of restlessness under authoritarianism. By temperament the voluble Balkan people were as much geared to fighting as to talking, their motivations steeped in poverty as well as guided by political and psychological traditions. Western Europeans enjoyed a far higher standard of living than the Southeastern people: the poorest of French peasants was rich by comparison with his Balkan counterpart, who as often as not lived in squalor off barren uplands. Many agrarian Yugoslavians had learned from bitter experience that, with nothing to lose, it was often essential to fight for what was quite unobtainable by peaceful means. Even in peacetime they lived close to the boundaries of intolerance, and enjoyed a reputation for banditry.

Then came the Germans and their Bulgarian, Hungarian and Italian allies with all the trappings of the ultimate police state, committed to dismember Yugoslavia and subjugate Greece with a tempestuous thoroughness which made the storm they raised over Western Europe seem like the gentlest zephyr.

Faced with the threat of invasion it had been the immediate reaction of General Simovic (who led the revolt against the young King Peter's government when it agreed to let the Germans in) to propose "establishing a Salonika front and at the same time sending men to the mountains to fight the Nazis." There was insufficient time for this, of course, since the invasion came but a fortnight after the revolt and swept all before it. Nevertheless some hasty instructions sent key men into the wilds to lay down widespread arms caches at the same time as the regular forces were surrendering.

In political leadership Yugoslavia was both fortunate and unfortunate. Supreme in strength of character and the art of command, Josip Broz combined diplomatic insight with soldierly prowess. Trained in revolutionary tactics by the Comintern during the 1930s, he had run the "underground" from France into Spain during the Civil War, and then assumed leadership of the underground Communist Party in his own country—an organization which, for twenty years, had thrived in the fight for survival against suppression and learned its trade along with the Republican forces during the Spanish Civil War. It was Broz who first formed partisan bands—a political hierarchy already well practiced in defying and evading authority. But the brigands of Montenegro, who, in the First World War, had conducted a prolonged campaign against the Central Powers and were the first exponents of anti-Axis guerrilla warfare, tended merely to form armed, mountain-village communities, geared to self-protection and local raiding rather than a unified struggle for Yugoslavia.

There was also a hastily formed party of Royalist officers who grouped themselves under Colonel Drava Mihailovic, established "cells" in the mountains and forests and named themselves Cetniks, after the original organization which, after 1918, had helped consolidate Serbian influence in non-Serbian areas. Mihailovic was a military bureaucrat rather than a commander, lacking the immense strength of character which Broz had acquired in hard times. Mihailovic's wild beard concealed a softer spirit, more attuned to the office desk than the rugged field of war. He could deviously intrigue among the plethora of provincial political splinter groups which appeared in the Axis wake, but his military purpose was ambiguous and, therefore, the antithesis of the demands of successful guerrilla warfare.

May and June were months of search and discovery. Mihailovic started from nothing, sending out emissaries in the name of the old government with appeals to form Cetnik bands and then prepare for the day "when the time is ripe." Cetnik strategy was geared to waiting, not combat—the opposite of Broz's intentions. Even Broz admitted that the need to strike at the earliest moment had to be tempered at first by the demands of training. All agreed that premature insurrection might be fatal to future chances. The time was thus best spent in making propaganda, raising the morale of the people by exhortation, acquiring an arms factory at Uzice and forming small squads trained in sabotage. Nevertheless Broz's Partisans firmly adopted the unwritten dictum that the best training was to be found in heat of battle, that expansion would come with success and that fervid patriotism had to advance in conjunction with a readiness to suffer in the service of future unity and the Communist cause. Compromise was anathema to them.

The Hungarians, Italians and Bulgarians were intent on dividing the spoils while the Germans hastily redeployed for the forthcoming invasion of Soviet Russia. The latter contented themselves with taking control in the key areas—Slovenia, parts of central Serbia, Macedonia and along the main arteries leading to Piraeus (this port supplied conquered Crete and, thence, the Axis forces in North Africa) those places which, above all, provided essential minerals, such as bauxite. The rest was handed over to their partners to govern as they wished, though on the clear understanding that, as a nation, Yugoslavia must cease to exist. Croats were to be played off against Serbs, religious bodies set in mutual opposition, Jews and political parties exterminated, along with the intelligentsia. The population was to be reduced to starvation. This may have symbolized Hitler's contempt for all racially inferior species, but it ignored the reaction of combatant human beings who happened to live in spacious, complex terrain that was ideal for guerrilla warfare. Nevertheless while the Ustase, a Croatian Fascist organization, indulged in genocide against the Serbs, the soldiers of Italy and Bulgaria casually made themselves at home. In Greece, where the Italian Eleventh Army became known as the "S'agapo army"—meaning "I love you" (in reference to its convivial relationship with the local populace), there were marriages between soldiers and Grecian women: in the Italian sector, insurrection was held at a lower temperature than in the German, where sabotage was sparked off by the Communist EAM.

Discontent was quick to crystallize wherever the Germans happened to be. It began slowly and diplomatically in dealings with the Italians over mutually satisfactory boundaries of occupation. It rapidly blossomed into violence from Tito's Partisans (as Broz was now better known) on June 22, when the invasion of Russia began. That day Tito received a signal from the Comintern calling for guerrilla attacks against the German lines of communication, a desperate proposition which could little affect the main campaign. Nevertheless, on July 5, Tito addressed a pamphlet to the Yugoslavian people. "Now is the time, the hour has struck to rise like one man in the battle against the invaders . . . killers of our peoples. Do not falter in the face of any enemy terror." At once came the first shots from an ambush in Serbia, aimed by a student, Savatije, an electrician called Steva and another man called Srecko. They killed two Germans and forced another to surrender.

To understand the nature of the partisan warfare which broke out in the Balkans it is essential to relate the density of Axis forces to the size of the country—a crucial factor in every guerrilla war, but particularly so in mountainous and wooded terrain. Yugoslavia, Albania and Greece together measured some 160,000 square miles. There, in July 1941, lay eight German and the equivalent of ten Italian divisions plus elements of a Bulgarian and an Hungarian corps in addition to gendarmerie and Ustace. They could hold the centers and lines of communication but not the interior, which, for most of the time, was unpoliced. Hitler and his diplomatic advisers paid scant attention to human decencies, while the Wehrmacht High Command (OKW) went to war lacking a prescribed antiguerrilla policy. But the German Army, following the tenets of self-protection, trained each man and unit to take care of itself, and the same could be said of its allies. To them all the outbreak of guerrilla warfare in the Balkans came as a shock since it was in such contrast to their experience in the West. Moreover it presented the army with the task of mounting countermeasures, since Himmler's forces were committed already to digesting occupied Russian territory. In the Balkans retribution was improvised and became uneven. While the Italians, hotly engaged in August by a furious Montenegrin rebellion, were hard pressed to maintain a foothold, the Germans laid down an arbitrary rate for the execution of hostages at three hundred for each German killed.

It was the speed and intensity of the Montenegrin uprising, linked to its location in the most inaccessible part of the country, which embarrassed the Axis. Nor was it coincidence that the Montenegrins struck first, for not only did their territory contain the choicest arms caches, but their opponent was vulnerable. The Italian army of occupation gave up in profusion—four thousand of them, with all their weapons—and the revolt spread wider to Serbia, where Partisans and Cetniks liberated entire districts, cut the Axis lines of communication, and set up arms manufacturing plants as it became doubtful if aid could be expected from either the Russians or the British. Montenegrin losses were high and, suddenly, for political motives, as much due to Cetniks as to Italians; for the latter now agreed to leave the hills to the Cetniks who, disenchanted with Tito's Communists, for reasons that are explained below, undertook to control the Partisans. By mid-September, the fighting had spread far and wide, to include an outbreak of strikes and isolated sabotage by the Communist EAM in Greece. The Axis was compelled to institute sterner countermeasures than the simple police actions which had quelled Holland in February. By opening an antiguerrilla offensive they admitted, by implication, that the Balkan campaign had never really been completed.

This drift into guerrilla war polarized the relationship between Tito and Mihailovic. The swift expansion of the original Partisan bands into seventy thousand rabid combatants spread loosely around the country may well have struck Tito as dangerously premature, but in the circumstances he could hardly douse its enthusiasm without damaging Partisan morale. Events had escalated more quickly than he had expected, though it was encouraging to find national unity reflected in the number of Cetniks fighting at his side. To Mihailovic he proposed a pooling of their resources and a common strategy, pointing to the danger of accidental collisions between separate bands working independently towards the same objective. But Mihailovic took his orders from Simovic and the Royalist émigré government in London, and their policy was the same as Churchill's and Dalton's SOE—evasion of battle and conservation of strength for a supreme moment—a view which Mihailovic put to Tito when they met, for the first time, in September. It was a disturbing time for Mihailovic since not only were the Germans beginning to react strongly against his Cetniks, but he recognized in Tito's Communists, with their Red Star badges, a group which preached the abolition of the monarchy and which posed as great a threat as the Germans to what he stood for.

The outside world was ignorant of these events because it was not until September that Mihailovic was able to establish external radio contact, and not until September 16 that SOE Cairo landed "blind" its first mission from a submarine on the Montenegrin coast. This party, twelve strong and led by Yugoslavians, included a thirty-year-old British officer called Captain D.T. Hudson—a civil engineer who lacked military or diplomatic experience but who had worked in Yugoslavia before the war.

The tardiness and halfheartedness of the British intervention was only partially explained by transport shortages similar to those which hindered SOE London. SOE Cairo also suffered from weak internal organization (which then and later rejected the London system of running a subdepartment for each nation) and hostile relations with GHQ. Not that General Wavell, who handed over as Commander-in-Chief at the end of June, had been averse to irregular warfare—quite the reverse; Wavell, after all, was a general who admired Lawrence and who had sponsored the Long Range Desert Patrol, the SAS and the raising of Gideon Force to wage guerrilla war in Abyssinia under Orde Wingate. The trouble arose from the attitude of established politicians and staff officers who resented a rapidly expanding interloper moving among the older, secret departments; they attempted either to eliminate SOE or bring it under GHQ control. SOE was young and brash, the antithesis of the older services; neither side was innocent of intrigue. Charge and countercharge seemed at times to take precedence over prosecuting the war just when the British were most hard pressed in the desert and resisting semisecret Axis incursions of an SOE nature into the Levant. It took a special mission from SOE London, in July, to restore working relations by changing the heads of SOE departments and making SOE Cairo operationally responsible to GHQ. But the new system had to be adjusted, and in the meantime the Balkans imbroglio would not wait. When Hudson at last arrived it was to find acute radio communication difficulties with London, Cairo and Moscow (through, at the most, two sets) while there was only one aircraft and occasionally a submarine available for the support of clandestine operations. Hudson could hardly instigate swift investigations. It was many days before he was taken to Tito and October 28 before he met Mihailovic. Tito and the Partisans impressed him, but it was Mihailovic who laid claim to be the sole representative of the Yugoslavian people and sent fulsome reports of his prowess and requirements to London, while doctoring Hudson's messages and forbidding the Briton to join him in talks with Tito. He claimed he could raise an army "in a few days" and stated that an accommodation with the Partisans had been reached. This was quite untrue. Early in November Tito's men had unsuccessfully tried to capture Mihailovic and on November 11 Mihailovic was engaged in talks with the German staff and collaborating with the Italians.

At a time when every possible aid was needed, to take pressure off the Russians even more than the British, the latter were in a dilemma and the former inflexible in their preconceived notions. The British, faithful to their pledge of support to resistance anywhere, provided it was through the agents of a *de jure* regime, could hardly reject Mihailovic's well-formulated reports in favor of Hudson's garbled messages. In September they had opted to support Mihailovic because he represented the *de jure* government, a sign of intent rather than concrete aid, as it happened, since neither the stores nor adequate transport were available. Nevertheless, towards the end of October, when Mihailovic and Tito met a second time, Hudson managed to report that Cetniks were fighting Partisans and suggested that British aid should be withheld. The Russians, meantime, were giving wholehearted propaganda support to the Cetniks, whose government they recognized, to the exclusion of Tito's Partisans; they had no liaison mission in the country at all, nor did they give much credit to Tito since he had failed to impress them during his Comintern course.

Mihailovic settled for collaboration with General Nedic's pro-Axis Serbian government rather than Tito's Communists. On December 2 he told London that he had started "complete guerrilla warfare" against the Germans but next day ordered an attack on the Partisans, even though the Germans continued to harry his Cetniks. He bowed to temptation when information reached him that internecine warfare had broken out between Communist extremists in Montenegro and Macedonia, weakening Tito's position. But Mihailovic's Cetniks came under the pressure of the Axis First Offensive which started late in September, and by December was closing in on the Partisan bands near Uzice.

This offensive was not only a remarkable demonstration of German strength when the campaign in Russia was at the peak of the drive against Moscow; it was the one coherent act in an involved situation. With France pacified, Greece uttering only a low murmur of discontent and victory seemingly imminent in Russia, it was permissible to extract a division from each of those countries and send them as reinforcements to Yugoslavia for a systematic purge of the lines of communication, followed by a sweeping envelopment of the mountains surrounding Uzice in the area east of the River Drina. It was a classic antipartisan operation of the sort von Seeckt had directed in China, fought by one hundred thousand well-equipped men with tanks and aircraft against thirty thousand ill-armed, squabbling guerrillas. It was thus the moment for the classic guerrilla defensive gambit of dispersion into space—executed with commendable skill by the Partisans but bungled by the Cetniks, who virtually disintegrated. By the end of December the Germans claimed two thousand guerrilla casualties at scant loss to themselves.

In the heat of battle the diplomatic exchanges ceased. Hudson lost contact with Mihailovic and therefore with the outside world too, but whereas Mihailovic managed to reestablish radio contact a few weeks later, Hudson was unheard of for six months. In consequence the British and Yugoslavs in London could only maintain tacit support of Mihailovic while abortively seeking corroboration of Hudson's last transmitted doubts—a search which was hampered by the utter failure of four successive missions to reach their objectives.

In the meantime Tito's Partisans were at war with everybody in sight and befriended by none, fighting a battle of retreat and evasion with arms that could be found only from the enemy. For the factory at Uzice, with its output of 450 rifles a day, was quickly lost, and the Cetniks became sworn opponents instead of voluntary allies. Vladimir Dedijer described in his diary how, at Kosjeric, a gendarme and his assistants "killed seventeen comrades, including girls. . . . The girls were first raped, then Ajdacic roasted them to death." True or false —and there is no reason to disbelieve Dedijer—these were but tiny steps in a mounting bestiality. At Krguyevac on October 21 over two thousand men and boys were shot by the Germans helped by Ustace—an incident of some importance since it strongly persuaded Mihailovic to acquiesce in Axis countermeasures. The wholesale massacre of the populace had begun, accelerated by Field-Marshal Keitel of OKW when he signed an order which stated, "In reprisal for the life of a German soldier the general rule should be capital punishment for fifty to a hundred Communists. The manner of execution must be arranged to have a deterrent effect." Aimed primarily at Russian partisans, it settled on a rate for hostages where none had existed before—and Yugoslavia was the first to feel its full weight in a genuine guerrilla context. Almost the first hostages to go were the Serbian élite to which Mihailovic belonged, and as a result, his local leaders were eager to make an accommodation with the Germans by turning on the Partisans. In December Tito was compelled to desist from attacks on the Italians (a lucrative source of arms) by the needs of defense against the Cetniks. Civil war, the predatory companion of guerrilla war, and the most morally degenerative of all conflicts, had begun.

In deep complexity the guerrilla war raged in the mountains as

Tito and his followers sought safety on the run; moving sinuously through snowbound passes; staging from village to village and from peak to peak; dodging the bombers; fighting rearguard action after rearguard action; holding off Cetniks and Axis; succoring the wounded; sorrowfully abandoning the aged and the young to the viciousness of a hotly pursuing enemy; saving what they could from the carnage—but losing three thousand Communist Party members alone in two months of being hunted until at last they reached temporary cover at Foca in Bosnia.

Two years had passed since the invasion of Poland and only now in Yugoslavia had full-scale partisan warfare broken out in Europe. In Yugoslavia alone every element of the classic guerrilla struggle was to be found on a nationwide scale—the disruption of factions into civil war, anarchy, utter ruthlessness, the lie and counterlie of propaganda, the ragged, ill-armed bands with their indistinct uniforms, the women marching at their men's side, the swift cut and thrust between closely coordinated regular forces and loosely organized bands which gradually coalesced only to be flung apart. Above all the hideous hatreds which were to poison the years ahead.

Within the Yugoslavian movement, however, dwelt a unique spirit unknown in past European guerrilla warfare (except, perhaps, among the Irish patriots of 1920), detected in a flash of insight by the German representative in Belgrade. "I get the impression that even news about the surrender of the USSR would not result in the capitulation of these bandits who are as tough as the devil," he had written in September on the eve of recommending the all-out Axis offensive. It might have been a just comment on formal warfare, too, for this partisan force was, in organization and effect, converting itself tentatively into a new national army with ambitions far outreaching those of simple sabotage bands. This was a disciplined force which bravely thrived on adversity rather than cautiously blossoming only in victory.

CHAPTER FIVE

Reluctant Partisans

On July 3, 1941, Josef Stalin reversed twenty years of Soviet military policy when, in a radio broadcast to the nation, he called for the formulation of partisan units to "blow up bridges and roads, damage telephone and telegraph lines, set fire to forests, stores and transport." By demanding that the enemy must "be hounded and annihilated at every step and all their measures frustrated," he admitted the inability of the Red Army to secure the frontier defenses or hold the hinterland.

Hitler correctly interpreted this as a cry of despair. He could assume, in a summer overburdened by optimism, that the absence of guerrilla warfare in the other theaters of war would set the trend in his newest domains. He would hear his generals recall how Russians surrendered in droves to a handful of Germans in the First World War. Yet since he was among the enlightened who recognized that times had changed along with methods of persuasion and propaganda, he might have taken warning instead of encouragement. Abroad, Stalin's plea was plainly heard and understood—and not only by Tito. Every Communist movement in Europe listened and overnight turned from neutrality to open aggression against the Germans, obeying the request from Russia. A fresh power of incalculable potential was added to the opposition against Germany, a force which denied any sort of restraint in the struggle. Until Germany attacked Russia each nation she had overrun had been careful to minimize loss of life, fearing a repetition of the slaughter of the previous war. Germany, too, had aimed at short, inexpensive campaigns but now, for the first time, she encountered an opponent who was prepared to suffer immense losses, whose leaders were calling for absolute war cloaked in a struggle between the fundamental conflicting ideologies of Communism and Fascism—demanding religious war, one of the most pitiless conflicts of all. There had been nothing quite like it in Europe since the Thirty Years' War.

Yet, on the Eastern Front itself, the immediate partisan threat hardly showed during the twelve days' orthodox campaigning that led to the destruction of the Soviet frontier armies. A German advance of 275 miles from East Prussia through Lithuania and Latvia, and another of similar distance towards Minsk, had caused disintegration. In the Baltic States, with no place to hide, the Russians surrendered piecemeal, and in the Minsk sector thousands took shelter in the abundant forests there supinely to await their fate. Official Soviet descriptions of their initial resistance are grossly exaggerated as well as contradictory. When they have been willing to admit shortcomings in overall preparedness against the German attack (of which they had received ample warning both from their own intelligence and that of the British), they can hardly be credited with possessing a well-founded, prewar partisan movement. No doubt there had been planning of a conceptual nature but of coordinated execution there was none. Not that failure arose out of departmental indifference; it stemmed, in fact, from the indigenous people's distaste for rule by the Greater Russians, from their hope that a new autonomy might extinguish rule by foreigners—be it from Moscow or Berlin.

The Balts—the Letts, Estonians and Lithuanians—had only recently, in 1940, lost their short-lived independence (virtually won for them by the Poles in 1920) to the Soviets, and shared the fate of the East sector Poles. First among the Soviet states to suffer the German invasion, the Balts were virulently anti-Soviet—and furthermore had been quite closely politically linked to the Germans in the past. Further east, the White Russians adopted their customary opportunism. They were willing to accept a German presence, recollecting that the German occupation in 1918 had been less severe than that of the Soviets, and that Stalin's liquidation of the kulaks, allied to collectivization in the 1930s, had done nothing to improve their lot. Then to the south waited the Ukrainians, ready, like the Balts, for pro-German activity, spurred on by the local adherents of Canaris whose recruitment of Ukrainian dissidents had begun long before Hitler announced the eastward drive. Perhaps they would fight as hard for independence in 1941 as they had in 1920. Certainly the Germans were entering zones all of which were potentially more favorably inclined than any they had attacked so far. It is no exaggeration to say that the indigenous population welcomed them as liberators, ready to help rather than hinder the conquest, while the Red Army fought its opening campaign under a far greater threat of guerrilla resistance than did the Germans.

Yet Hitler allowed neither political nor humanitarian considerations to take advantage of this condition. His preconceived ideas rode roughshod. In March he told the army that commissars were to be treated as criminals and could be shot on the spot by troops. The orders for Operation Barbarossa stated that trials of guerrillas would have to be excluded for lack of judicial staff and time. The troops were to take "ruthless action themselves," both in the narrow belt of the operational zone and across the rear army area established for the task of administering and guarding the supply services. Afterwards would come the imposition of the Nazi system—the creation of a Zone of the Interior governed by Reich Commissioners, with the assistance of the Wehrmacht, under the overall direction of the SS Reichsführer, Heinrich Himmler, and executed by Alfred Rosenberg as Reich Minister for the Occupied Eastern Territories. And within the Wehrmacht zones, too, elements of the political SS were to operate under the aegis of army groups. Four Einsatzgruppen composed of SD, Gestapo and Waffen SS, were formed for "the extermination of undesirables"—anything from Jews to gypsies, lunatics to commissars. Yet experience at last had taught even the SS that undisguised bestiality was as abhorrent to normal, decent Germans as to the defeated, so the task of the Einsatzgruppen was thinly disguised under the cover of "antipartisan or antiguerrilla action"—a term which embraced a multitude of sins.

Who began the partisan war on the Eastern Front it is difficult to ascertain. There is record of activity on June 23 in Lithuania by five hundred Russians, many of them Red Army men who had changed into civilian clothing. This band was composed largely of Greater Russians, many of whom may have been on leave or in course of mobilization: their action was that of normal, disciplined troops in defense of a forest position. The Germans were in error to consider it a deliberate partisan attack. It is certain, however, that, on the same day, Einsatzgruppe A covertly started to set one section of the Lithuanian population against another until, between June 25 and 26, Lithuanian bands were murdering fifteen hundred Jews in what were known as "self-cleansing operations." Thus began German stimulation of resistance where none need have existed at all. By these repulsive methods they could hardly have done more to raise opposition even had it been their deliberate policy to do so.

A report by Einsatzgruppe A claims to have liquidated 37,180 Jews and Communist leaders up to October 31, 1941, on the northern front, mostly before the first signs of an organized guerrilla resistance had appeared. There is a report of eight juveniles from a children's home who hid "three heavy machine guns, fifteen rifles, several thousand rounds of ammunition . . . and several packages of poison gas Ebrit in the woods." They were shot, the victims of a confidence trick by the Russian agent who persuaded them to do the job. Incidents of this sort were commonplace. Every arms cache was at risk, however, when members of the local populace were ready to loot or report their location to the Germans, and, by the autumn, special equipment for guerrilla warfare in the German rear was in short supply.

In the flush of their sweeping advances and seemingly all-embracing encirclements the German High Command imposed a dilemma upon itself. Modern mechanized armies achieve security by constant mobility. They fail when supply lines are cut or if a defeated enemy rabble cannot be captured or neutralized swiftly. By the first week in July, with a broken foe before them and a mass of undigested and disorganized enemies cluttering their rearward zone, the Germans lacked sufficient strength simultaneously to garner the fruits of victory and continue the advance. Hostile acts by isolated Red Army units far behind the so-called front played but a small part in disrupting the German plans and were indistinguishable from conventional action on a fluid battlefield, but their presence acted as a deterrent to further advances until they could be eliminated. Ironically the Germans were deprived of victory by the magnitude of success in battle, the reality of their proportionately meager resources being woefully inadequate for the total subjugation of Russia. Even after the enemy groups had been dispersed, either into prison camps or because they had escaped in droves to the east, a profusion of equipment was left lying about because the Germans had not the capability to collect it.

In July and August, fascinated by a campaign to delight the hearts of orthodox soldiers, the German generals turned a blind eye to what went on in the captured zones. There is as much evidence to say that the army shot commissars as to suggest that the generals circumvented the Commissar Order. No doubt some among the officers were deluded by the antipartisan device which concealed the real work of the Einsatzgruppen, while the rest either surmised what went on, condoned it or were afraid to protest. They can hardly have been indifferent. By mid-September, however, guerrilla warfare in the rear had become a reality that could no longer be ignored—hence Keitel's instruction of September 16 which, as we have seen, bore down harshly upon the Yugoslavs. Not that the activity was so intense as seriously to deflect the German offensive effort—the difficulties of moving supplies along mud-gutted roads and of repairing equipment that broke down in the longest mechanized campaign yet experienced far outweighed the distractions of a few pinprick raids and insurrections. In fact the vast majority of the west Russian indigenous peoples were collaborating with the Germans, despite SS racial atrocities. As the railway gauge was altered to accept German rolling stock the local populace willingly did much of the work and operated the system. Money had to be earned, after all, and the harvest gathered and distributed to prevent famine. It was village headmen who persuaded the people to cooperate with the Germans since, with the Soviets on the run, it looked as if the invaders were going to be the victors.

The Soviets' title for the Second World War is the Great Patriotic War—which, in so far as their partisans were concerned, amounted to rich Orwellian doubletalk. Undeniably, patriotism was extolled by their propaganda and indubitably inspired sections of the Communist hierarchy—above all the commissars—who had everything to lose if the regime collapsed. But the battle front had shifted deeply into the hinterland before a coherent resistance movement took shape—a measure in itself of Soviet unpreparedness. First there had to be an organization where none existed, then cells (based upon territorial regions) around which resistance would coalesce.

In July the parachuting of small sabotage groups behind the German southern front was a purely military operation in an area untouched by severe fighting, not part of the all-embracing political force being planned in Moscow under Marshal Voroshilov. For the Soviet leadership envisaged partisans as a body separate from the Red Army. A week after Stalin's plea there came into being, under the Central Committee of the Communist Party Organization, a special Partisan Force with tentacles thrown downwards through the Administrative and Propaganda Department of the army and outwards through the Departments of State Security (the NKVD and NKGB). At the lowest level political officers formed guerrilla bands which varied from seventy-five to one hundred and fifty men and whose primary task was to provide antiparachutist units to guard the Red Army rear, going "underground" after the Germans arrived in strength. In addition, small units were based on factories and farms, and within the railway system—an expedient very similar to what had been done in Britain in 1940 by the formation of Local Defence Volunteers (later known as Home Guard)—and just about as potentially ineffective, even though the British put the LDV under the War Office instead of the Home Office.

The orders to the partisan units emphasized Stalin's original concept—attack on the enemy logistical systems. Only the smallest enemy detachments and individuals were to be harried since it was realized how little could be achieved in open battle by ill-trained men—one of the fundamental differences that existed between the reluctant partisans of Russia and the enthusiastic patriots of Yugoslavia. Shortages of ammunition and deficiencies in training were perennial. A celebrated

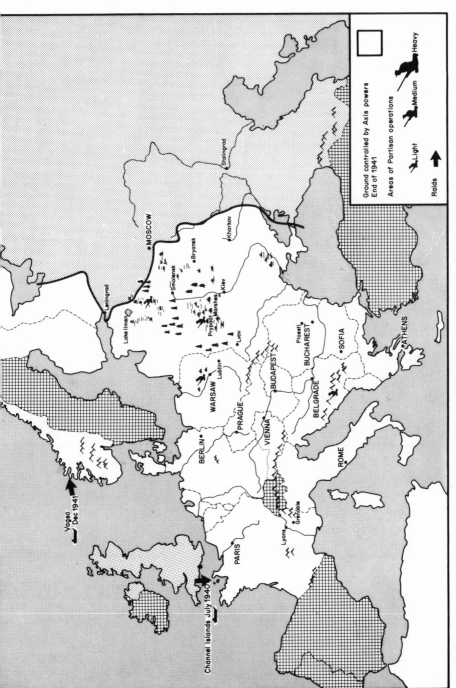

Early pin-pricks—the limited extent of raiding and European partisan activity as the time of maximum axis expansion approaches at the end of 1941.

Russian guerrilla leader, A. Kovpak, describes digging for abandoned ammunition in the snow as if it were gold. He also says, "Time could not be spared for training—it was combined with the execution of battle tasks. . . . Three men would be assigned to guard duties, one with an automatic rifle and two riflemen. One rifleman would keep watch while the other, in reserve, would sit in the bushes nearby with the automatic-rifleman, with whose assistance he would study the automatic." There is scarcely mention of target practice: indeed, partisans were notoriously bad shots for that very reason. Operations aimed point-blank at the enemy would always take second place to the long-term aim of reestablishing Soviet rule where it had been broken by the German presence. Soviet propaganda was endlessly directed towards patriotic motives and undeniably won its successes by stimulating the emotional streak in the young and among a few intellectuals. On its own, however, propaganda was not enough. It had to be backed by credible news of success by the Red Army, deliveries of weapons, positive contact with a central authority and, above all, a strong and imaginative command and leadership.

As a symbol of success the Red Army was of negative value until December 1941 when, at last, the German Army came to a standstill in front of Leningrad, Moscow and Rostov—as much out of its own exhaustion as from Russian resistance. From the Russian counter-offensive, when it began on December 6, the partisans drew real encouragement: their activities at once increased even if they were hampered by a shortage of arms. By then, of course, contact between the partisan bands and the higher direction from within Russian-held territory had begun to coalesce—though inefficiently. As early as August the German intercept service had begun to detect radio traffic directed at partisan bands and from this was able to assemble an order of battle, locations and tentative warning of hostile intentions. Communication by couriers with the bands through the German lines was never very difficult, for enormous gaps yawned wide for them to come and go more or less as they chose. Radio had to be used, however, because it brought immediate response whereas couriers took far too long.

At the end of 1941 many of the weapons recovered from the débâcle were either breaking down or falling into German hands. Bulk supply by land was unreliable and so the Russians turned at once to air transport, though at first in a very haphazard manner, and in low numbers due to a dire shortage of aircraft as a result of heavy losses. Nevertheless, during the winter of 1941–42 a special air army came into being for the support of partisans, using practically every type of airplane in the Russian Air Force but depending principally upon the little single-engined, twin-seater U2 training biplane which could land and take off in short spaces and was not in the least hampered by its short range since it flew to its objectives from airfields located close behind the front. In the matter of air support policy the Russians had, therefore, arrived at a diametrically opposite solution to that of the British. While the latter gave preference to strategic air forces, as the best means to attack the enemy's homeland and back areas, and thus starved their partisans, the Russians rejected strategic air forces in favor of support for the field armies. They preferred explosives to be carried by agents into the enemy rear, but by so doing left the German homeland inviolate. Only by chance did Germany's foes arrive at a comprehensive system of attack against every corner of the Third Reich, yet this not only had a crucial impact on economic warfare, besides guerrilla operations, but also raised conflicting moral issues in connection with noncombatants.

The volume of air support fundamentally conditioned the scope of partisan activity. The slow and hesitant infiltration of agents into Poland, Yugoslavia and Western Europe retarded partisan evolution there. For the arrival of aircraft from afar enhanced guerrillas' morale since, if they brought supplies, that was useful; but, if leaders with radios, it was a portent of intensified activities—a declaration of intent, military or political, from the highest agencies of all. In Russia the presence or arrival of a strong leader was crucial, particularly where the mass of people waited supine and inert. The first Russian partisan leaders had primarily to turn the people back from the Germans towards the Soviet ideology before military action by civilian bands could be undertaken.

The experience of the partisan leadership in Kharkov, in an area generally unfavorable to the Soviet cause, is revealing. There was little success in recruiting bands before the German arrival on November 6. Only the Communist Party foundation existed as a viable element of resistance. As a first step, therefore, the leaders concentrated on punishing those thought unsympathetic to the Soviet cause by the instigation of a reign of terror that far outrivaled that of the Germans. The selection of the head of the local movement was, of course, crucial. The man chosen—a former chief of the Cheka (the agency used for counterrevolutionary activities within the Soviet Union)—was the epitome of a guerrilla chieftain. Sayenko was fifty-one years of age in 1941 and, despite excessive drinking, described as, "physically strong and in good health, about 5 feet 8 inches tall, broad shouldered, brutal and tough. His little eyes of indefinite color under a projecting forehead were very characteristic. His face revealed . . . inexorable cruelty and obstinacy in obtaining his aims." He is said to have been a convinced Communist though not an ardent supporter of Stalin—a crafty realist who understood best how to enforce iron discipline. He was outstandingly courageous—too brave in some respects in the way he indulged in risky operations without taking proper care of secrecy. He controlled his organization through a few specially selected lieutenants, developed a small technical staff and gained information from a network of spies. It mattered little who did the dirty work—anybody might be coerced with women and children recruited to carry messages and arms, steal equipment from the enemy and execute acts of petty sabotage.

On November 9 a house containing rare birds in the zoological gardens was blown up and the keeper, who tried to prevent it, murdered. In December two boys aged twelve and fourteen were persuaded by an agent to set fire to a warehouse containing horses and transport belonging to the German Sixth Army. The boys were caught, so their fate was never in doubt. Most subtle of all, small red worms were fed into the town's water supply—but the timing was faulty since, if they had been introduced in warm weather during the breeding season, instead of the winter's cold, an acute health hazard would have arisen. It is said that the Germans were impressed by this act. More to the point is the fact that the main sufferers would have been the local populace, not the Germans. Indeed acts of this kind caused a backlash against partisans everywhere. Petty annoyances do not pay. But Sayenko was desperate to make a quick impression despite a severe shortage of resources and was prepared to waste the one surplus commodity available—manpower. Loss of human lives meant nothing and they could always be traded for a few extra arms or some trivial experiment in sabotage, provided it affirmed the long memory and arm of the regime. The system thrived on intimidation—the repeated threat that, once the Red Army returned, all who had collaborated with the Germans would be liquidated; the murder of anybody who claimed that working for the Germans was more rewarding than for the Russians; the restriction of industrial reconstruction and transport services by threat and assassination. If these methods induced starvation they were rated worthy of the cause in the long term even if disastrous at the time. Sayenko had a nice sense of the macabre—his first secret headquarters were established in the cellar of the local crematorium.

Men such as Sayenko were of course the lifeblood of the movement. They were also somewhat rare in 1941. Many so-called partisan leaders turned their backs and allowed the membership to decline or revert to

German control. When bosses were killed whole bands disintegrated and even if the bands survived these early days in sufficient strength to carry them over the nadir of Red Army fortunes, the damage they inflicted was only slight and so scattered as to be of nuisance value alone. A few score bridges destroyed in Army Group South's vast zone was trivial and little more than a condemnation of the Red Army's failure to devastate the lines of communication as it withdrew to the eastward. Chaos there certainly was on the railways, but it largely stemmed from German inefficiency and lack of foresight. They had omitted to make provision for rolling stock on the wider Russian gauges and tried to use locomotives which, in winter, could not withstand extreme cold. But loss of the railways was not wholly fatal logistically since road transport kept the German armies mobile and the Russian guerrillas did far less harm to that than to railways.

Paradoxes abounded. The older men who populated the German administrative and rear area security units tended to feed the local populace, among them active partisans. Civilians were allowed to move about freely and social intercourse became commonplace. Village headmen were kept informed of impending antipartisan operations and this simplified defense against their fellow countrymen. Sometimes, of course, they passed information straight to the partisans—but not invariably.

Partly in answer to the question of patriotism came the rapid collapse of the politically based Soviet partisan movement and with it a condemnation of the Communist Party's conduct of operations. Evidence is scarce on the subject, but there is little doubt that, at the turn of the year, a power struggle broke out between the Party and the Red Army when the latter began to win battles and push the Germans back. At all events it was the trained Red Army leaders, infiltrated through the lines to take charge of the bands, who made the greatest guerrilla impact—not the Party's men. As often as not, entire Red Army units operated in the German rear in the role of disciplined, raiding commandos. Throughout the winter amateur partisan bands were being replaced by professionally regulated Red Army units operating in the gaps between the German redoubts and as far to the rear as they dared—actually to the extremity of radio contact. In this period partisan operations contrived an improved, coordinated military format, shedding though never losing their political element. Political figures of the first grade played their part in the councils at the front—A. Zhdanov in the Leningrad sector, P. Kalinin in White Russia and N. Khrushchev in the Ukraine—all of whom one day were to reach the highest echelons of the Soviet government.

In Moscow, however, the threat of Red Army predominance

frightened the political hierarchy. Marshal Voroshilov, who had commanded the partisans since the early days, was replaced by another strong Communist, General B.K. Ponomarenko, who, from this moment onward, ruled the Central Staff of the Partisan Movement as a separate service—a Fourth Arm such as had been envisaged by Hugh Dalton in England. Cooperation with the Red Army would be encouraged, but it was to be a case of first among equals insofar as the Partisans were concerned.

The early spring of 1942 brought a steady strengthening of air transport support, the injection of qualified Red Army officers to train and guide the ragged bands, and encouragement by the hope or fear generated by renewed Russian offensives; for the Red Army persisted in its attacks well into May, overtaxing its strength long after the German Army had recovered from its setbacks before Moscow and in the Ukraine. Confused loyalties split the nation and the Communist Party. Though popular support for the Germans was on the wane, as knowledge of racial depredations and wholesale looting became widespread, whole communities remained violently opposed to the Stalinist regime. Cossacks joined the German Army and formed antipartisan units; peasants, who longed for tranquility, rejected the Russian partisans, judging their interference and persecution as somewhat worse than the presence of Germans. Intolerably severe conditions in the German prisoner-of-war camps drove hordes of uncommitted Russians to enlist in the German police or the Wehrmacht. In September 1941 the deputy mayor of Smolensk appealed for concessions of the sort he felt sure would swing the entire peasantry the German way, concessions such as would liberalize trade as well as increase personal freedom and thus raise living standards far above the common low of the monolithic Soviet system. This might have attracted over half a million uniformed volunteers besides engendering goodwill just when serious German manpower shortages were being revealed. But Hitler saw no need to give racial concessions when victory seemed assured. He was more concerned with tightening the screws on all occupied territories, draining off their resources into the German Fatherland.

A genuine ethnic Russian antipartisan unit had been formed that autumn in the heavily forested region of Bryansk—the stamping ground for so many partisan bands of Soviet sympathy and a vital communication center too. Over a thousand strong and led by B. Kaminsky, an engineer of Polish extraction who had served an imprisonment term in Siberia, this band had as its declared aim the overthrow of the Stalinist regime. Its uniform consisted of a white arm band bearing the cross of St. George. It was better armed and disciplined than any Soviet partisan band and therefore effective in protecting the German lines of supply to the Bryansk front. Backed and equipped by the Germans, Kaminsky had recruited nine thousand men by the summer of 1942. By fighting the Soviet partisans in their own way, they neutralized, if they did not wholly destroy, all the local guerrillas just when the Germans were at full logistic stretch, preparing for the summer drive that was to take them to Stalingrad and into the Caucasus.

Yet Kaminsky was small fry by comparison with another star discovery made by the Germans in the summer of 1942. In the Leningrad sector, despite desperate Soviet resistance that had not wholly been directly supported by the vaunted partisans, they captured the commander of the routed Second Russian Army—Lieutenant-General Andrey Vlasov. Vlasov was of peasant stock, a brilliant soldier, Soviet hero and patriot—but utterly disillusioned with Stalin and his works. To Hitler he offered his services "to fight as Germany's ally for a socialist Russia and to rid my country of Stalin's system of terror." Here was an ally of incalculable potential, one who could ensure a shift of the balance of power Germany's way. He arrived, too, on the eve of the offensive into the Caucasus just as the Germans were tacitly demonstrating their weakness by undertaking only a single major thrust instead of a repetition of the multipronged advances of 1941. But unfortunately for Vlasov his negotiations coincided with the latest Nazi successes as the Red Army again broke down and the partisan movement once more receded in the face of German success. Racial purity mattered above all to Hitler when he was winning; so Vlasov was kept waiting.

The prologue to the Caucasus offensive nevertheless demonstrated German comprehension of the changing pattern of warfare in the East. All the supply lines to the front, except those in the south, were permeated by Russian forces which oozed among the armies. They could not be ignored. The Central and Northern fronts from Bryansk to Lake Ilmen were seething with guerrilla activity. Sometimes entire armies were severed from flank contact: regularly divisions lived from hand to mouth, supplied in their isolation by air. It demanded combined operations to crush the enemy forces which had interposed themselves, operations of a magnitude that exceeded the antipartisan requirements.

At the end of May 1942 some fifteen thousand Russian so-called irregulars under General Belov dominated the terrain between Vyazma and Yelnya, and the Germans had been forced to yield everywhere except for the vital communication centers and road and rail links. To eliminate this major Russian presence, whose armament was not much worse than that of some regular troops, as then equipped, a Panzer and an Infantry Corps, including three panzer and four infantry divisions, two Security Divisions and a special Police Regiment had to be employed under an SS officer called von dem Bach-Zalewski. Helped by the Luftwaffe, they carried out a far from entirely successful sweep of an area of some four thousand square miles. This was Operation Hannover. An attempt to kidnap Belov failed and what remained of his force (which dispersed under pressure) eventually escaped southward, a fortnight later, through the weakest link in the net—a sector held by one of the low-grade Security Divisions. The casualties of both sides indicate the scale of the operation. Out of their forty thousand men the Germans lost two thousand dead and wounded. The partisans seem to have lost anything up to ten thousand although many of these may well have been innocent bystanders.

As a corollary to Hannover the German Second Panzer Army launched Operation Vogelsang near Bryansk early in June as the escapees from Hannover bolted in that direction. Here a single infantry division killed or captured nearly fifteen hundred Russians and forced the residue of a strong force to evaporate westwards into the deep forests, leaving behind small cadres upon which to reform later. In sum these two major engagements complemented the defeat of the Red Army's attack at Baravenko and brought to an end the overall Russian offensive which had begun before the warm weather. The Russians had exhausted themselves by overambitious operations. The Germans had strengthened their condition in all departments, both at the front and behind the forward defense zones. Indeed there were Germans who held that antipartisan operations gave the best possible training to troops under live conditions, forgetting perhaps that fighting men, most of all, need rest and relaxation.

The Soviets had now to concentrate again on survival. Every element—regular and irregular insofar as one could distinguish them —now began to melt away while waiting for the German offensive into the Caucasus to spend itself. Risky as it might have been to surrender so much territory and forsake offensive action at the expense of morale, the Soviets, with time and space to spare, put survival of the Communist Party above all else. The army and the people must suffer. An example of the effects of this Fabian strategy can be obtained by a study of German stupefaction in their Sixteenth Army sector to the south of Lake Ilmen. Here, throughout the winter, lines of communication were constantly cut by marauders, and the front so thinly held that no reserves could be spared to combat the partisans. Hence an area of swamp and forest, some three thousand kilometers square, was totally devoid of a German presence and wholly under partisan control. Not until the warm days of June, when a lull at the front permitted a regimental group to come into reserve, could anything be done. A sweep was ordered, aimed at the partisans amid a complex of villages, said to contain a central supply dump. Intercepted radio messages had provided information which sounded authentic. Assembling in secret, a night's march from its target, the regiment moved in darkness to its start point and deployed at dawn—plunging deep and unopposed among the forest and swamps. Nothing happened. The place seemed deserted except for a few old men, women and children herding cattle. And when the Germans reached the objective it was again to find nothing—the radio traffic had constituted a deliberate deception. Nevertheless the partisans were present and in strength—carefully concealed in the dense undergrowth, slipping aside to let the Germans pass, hoping they would depart by nightfall when urgently needed supplies were expected by air. But the Germans took root, resting uneasily in clearings at the end of a fruitless day. Then they heard aircraft approaching and, to their astonishment, saw flares mount up all around them as the partisans tried to attract the air drop into their hands. But the Germans also fired flares and they too were rewarded by a delivery of ammunition and food from above. Yet still no partisans were found.

At least the mystery of the vanished partisans had been partly solved and now it was for the Germans to prosecute an intensive search, looking for scattered supply dumps while the partisans stepped deftly out of the way and attempted to herd their cattle to safety in the south. Aircraft joined in the search by daylight, yet not until the fourth day did the Germans at last discover a major food dump and ambush its guard. From these men they learned of the partisan intention to avoid combat and safeguard food in readiness for the winter. The next fortnight witnessed a yet more subtle kind of harassment; the shooting of every animal in sight by Luftwaffe aircraft quartering the area, an attrition bearing hard on the partisans' future existence. Their supplies were in jeopardy, their morale drooping; there was no alternative but retreat into fresh pastures. One night, nearly a thousand strong, they shifted bodily northward—into the territory of the German Eighteenth Army, whose problem they then became. Then, once more to the east, the main battle flared again and the German regiment had to return to a contest more conducive to its nature—combat against a recognizable opponent who stood to fight, face to face.

Maybe a winning game of hide and seek strengthens the confidence of partisans, though it is wrong to equate the semitrained civilian with his better-conditioned military counterpart. The civilian under tension and fear is more liable to relapse into torpor or turn against his leaders, preferring home comfort to battlefield rigor if home is nearby; the trained soldier imbued with a corporate discipline and, likely as not, divorced from local emotional involvements would be more insensitive. Young partisans—mostly in their teens and few over thirty—were shielded from disillusionment by the witless enthusiasm of youth. Pity was to them an afterthought—their heartlessness an inoculation against hardship in a cruel environment. Always on the move, hunted like wild animals, the distances they covered were often quite tremendous, particularly when it is realized that they carried practically everything with them. Fresh food was rarely in short supply because they took it from the villagers (who starved instead), but meals had often to be served cold, since cooking fires might attract hostile attention; salt was scarce and there was an imbalance of diet which sometimes led to scurvy and other afflictions. Demoralization by squalor might be offset by the stimulation of danger; on the other hand the prospects of survival, if captured or wounded, were so remote as to create tremendous tensions. The wounded, if lucky, might be flown out to hospital, but as often as not had to be treated in primitive conditions by rudimentary methods. Capture was tantamount to a death warrant.

Morale could as well ascend in the aftermath of a successful raid as it could sink with a setback; guerrillas relished life quite as much as other people—including the most fanatical among them. One enthusiastic eighteen-year-old gave almost as much diary space to his amorous enterprises as to his guerrilla adventures and obviously, in a cosexual organization, women played a subtle role. It is on record that the rank and file objected to manifestations of petticoat influence over their leaders; it is also known that, at German instigation, wives played Lysistrata and coerced their husbands into returning from forest to hearth. The young diarist reveals a savage aspect of family life among the guerrillas commensurate with his own callousness: "Shot a traitor. Morale good! In the evening I went to do the same to his wife. We are sorry that she leaves three children behind. But war is war! Towards traitors any humane consideration is misplaced." This passage underlines the strain under which a partisan lived—the constant fear of being betrayed, the knowledge that any hand might be against him at any moment, the impulse to live every minute, the invidious task of driving a wedge between people who wished to live in peace and in harmony with the Germans.

Among the ranks were those thoroughly engrossed in the turgid propagandist ideology upon which they were fed. A tract headed "Death to the German Occupiers" and prefaced with, "We partisans took up arms to defend the honor, freedom and independence of our native country—the Soviet Union! We are defending our people from destruction and slavery; we are defending our blood-soaked soil and the descendants of our fathers and children," could not fail to appeal to the minds of a simple populace with inherent patriotic tendencies. At the same time the normal discontent of impressed soldiers in every land was invariably to be detected: "If only the war would end quickly," one wrote, "I would find myself a lifelong position, either as a locksmith or as a guard in my beloved North Park in Vitebsk—a good, merry and secure life." To men such as that sergeant the prospect of becoming a hero held no attraction. He would have been skeptical when he read about a young man who had been awarded the Order of Lenin for reputedly destroying "forty Hitlerites with a bayonet and hand grenades in one battle alone," knowing, from experience, that exact counting in combat was impossible and that reports from scouts and individuals were prone to great exaggeration and inaccuracy. The conventional, half-willing partisan might well have echoed the sentiments of Bilbo Baggins in moments of fatigue after strain, "thinking once again of his comfortable chair in his favorite sitting-room in his hobbit-hole, and of the kettle singing." The Russian peasant was no fool, no blind martial addict, but a man who preferred stability even at the lowest level of subsistence.

Because the partisan lived in a state of constant flux and uncertainty, invariably under pressure and beset by doubts that were only momentarily assuaged by constructive action, the bands suffered badly from desertions. The partisan resented the party machine for eroding his will and putting greater emphasis on the prolongation of Communism instead of defeating the enemy, which came last in many exhortations. He would know there was as much a hidden menace from his comrades as from the enemy and that, in battle, he would encounter an opponent who was far better armed and trained than himself. In summer his lot might be bearable but in winter it could be intolerable when the enemy drove him from shelter to die of exposure in the frozen wastes. Even if the small hierarchy survived there was often, at best, decimation among the lower ranks.

CHAPTER SIX

The Extremists

When Reinhard Heydrich, Himmler's deputy leader of the SS, was appointed Protector of Bohemia and Moravia in place of the ailing Konstantin von Neurath in September 1941, it can scarcely have entered Hitler's mind that this would attract guerrilla warfare close to Germany's doorstep. In Hitler's view Heydrich was "a man with a heart of iron," and in this spirit he tackled the task of completing the Germanization of what had once been the heart of Czechoslovakia. Czech resistance, at this time, was supplying useful information to the Czechs in London under Dr. Benes, but refraining from sabotage because aid from SOE was practically nonexistent. The atmosphere was taut but outwardly calm. This Heydrich changed within a month by rooting out ten thousand people to make room for Germans, incidentally thinning the resistance movement and, quite by chance, eliminating the one remaining radio transmitter. At a stroke Czechoslovakia was cut off from the outside world.

In November the longer winter nights made flights from England to Czechoslovakia and Poland possible again—the first parties parachuting into Czechoslovakia in December. They brought radios and arms, but also men of action—two agents who were briefed to kill Heydrich. This blow, it was claimed, would strengthen the failing resistance movement. Others, including Sokol, argued that it would have quite the opposite effect; that to assassinate so important a person would solve nothing and, in fact, aggravate the reign of terror. But it was the need to regain the political initiative within the resistance movements which probably determined the London Czechs upon this act—the desirability of reasserting their predominance as the party of action against the competing activities of the Communist movement, which was operating independently upon orders from Moscow.

On May 27 a bomb was tossed into Heydrich's car and a week later he died of his wounds. Nazi vengeance—the execution of nearly 2,000

84

people and the erasing of Lidice from the map—to join the list of Russian and Balkan villages already expunged—needs no description here. Of crucial significance for the future of Europe was the awful impact of the assassination upon Hitler's mind and the morale of his entourage. In a flash their delusions of invincibility were shattered. Coming so promptly upon the entry of the USA into the war, when issues were keenly balanced on the Eastern Front, they became haunted by fears of a recurrence of the old anarchy of the 1920s. Like wild beasts they reacted with a viciousness comparable only to that of the Communist-style guerrilla leadership they feared.

The summer of 1942 was the turning point in the war. In May the German Army in the East was 625,000 under strength. In June the Americans had destroyed Japanese naval supremacy at the Battle of Midway; in Egypt, in July and August, the advance against the Suez Canal was halted—forever as it turned out; at sea the war on commerce, though running still in Germany's favor, was becoming increasingly hazardous to the U-boats. On May 30 over a thousand British bombers struck a highly concentrated blow at Cologne, ushering in a new era of saturation bombing against German cities. Machines and manpower for the land battle were being destroyed faster than they could be replaced; on top of that the Germans were forced to double the strength of the fighter defenses of the Reich itself and pour effort and manpower into the radar and antiaircraft gun defenses—to the further detriment of the already overstretched ground forces at the front. The pot remained on the boil in Yugoslavia, too, pinning down formations which would have been invaluable elsewhere.

Fear of an unfathomable future stirred the German leaders to drastic measures aimed at rectifying a chronic manpower shortage and redoubling industrial output. They realized, at last, that they were committed to a long war despite having budgeted for a short one. On March 21, 1942, Hitler decreed "unified direction" of labor "including hired foreigners and war prisoners"—a system far transcending the one which had been dropped in Belgium during the previous war when it threatened trouble. Fritz Saukel, the minister responsible, was instructed to aim for a target of 6 million foreign workers (1.6 million of them Russians) to "force them to large-scale production." Suddenly, in all parts of Europe, people began abruptly to disappear as they were herded into Germany and set to work. No other measure did more to set Europe ablaze against the Germans; no longer was it possible to be indifferent and escape the issues involved; no more could people wear the mask of anti-Semitism on the pretext that only the Jews were being removed. Anybody might now be kidnapped without warning. Everybody now had a reason to fight for survival like the Slavs.

Only in Western Europe, however, were the Germans able to economize with occupation forces. The Abwehr and SS agencies, supported by a small élite and a few second-grade occupation divisions (some in process of rehabilitation from Russia), were easily able to maintain order in the hinterland and along the coastline. Yet even this state of affairs was under erosion. The first commando raids on Norway were followed in February 1942 by a parachutists' attack on the radar station at Bruneval, and on March 28 by the naval and commando attack on the St. Nazaire dock gates. Then came the assault on Dieppe on August 19 in which the equivalent of a division came ashore and gave rise to momentary suspicion of a full-scale invasion. And in addition to these major incursions there occurred a succession of minor coastal raids in late summer and autumn, undertaken by Combined Operations with the object of killing a few Germans, picking off prisoners—perhaps provoking the Germans into some indiscretion against the local populace. Official British policy may have been against harming the people unnecessarily, yet it welcomed violence by them and spread exaggerated reports of a French uprising at St. Nazaire after the raid.

Surprises and distractions, crowding one upon another, led the Germans to make a wholesale reappraisal of their counterinsurgency measures. It was recognized that the army alone was inadequate to deal with a threat to the Reich's structure. Comprehensive OKW regulations were required to establish a uniform doctrine that would harness every agency to the fight. Not that OKW ever totally disassociated itself from antipartisan policy—its chief, Keitel, had issued orders in September and the deputy chief of staff, General Warlimont, states that army orders on the subject had to be vetted by OKW. For example, the instructions issued by Commander-in-Chief South East for the guerrilla war in the Balkans were handed as of routine to OKW for examination and approval. But in August 1942 comprehensive OKW orders were issued and broke fresh ground. They brought antipartisan measures under one man, making Himmler the clearing-house for all partisan information (though stating as unequivocally as ever that the "harshest measures" were to be used) and demanded political, economic and military integration to suppress the enemy, whether at the "front" or in the "rear." Redoubled emphasis was laid upon the need to win the support of the conquered people, to harness their ancient political allegiances and draw them back to the German side. Even Himmler was clear about that and contradicted Hitler when he said, "I must be careful I don't spread guerrilla activity and drive off the entire male population." But diplomacy in the autumn of

1942 came a little too late. His SS were given the specific antiguerrilla rôle and as they were trained in every aspect of coercion, they were incapable of adapting themselves as peacemakers at the height of an increasingly ferocious guerrilla war.

In any case Hitler remained averse to appeasement in any form. He insisted that "whatever succeeds is right . . . annihilating guerrillas is an overriding duty." And he imagined himself in the place of the soldier facing guerrillas: "Let's say the bastards go into a house and barricade themselves in it and there are women and children in the house. Is the chap to set the house alight or not? . . . No question about it! He must set it alight." So the new OKW policy went out from a hierarchy that was divided more widely than ever before.

In October came yet a deeper plunge into the realms of stupid illegality. During a British raid on Sark, on October 3, five Germans had been taken prisoner and four killed when attempting to escape; next day one was found, hands bound, stabbed in the heart. Associating this discovery with captured Canadian instructions concerning unarmed combat, Hitler at once ordered the manacling of Canadian prisoners captured at Dieppe—to the alarm of some among his generals who feared retribution against their own men. But on October 18 Hitler went further and issued what is known as the "Commando Order." In this he declared that all sabotage parties, whether or not they were in uniform, whether armed or unarmed, in battle or in flight, were to be "slaughtered to the last man." It accorded right of judgment and execution to any soldier—and it was acted upon both retrospectively and in the future, in spirit and to the letter. Of a party of ten uniformed Englishmen and two Norwegians who had shot a German sentry and blown up the Glomfjord power station on September 21, seven, who had been captured while trying to escape to Sweden, were shot on October 30. The same fate awaited a man captured after trying to mine the battleship *Tirpitz* at the end of October, and six more captured in mid-December after mining cargo ships in the River Gironde; all were shot in March 1943. There was no trial; Keitel significantly reflected at the time, "I am against legal procedure. It does not work out."

This—for which several of those Germans responsible were later tried and punished—was the murky behavior conditioning partisan warfare after 1942—a standard of escalating viciousness linked with the flight from law to which the Germans allowed themselves to be driven. Although ruthlessness stemmed principally from Hitler, it was also the product of history. When Hitler dilated upon antipartisan measures, he recalled Red violence in 1918 and 1919 and his own small part as a corporal in suppressing it. And when German generals such as von Reichenau, commanding the Sixth Army in Russia in October 1941, wrote about the annihilation of revolt in the hinterland, "which, as experience shows, has always been caused by Jews," he not only reflected Keitel's order of September but underlined the deep misgivings of an influential part of the German officer class which genuinely believed that the Jew Karl Marx and his successors, such as Rosa Luxemburg, were cancers that had to be eliminated. In reality the number of Jewish partisans was only in proportion to the population as a whole—despite the extremes of provocation against their race.

The threat of undermining military discipline by licensing soldiers at the lowest level to kill prisoners with impunity seems hardly to have been taken into account at the time. The Wehrmacht's leaders disputed the case against the Commando Order with greater asperity than usual—yet timorously based their arguments on the fears of reprisals and the loss of valuable information such as might be gained by interrogating captives. Their most effective resistance was indirect, expressed in the difficulty of giving practical definition to an hysterical edict. Somehow a line had to be drawn between "clandestine operations" (said by Hitler to be punishable) and "open battle," when the normal usages of war prevailed. Order and counterorder on this litigious subject brought confusion to the ranks, who scarcely had time to study precedents in the heat of battle. In outcome the Wehrmacht tended to ignore the Commando Order (though not absolutely). But the SS were its most convinced exponents and by their excesses infected the conventional battlefield with the merciless brutalities of antiguerrilla warfare, earning un unrivaled reputation as butchers who had to be exterminated in return.

The escalating severity with which the Germans treated hostages most clearly illustrates the decline in moral standards that began to act as spur rather than curb upon guerrilla warfare in all the occupied countries. For shooting a German officer in Nantes and another in Bordeaux in October 1941, 48 hostages were shot. In September 1942, after an attack upon German soldiers in the Rex cinema in Paris, 116 hostages were shot, 46 of them taken from the fortress at Romainville and 70 from Bordeaux—indicating that the reprisal was at random and not in the least associated with the crime. In September 1941, General Stülpnagel, the military governor of Occupied France, specified that the burial of large numbers of those executed in a common grave in a particular cemetery must be avoided "since this would create a shrine for pilgrims which now or later might become a center for the stimulation of anti-German propaganda." But in July 1942 there was no longer any attempt to conceal the measures being taken. A notice in the *Pariser-Zeitung* proclaimed: "Near male relatives, brothers-in-law and cousins of the agitators above the age of eighteen years will be shot. All female family members of the same degree of relationship shall be condemned to forced labor. Children, less than eighteen years of age, of all above mentioned persons shall be sent to a house of correction."

To this had the Germans fallen since February 1940 when OKW had ruled that "Hostages shall . . . be chosen from sections of the population from which a hostile attitude may be expected. The arrest of hostages shall be carried out among persons whose fate . . . will influence the insurgents." This had certainly come closer to the meaning of Article 50 of the Hague Convention than any subsequent OKW order, but Article 50 was anything but precise about hostages, merely stating, "No collective penalty, pecuniary or other, can be decreed against populations for individual acts for which they cannot be held justly and severally responsible." As the British prosecutor was one day to admit, during the trial of Field-Marshal Kesselring, hostages had often enough been taken by the British in curbing insurrections of the past. Indeed, it would have been hard to find any other nation that could claim innocence, but few allowed the matter to get out of hand as did the Germans by the summer of 1942.

The concept of harsher treatment of people, whether hostages, prisoners or forced laborers, barely harmonized with an OKW policy based on wooing the populace to the German side. A shift in strategy which discouraged the passive guarding of vital points in favor of attacking the partisans whenever they could be detected seemed, at any rate, militarily realistic since it seized the initiative, which, till then, had been left to the partisans. It at least adapted itself to the situation instead of battering away at a doctrinal brick wall, but it came far too late. Offensive action demands reserves and most German reserves were committed to the battle fronts in the East, in North Africa (where the British victory at El Alamein and the Allied landings in November began a series of crippling German reverses) and in the Balkans, where another revival of Partisan activity had to be combatted. It was all very well for OKW to redeploy army training schools and Luftwaffe ground organizations into the partisan regions, along with the injunction that there were to be no Germans left in the bandit-infested area who were not engaged either actively or passively in the antipartisan campaign; it was another thing if these same units, plus the other lines of communication guard units (such as the Landesschützen battalions of the Security Divisions), were filled by the middle-aged reservists whose battle prowess was invariably suspect:

that was simply sending the blind to help the lame. It was equally dangerous to redesignate partisans as "bandits," for even if it employed a term which, to the Russians, meant "freedom fighter," it did nothing to alter the estimation of the German soldier for his adversary—be he in or out of uniform. In point of fact the German soldier felt more at ease fighting the Red Army at the so-called front than the stab-in-the-back kind of Red Army. In any case the special Security Divisions were in a hopeless position—one, for example, in the Minsk region, was responsible for forty thousand square miles, an area larger than Austria.

The integration of all elements—Wehrmacht and SS—into the antipartisan struggle undeniably had a rationalizing effect as the German armies came to a halt in the Caucasus and stuck fast in the environs of Stalingrad. The enforced thinning out of the rearward zones, due to manpower shortage as the area of occupation extended, was partly offset by more economic use of communication arteries, the reduction of guards, plus improved efficiency due to better intelligence about partisan intentions. Intelligence was, of course, as essential to antipartisan units as to formations in the main battle—perhaps more so. In the land battle the presence of an enemy mechanized mass was quite likely to be discovered by air reconnaissance, while the same agency only rarely located a guerrilla band. The most prolific source of information about partisans naturally came through informers, whose news waxed and waned in sympathy with German success and failure, not only at the front but in their relations with the local populace.

Next in importance was radio interception. From the Morse and chatter which filled the ether, day and night, the German monitoring and direction-finding stations, scattered the length and breadth of Europe, were able to disentangle these frequencies given over to specific types of operation. They could separate diplomatic from military traffic, the speech of soldiers, sailors and airmen from each other —and in due course were able to piece together the rising volume of clandestine traffic associated with guerrilla warfare—active and nascent—throughout the occupied territories. From North Cape to North Africa, Brest to Stalingrad, they unraveled a tangled network which told of new clandestine radios being set up on the most enormous scale. In a matter of minutes they could give a rough indication of a transmitter's location; within half an hour they could identify it closely. In the East and the Balkans it was operational talk plus information which they heard; in the West it was mainly a tale of supply and reinforcement by SOE groups making contact with determined patriots in readiness for when the time was ripe. Nearly everything was sent in cipher or code; some the Germans could read, others they could not—it depended on whether they had captured the keys or infiltrated the system. But frequently they were able to pinpoint a target and raid it, or at least assemble a picture of the scale of opposition. For example, in February 1942 German agents infiltrated a Russian band and captured a sabotage detachment near Tosno. The Russian radio was intact and so too were the codes. Interrogation persuaded the operator to divulge details of the impending arrival of an aircraft, and he was made to send a signal giving it clearance. When the aircraft arrived it landed in an area surrounded by troops, and this resulted in the capture of the passengers though the pilots shot themselves.

It was assumed by all sides that intelligence circles and partisan bands would be penetrated by an enemy. Russian partisan bands which took in German deserters—as some did—incurred severe risks, for the Germans frequently introduced *agents provocateurs* or employed pseudo gangs to associate with the real bands and then betray their presence. SOE, as the Germans eventually discovered, protected its radio networks by providing radio operators with a security check based upon a system of deliberate mistakes in specified places (for example, the displacement of letters at agreed intervals in a message). Later SOE supplied a bluff security check in addition to the real one so that the operator might deceive the Germans with the bluff and still introduce the real one if he was invited to transmit bogus messages. The system was far from foolproof; it was easily compromised and sometimes, even after a captured agent had sent the warning check, he was not believed at home, particularly if the message arrived, as so many did, in jumbled order. Radio war lay at the heart of partisan warfare, described by Gubbins as "the most valuable link in the whole of our chain of operations." Again and again radio warfare's coups and fiascos demonstrated their advantages and disadvantages. Yet, hazardous though it was, radio communication could not be discarded.

German antiguerrilla measures also depended, to a limited extent, upon aircraft, even though, on the Russian front in particular, the nature of nightly intrusions by liaison and supply aircraft were partly assessed from radio intercept. The Russian aircraft invariably navigated along prescribed and well-known corridors in an effort to separate supply and courier aircraft from antiaircraft zones. Nevertheless German night-fighters only occasionally tried to tail the intruders, and rarely scored kills. In fact almost every German night-fighter was already engaged in trying to stem the British night-bomber offensive: once more partisan warfare took low priority in German estimation. Meantime, in the West, so few Allied aircraft were being used for SOE missions that they were not considered worth special attention—in any case they were often swamped on the German air-defense plotting tables by the preponderance of the bomber force.

Nevertheless the Germans, like the Russians, used obsolescent aircraft for direct attacks against the Russian guerrillas—when they could find them. Old Arado 66 training biplanes were to be found in company with antiquated Heinkel 145s and Henschel 126s, backed up by an assortment of types which had passed their operational peak of efficiency in 1941. But if the air war against the guerrillas was an isolated sideshow, divorced from the main battle and fought by a quaint assortment of ancient aircraft, it was controlled, nevertheless, by experts who specialized in the work—the first Night Ground Attack Group with five squadrons, Combat Command Liedtke with three squadrons and Special Squadron Gamringer.

In fact, the German approach to antipartisan warfare after the autumn of 1942 became a specialized business—duly recognized in December by the appointment of a chief of Antipartisan Units, that rare bird, a Prussian aristocrat in the SS—Obergruppenführer Erich von dem Bach-Zelewski. He was a professional soldier with a first-class record as a fighting man in the First World War, a member of the élite one-hundred-thousand-man army which had been imposed by the Treaty of Versailles who had joined the General SS in 1931, and become a Nazi member in the Reichstag in 1932. Since the invasion of Russia he had been the Higher SS and Police Leader in the Rear Area of Army Group Center, directly responsible to Himmler but subordinate to the Wehrmacht for antipartisan operations in that heavily infiltrated forest sector. This rather uncharacteristic SS officer had already gained experience in the partisan struggle during Operation Hannover—but now he was primarily to be employed as a coordinator of policy, though often going forward to conduct some special operation. Let there be no doubt that Bach-Zelewski possessed the attributes of the essential SS man, fully conversant with the extent of Einsatzgruppe work and everything else that was vile; well versed in the ruthlessness of the Nazi cult—and yet exhibiting a veneer of chivalry and charm when the need arose. He bent the antiguerrilla forces towards standardized methods, frequently frustrated though he was by the varying shades of opinion and prejudice amongst the motley staffs and units that came within his ambit. The execution of his schemes was at the mercy of entrenched Wehrmacht practice (and its units were in the majority), SS excesses and the violence of such formations as the so-called Dirlewanger Brigade, composed for the greater part of so-called poachers, burglars and murderers.

From Bach-Zelewski's office, in May 1944, was to be published

"OKW Regulations for the Fighting of Bands"—a much milder technical manual than previous OKW documents on the subject; and from the man himself comes insight into the German attitude to this kind of warfare. Like all of his kind he was to blame the unnecessary killings of large numbers of the populace upon the lack of specific orders and shift as much responsibility as possible upon the generals whose task it often was to fight the guerrillas. During his period of office, in fact, the tide of violence rose and guerrilla warfare did anything but abate—though that was hardly Bach-Zelewski's fault. German antiguerrilla operations drifted into a pattern of brutal aggressiveness that fitted means to the ends. Cordon, search, kill and burn with scant regard to legal precedent became the order of the day, to match an expanding volume of internal opposition within all the occupied territories. Yet Bach-Zelewski's regulations prescribed: "All bandits in enemy uniform or in civilian clothes who are captured in combat or surrender in combat are in principle to be treated as prisoners of war. . . . Bandits in German uniform or in the uniform of an allied army are to be shot after careful interrogation. . . ." And: "The administration must see to it by just treatment, planned and energetic government, and thorough and purposeful enlightenment, that the population is brought into the right relation to ourselves." But by May 1944 all hope of implementing the spirit of these belated regulations had passed; only the military techniques remained valid—academically.

The encircling movements executed against Tito in winter 1941, the "partridge drive" in the swamp near Lake Ilmen in June 1942, the application of air power, and every sort of intelligence agency and pseudo gang were to be faithfully reproduced in the regulations' pages. Subtle aggression was to be the theme, and if it could be applied by adopting partisan methods, so much better the chance of achieving success. Yet the manual merely consolidated what all had known but few remembered to put into practice when normal military instincts in a tight spot prevailed. It was, in the main, a record for history and for study by others in the postwar future.

Emulation of partisan methods enhanced by superior armament and mobility could pay off. Bach-Zelewski rarely despised his enemy—his definition of a partisan was "a man carefully selected and trained by the enemy . . . also very well armed." To match combatants such as that, the Germans themselves had to live like partisans in the wilds. Those who based themselves in comfortable villages sacrificed secrecy from the outset: everything they did or said could be reported to the bands. But, for example, a highly trained ski unit which, in the autumn of 1942, adopted the rather unpopular measure of living rough in snow-houses deep among the Bryansk forests at once achieved success. Because the partisans were deprived of information, they made the error of ambushing a train carrying men on leave in close proximity to a ski company. The noise of firing by the leave party drew the skiers to the spot; they caught the partisans as they were in retreat from a hot reception and cut them down in the snow. Likewise, that same day, another company came to the rescue of a bridge guard that was under attack, slaughtering partisans who imagined they were dealing with an isolated detachment.

The best guerrilla or antiguerrilla was the trained, self-sufficient man armed with an automatic weapon—and here regular soldiers provided with ample ammunition and opportunities for target practice always held an advantage over partisans who were chronically short of ammunition and rarely able to practice shooting, for fear this might disclose their location. In practice, partisans were nearly always outgunned. They only rarely possessed mortars and artillery and hardly ever drew directly on air support. The Germans employed heavy weapons as a matter of course and, at times, to excess by reducing the pace of their reactions to a fluid situation in their anxiety to apply fully concentrated fire against some transitory target.

As 1942 drew to its end, Bach-Zelewski had but recently moved into his new office and his regulations were barely a notion. The partisan war was meantime crossing its watershed, not because the opposing guerrillas were more proficient than six months previously but because the crucial battles at the fronts had been decided. The Germans were surrounded at Stalingrad and in retreat in Africa. Indigenous peoples were taking stock again as beguiling news filtered through.

Oil storage tanks in the Lofoten Islands burn after the first raid by British Commandos in March 1941.

German infantry—the principal anti-guerrilla fighters of Europe.

Russian infantry in 1941. The variety of uniforms and weapons shows how easy it could be to confuse regulars with irregulars.

A Russian partisan band hears news from home.

Germans searching for partisans in Russia.

Tito—a master of guerrilla warfare—in play.

Heydrich's car after the attack by Czech partisans.

Russian partisans planning a raid.

. . . not many Russian partisan
bands were as profusely armed
as this.

The aftermath of a railway demolition job.

A heavily armed British SAS jeep party. Notice the long-range petrol tanks and the spotlights.

A Lysander mission behind the Italian front in April 1945. Only when the Germans were utterly defeated was this possible in daylight.

US Flying Fortresses deliver supplies to the French Resistance during Operation Carpetbagger in June 1944—another example of the advantages of air supremacy.

Members of the FFI with British and German weapons.

The Commander of the Polish Home Army during the Warsaw Uprising, Bor-Komarowski.

At the Warsaw barricades during the Uprising in 1944.

'olish youths armed with petrol bombs during the Warsaw Uprising.

German troops taking cover behind the colonnade of Warsaw's Opera House during the Uprising.

Zervas' Greek guerrillas use a captured enemy gun.

A British sniper lies in wait for the ELAS in Athens.

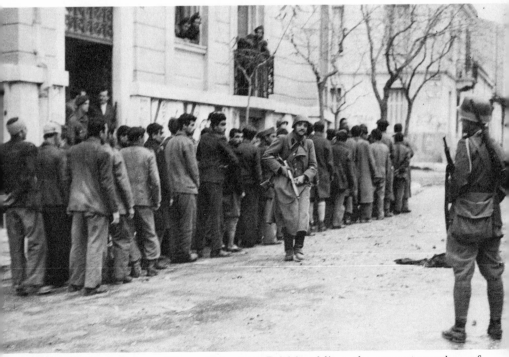

Captured guerrillas in Athens. The onlookers are British soldiers, the captors members of the Greek National Guard still wearing the Axis uniforms of their previous employers.

CHAPTER SEVEN

Discord and Unification

It was a measure of SOE's embarrassment that its 1942 directive from the British Chiefs of Staff was not published until May. If the delay reflected something more than the strategic uncertainties of 1941, as the war dramatically changed shape when new and powerful allies were brought to Britain's side, it also epitomized official misunderstanding and doubt about an organization which was mushrooming into the size of a Department of State while producing a series of painful failures offset by a few trivial gains. Political and military attitudes responded to swings in the strategic balance. Logistic problems, above all shortages of equipment and transport, predominated. It was the transport famine—real or simulated—that most severely restricted SOE's activities—particularly when overall priority was invariably given by orthodox military leaders to conventional operations. Even if it improved its organization and methods, SOE had to mark time until it was given the means to lift large numbers of men and matériel into the occupied countries.

There were several MTBs available to take parties across the English Channel, but this traffic declined when German E-boat patrols made it too dangerous. In all theaters, there were submarines for random use on the strict understanding that primary naval missions took first place. And from Gibraltar a pair of feluccas, manned by intrepid Polish crews who were described by General Sikorski as "too rough even for the Polish navy," ran agents into Southern France. Apart from that everything had to go by air.

Of RAF aircraft only five machines were available in the United Kingdom up to August 1941, and fewer still in the Middle East. None had long range and a large cargo capacity. That year a mere twenty-two sorties were flown to France carrying just one and a half tons and thirty-seven agents—and France received the lion's share compared with the rest of Western Europe. Dalton's purpose of applying propaganda, sabotage and coordinated action by patriots was broadly reflected in the 1942 directive. But his concept of infiltrating three thousand agents to build a Secret Army which, in France alone, would be twenty-four thousand strong by the autumn of 1942 and which would demand twelve hundred air sorties for its accomplishment (and even then provide only enough "lift" to give each man a personal weapon and a few explosives) fell flat in the face of practical logistics. Furthermore there existed a profound contrast between the idealism of those who, in England, conjured up visions of Europe seething impatiently for liberation and those under the German heel who recognized the difficulties of subversion. Had Dalton and his staff been able to make a personal survey of each country they too might have been disillusioned. But while members of the French BCRA went to France in 1942, those in charge of SOE or its F Section never did.

Norway, with its mountainous terrain, was well suited to guerrilla operations. It was flanked to the east by a good escape route into Sweden (even though that nation was careful to maintain friendly relations with Germany) and its long indented coastline was relatively accessible to small boats and aircraft sorties—though parachute descent into the mountains was extremely hazardous. The Norwegians certainly generated their full share of anti-German propaganda, took a part in the sabotage campaign by receiving numerous small parties (nearly all Norwegian in content) and stolidly recruited an underground army, Milorg. But in September 1942 agreement was reached between the Norwegians and the British as a result of which their operations were jointly controlled and kept in a low key.

Of this the Germans neither knew nor much cared. Their purpose was to defend the country and the important naval bases against orthodox invasion and this, from 1942 onward, obsessed Hitler's intuition and his Naval Staff's calculations. They reasoned that Britain could not for long suffer so potent a threat to her sea communications.

General Falkenhorst was promised eighteen thousand reinforcements in the spring of 1942 and was told to form a new mountain division and an armored division. Simultaneously the battleship *Tirpitz* was sent, along with other major surface vessels, as a threat to the Atlantic and Russian seaways and also for defense. Tension grew on the German side as real as well as unintended Allied deception measures played on the fears of Hitler and his sailors. Rarely, however, were they disturbed by commando raids or scattered acts of sabotage against industrial plant and shipping, which had not the slightest bearing on the reinforcement plan—despite Allied propaganda claims to the contrary.

Norway possessed one of the most important industrial installations under German control—the hydro plant at Vermork with its capability of producing "heavy water"—a vital material, in the opinion of those German scientists engaged in research, for the manufacture of an atomic weapon. In 1940 the Germans had ordered production of heavy water to be raised to three thousand pounds per annum and in 1942 they increased it to ten thousand pounds. Norwegian agents informed the British of this and it was deemed essential to stop manufacture. But SOE relations with the *de jure* government in London were still tetchy. Therefore, although small Norwegian parties were active in the country, it was decided to ignore SOE and employ a special Combined Operations gliderborne mission composed largely of British engineers. They were to land on November 19, 1942, and assault the installation, blowing up its key parts. One tug-airplane was shot down, however, and its glider lost, while the second glider crashed and its occupants were taken prisoner. Yet the Germans failed to discover the glider party's real purpose (even though they captured a marked map) for the arrival of these uniformed raiders coincided with the issue of the Commando Order: all were peremptorily shot without undergoing the interrogation which would surely have revealed the secret. Therefore when a Norwegian party made the next attempt on February 28, 1943, the guard of one hundred was a minimum of that required. Moreover the opposition was nil because the raiders used a concealed approach. The work of destruction was executed by only a few pounds of explosive with perfect precision. Leverkuehn reckons that it was the only sabotage attack by Germans or Allies which was truly effective in the sense that an important installation was damaged with lasting effect. It was beside the point that the Germans were on the wrong track in their atomic research and that the heavy water was being misused. If they had been right and the heavy water left in production the outcome of the war might have been reversed.

Vermork apart, however, minor sabotage in Norway, carried out with enormous courage by individual patriots who were trained in England (and who preferred to wear uniform as often as possible within their own country) played a significant part only in stimulating political propaganda. Milorg, at its zenith in 1945, numbered only fifty-seven thousand men, never went into action as an outright partisan army and was more preoccupied in preventing a premature uprising than stimulating one. Knut Haukelid, a great Norwegian guerrilla who led the Vermork raid, commented, with all the bitterness of a true man of action, that it was not until 1945 (when the war was virtually over) that the people were "more willing to fight if it should be necessary"; adding that they "had gradually come to understand that other values than higher wages were worth fighting for." That about summed it up. In the winter of 1944–45, while Germany was being submerged by invasion, a member of OKW described Norway as among the most peaceful places in Europe, in which some troops still kept Sunday as a holiday when suitable forms of diversion were considered to be "National Socialist Leadership courses or athletic competitions."

Holland too contained, in 1942, a potential partisan army, the conservative-minded Order Service—once described in its early years as "a General Staff without troops." Deterred by the German reprisals taken against earlier attempts at sabotage, it relapsed into a mood of self-preservation from which it rarely emerged except in the closing stages of the war. Resistance in Holland centered, therefore, upon the socialistically inclined—notably upon individuals to whom the Order Service's posture as an alternative to the *de jure* government in London was repugnant. This implied almost total reliance upon SOE's infiltration of individual agents, the slow recruitment of intelligence and sabotage groups and the gradual rebuilding of an élite armed force—all under duress in a country geographically unsuitable for guerrilla operations.

The first radio stations established by SOE agents from England had been detected in Holland by the Germans in the summer of 1941. A few weeks later one had been captured by the SS complete with operator and codes, but the opportunity to "play it back" to London was forfeited because the SS misunderstood the subtle nature of such an operation. By February 27, 1942, however, Major H.J. Giskes, the Abwehr officer in charge of counterespionage in Holland, had obtained sufficient insight into SOE's communication system to know exactly when and where sabotage material was to be dropped into Holland. On March 6 he was able to arrest an SOE radio operator, H.M.G. Lauwers, complete with his set and codes. This was the beginning of Operation North Pole, known by the SS as the "Englander Spiel." It has been described by both Giskes and Lauwers in Giskes's book *London Calling North Pole*—the most profitable radio "playback" ever.

In essence, Giskes persuaded Lauwers to operate the set under Abwehr instructions, thus allowing Giskes to control the network.[1]

---

[1] Giskes tried to sway Lauwers by appealing to his better feelings on the lines that, in introducing clandestine warfare with all its brutality, Lauwers was perpetrating an illegal act which could lead only to a blood bath for the civil populace. It was, in fact, the normal, self-interested anti-*franc-tireur* attitude quite sincerely held by many Germans—both then and to this day.

Lauwers consented since it gave him the opportunity to use his secret security check and thus allow London either to disown him or to play back the playback to their own advantage. Unfortunately London's suspicions were neither aroused during the first Lauwers transmission nor during subsequent sessions.[2] Messages began to pass freely between the British and Germans, deliveries of supplies and agents came to Holland as if nothing were amiss. Exactly how this was allowed has never entirely been explained. The prime error of ignoring or missing the security check was compounded by failure to make independent checks on circuits until far too late. The fact remained that Giskes's sham reception parties were able to receive each of the forty-nine agents as they arrived, talk to them and extract information in all innocence prior to their arrest a few hours later. Soon the Abwehr had acquired far more than the contents of every "drop" into Holland; they had learnt the inner workings of SOE in Britain—about its organization, personalities and policy. Armed with these clues, and every new radio and code which arrived, Giskes was enabled to widen his activities, increasing the number of links being played back to fourteen, intercepting over two hundred drops, making over four hundred supplementary arrests in a golden eighteen months during which the Allies fondly believed they were constructing a formidable resistance base in Holland. In fact, the Germans were blunting every penetration and learning the most intimate details about their opponents—the sort of equipment they were using for sabotage, the system of Eureka homing beacons that guided aircraft to the dropping zones, and the methods of encoding and security checks upon which the vital SOE communications depended throughout Europe.

With an ineptitude that is hard to credit, SOE allowed the Germans to substitute their own operators for the original SOE men and authorized newly arrived groups to contact each other, thus breaching the bulwarks of secrecy which were meant to immunize one group from another. The Order Service was penetrated via SOE: far worse, from the Allied point of view, certain courier links from Holland into Belgium and France and right through to neutral Switzerland and Spain came into German hands. In due course various SOE circuits in the other occupied countries were infected, and in Belgium the Armée Blanche was infiltrated. So complete was the German mastery of SOE in Holland and so detailed their knowledge of SOE (cheerfully displayed to captured SOE agents) that agents came to believe that the

[2] By no means an unusual error on the part of SOE. See *SOE in France*, pp. 329–32, for some more glaring examples, but also p. 344 for their counterpart.

SOE headquarters in Baker Street, London, contained a traitor. There is no evidence in support of this and Giskes denies it, though stating that he deliberately fed the belief into captured agents' minds in order to loosen their tongues under interrogation. In the meantime Operation North Pole continued undisturbed until October 1943 when, at last, two SOE agents escaped and gave the game away. But, as Giskes claims, the creation of a Dutch partisan army had been delayed for nearly two years. There were even longer-term effects. After the war there was speculation on the part of some Dutchmen that the whole tragedy of errors had been deliberately rigged by the British—an accusation which was never substantiated but which illustrated the emotional advantages politically motivated people could take in the aftermath of internecine war.

In Belgium there was political and constitutional confusion besides the difficulty of organizing partisans in a mainly urban country (only the wooded Ardennes provided anything approaching satisfactory guerrilla conditions). The king was in German hands and the Légion Belge (the most influential secret army, composed mainly of army officers) aimed simply to reinstate the king after the war rather than indulge in combat against the Germans. They emulated their neighbor, the Dutch Order Service, but they also diverged from the aims of the coalition *de jure* government in England as well as becoming anathema to the Communist-inspired Front de l'Indépendence which operated among the people in a manner appropriate to its name. In matters such as these both the British government and SOE trod on delicate ground. Their overall declared policy was the reinstatement of prewar systems of government in each occupied country. To the British, however, King Leopold of the Belgians was defiled, his part in the surrender to the Germans in 1940 interpreted as a betrayal of the British Army as it struggled to safety at Dunkirk. It was the Belgian government in exile which decided the issue, laying down, in July 1943, that the Légion should convert itself into the Armée Sécrète that should recruit fifty thousand men who were to come under Allied command as required—promoting what was later to become the constitutional struggle that ended with Leopold's abdication in 1951.

Throughout 1941 and 1942, however, a traffic in agents and supplies developed as and when limited resources and opportunities permitted. Sharing fairly between nations and between various organizations in days of shortage was an appalling problem. Clearly neither the British government nor SOE could disclose the ratio or quantity of supplies being provided, particularly since, in late 1942, greater emphasis was being placed on helping the highly active Balkan partisans instead of the semidormant Western European ones. Belgium contributed a prime example of a nation which harbored many resistance groups (twelve, it may be thought, was too many) and factions who were prone to squabble over allocations between each other. Indeed this became a universal disease as time went by and more resources became available. Political considerations were bound to intrude when one faction tried to outbid another: in France, for example, the Communists claimed a kill rate of 550 Germans per month—a deliberate exaggeration but one that was impossible to refute at the time. In fabricating such figures, however, the Communists had a political objective. By creating the illusion that only they were fighting, and that therefore they alone deserved supplies, they would ensure that they emerged as the dominant armed force which could impose its will upon the nation after the Germans had been driven out.

While Norway, Holland and Belgium indulged in moderated factional disagreements in 1942, France writhed in a terrible disarray, unsure of her destiny. The presence on her own soil of a legal government—Pétain's in Vichy—to which many Frenchmen patriotically gave allegiance—was something tangible by comparison with the apparently ephemeral Gaullist Movement or the destructively minded Communist Party. Of those few among the French who offered resistance, the young and the working class were predominant. The old had lost heart while the middle class had far too much to lose in a fight. Even those who were ready to give battle were sick of a chronic discord which SOE agents could report but do little to cure. Mistrust lay at the root of everything: of the Pétain government because it kowtowed to the Germans; of the Socialists, under Léon Blum, because they welcomed German Socialists in their midst, of the Communists because, having played at neutrality until Russia was invaded, they now wanted all-out aggressive action in order to prevent German troops from being transferred to the Russian front; of the Gaullists because they lacked both prestige (on both sides of the Channel) and strength to deal with such a massive problem; and of the police, of whom at least ten per cent were more gestapo than the Gestapo in their outlook and methods. As Hitler put it, in explanation of an affinity between French police and his own, "for the first time in their lives they feel authority is behind them. . . . Previously if there were riots in Paris and the police fired they got it in the neck."

A semblance of unification was France's most desperate requirement and in search of it came two men—Charles de Gaulle, who pleaded for and demanded it *ad nauseam* as his voice gradually assumed a more authoritative ring; and Jean Moulin, who, in 1940, at the age of forty-one, had been the youngest prefect in France. Beaten up by the Germans in June 1940 when he refused to sign a false declaration admitting French atrocities, Moulin attempted suicide rather than face another beating. Until September 1941, when he came secretly to England via Lisbon, he had been busy organizing three French political resistance movements and making contact through the United States consul in Marseilles with SOE. In Britain this rather inconspicuous man with the husky voice, open countenance and dynamic personality—and as well-developed a distaste for the Vichy régime and the Communists as for the Germans—met Colonel Buckmaster, the head of SOE's F Section, Colonel Dewaverin, the chief of the French Bureau Central de Renseignements et d'Action (BCRA) and finally de Gaulle. On January 1, 1942, he returned home by parachute, convinced that de Gaulle was the man for France, the general's appointed delegate-general entrusted with the task of bringing as much as possible of the French Resistance under the Gaullist flag. But Moulin was more than the emissary of an unenfranchised rebel and much more than an agent for SOE (which at that time maintained delicate relationship with the Gaullist camp while the general fought the Allies for French independence quite as fervently as the Germans); he was, above all, the leader of the movement against Communism. In a highly persuasive report on the state of Resistance in France he claimed that the attitude of his movement to the Communists was "collaboration at the bottom of the scale and goodwill and neutrality between the leaders—strictly within the limits of the struggle against Germany." But on doctrinal matters the movement called Liberté "has definitely ranged itself against the Communists." Moulin warned that those who feared the Communists were being driven, at German and Vichy instigation, into the Pétain camp and therefore support for Pétain was growing. He complained that communication between London and Vichy had been more coherent than between the mass of Frenchmen who wanted to fight the Germans —and it is certainly true that, until November 1942, strong links existed between Vichy, French North Africa and the outside world. Both the Americans and Canadians kept close diplomatic contact with Pétain as did the *de jure* Dutch and Belgian governments in London. Vichy maintained a representative in Pretoria. Secret missions passed between Pétain and Churchill, the latter stolidly hopeful that the Marshal would resist. But Pétain was in the hands of Pierre Laval and Admiral Darlan—the one pro-German, the other an Anglophobe. Unity on British terms was not to be expected from them.

Moulin demanded aid as prevention against the flight of hard-core resisters to the Communists. He wanted militancy in addition to a propaganda offensive, such as de Gaulle favored. He insisted upon increased sabotage and the formation of a secret army—and he had his way. By the end of March he was able to report complete allegiance to the Gaullist cause from all those groups he had by then contacted. Moreover he had discovered the man he thought fit to fill the role of commander-in-chief of the Secret Army—General Delestraint, an influential regular officer. But Moulin was also to find, as others were later to confirm, that the older regular army officers were conditioned by training and attitude against subversive warfare. They knew how to organize and administer, but their tactical concepts were conceived along straight lines and therefore were ill matched to situations that demanded extreme flexibility and mental agility. They trusted people in an environment where infidelity was the rule, and applied conventional military solutions (such as holding ground) when the unconventional (such as running away) supervened.

Delestraint posed an honest threat to security in conditions where deceit and secrecy were the keys to survival, a man who could not remember a password and preferred to use his own name instead of a false one. His concept of the Secret Army was real enough, founded as it was upon the original district command structure of the French Army, employing trained officers whose professional imperfections were accentuated by exposure to a random communications system. These regular officers were accustomed to holding open discussions at a moment's notice at a desk or by telephone. Divorced from these bureaucratic facilities and compelled to wait days, sometimes weeks, before they could meet an essential contact, they became impatient as well as careless within an organization which took its pace from opportune meetings. For example, in 1944 P. Fourcaud would endeavor to arrange ten meetings a day, finish with hardly anything accomplished, and yet be five hours late for his last appointment, having risked his and everybody else's liberty as he tramped from abortive rendezvous to rendezvous.

Delestraint thought hard about fighting battles for position, and in the summer of 1942 busily toured the countryside selecting terrain that might be held for protracted periods as bastions against the Germans. In July he came to view the elevated plateau of the Vercors, just to the west of Grenoble, and saw it, as did the Vichy General Staff, as ground suitable for his purpose. He dreamed of battle in the style of 1918 and linked his plans to the one existing French uniformed force—the ORA of one hundred thousand ill-equipped men that the Germans had permitted the French to keep in the Vichy-controlled zone. And yet the belligerence of the Secret Army was ever in some doubt, for the soldiers' political masters (and many of the soldiers too) tended to see the true role of the Secret Army in the same light as their neighbors in Belgium—as a takeover force when the Germans departed, not as a means to speed the departure.

Neither secret armies nor sabotage posed serious threats to the Germans in Western Europe, let alone France, during 1942. Nevertheless the delayed British directive, when it appeared in May, confirmed what Moulin had demanded and much that SOE had wished from the beginning. It looked ahead to "a large-scale descent on Western Europe in the spring of 1943," when the patriots' task would be interruption of enemy communications, prevention of demolition, attacks on enemy aircraft and air personnel and disorganization of rear services by the spreading of rumors. Stress was laid, however, upon the vital necessity of preventing a premature uprising by inadequately armed and trained guerrillas. Always there was this proviso.

Foot has shown, over and again, how careless security was mostly the cause of downfall to those agents who were captured. It would have been astonishing had it been otherwise. Both indigenous resisters and SOE agents were recruited from the full spectrum of society in their respective countries of origin and, like their commanders and staff officers, were new to the job—raw amateurs despite the care lavished on their training, which, itself, could only be empirical. Aristocrats and members of the upper middle class rubbed shoulders with industrialists and artisans. Couturiers and perfumiers found themselves cooperating with jockeys and valets. One thing placed them on another plane to their opposite numbers in Russia—they were genuine volunteers. Some, particularly those who had escaped from the occupied territories, joined by asking around for work of this kind; a great many more were simply recruited on the recommendation of those already in the organization—which is why, for example, prewar representatives of business organizations such as Courtaulds and Hambros predominated among the first trainees under Holland and Gubbins in 1939. The process of final selection could only be completed at the various national training schools where everything from parachuting, demolition, unarmed combat and coding to assimilation of current life in the occupied territories was taught. If an agent's defects went undetected there, he, or she, was passed fit for work in the field—and let it not be overlooked that many instructors were, themselves inexperienced in the field.

In the field, however, was to be found a totally different environment from that of some quiet country house in England. Agents had to survive in an atmosphere of hatred whipped up by the Germans as an antipartisan measure. Propaganda infiltrated every layer of society, turning friends into enemies and breaking down trust. For example, films that gave the German angle were presented as being French-made. Everybody became involved yet, remarkable to relate, scant effort was made to recruit the mass of organized French labor into the Resistance. An attempt in 1941 by SOE (on Dalton's insistence) to contact Léon Jouhaux, the French trade unionist, broke down when Jouhaux was arrested by Vichy police. And there for the time being the attempt rested.

It was left to the Germans to act as the best recruiting sergeants of the masses into the ranks of embryo secret armies. On top of the incitement to rebellion, implicit in every execution of hostages, there came the impact of the forced labor program. Against his will in the summer of 1942, Laval was compelled by Saukel to contribute fifty thousand workers—a figure which was raised to four hundred thousand by March 1943. This measure injected the same sense of desperation as in all other Europeans. It cut across political loyalties but, unlike the reaction in some other Western European nations, it drove a section of the French populace to migrate into the forested hills—chiefly among high ground on either side of the River Rhône. Here, purely as an act of escape and evasion, they set up camps. Only later did they begin to make a petty nuisance of themselves—and even then they were of so little account at first that the Germans barely took notice, rating as bandits what became known as the maquis gangs.

To Moulin and the Gaullists the maquis offered the cadre of a highly belligerent secret army. For the first time, Frenchmen demonstrated their independence by cutting themselves off from the shelter of everyday society and became almost unique among a population which did its best to carry on as usual. The maquis were to practice what the Communists preached—to learn the art of resistance by fighting in the open. Yet they also epitomized the guerrilla's inherent and fatal weakness: if they steered clear of important targets they could be ignored because of ineffectualness; come any closer to vital spots and they attracted irresistible countermeasures. Practice their art and they compelled retribution; fail to train and they would be useless. In weakness and solitude they were reduced to temporary sterility.

Unhappily for present-day French patriotic conscience there were few among them who had the urge to kill Germans during the Second World War. Many felt satisfied simply to inculcate a sense of fear and uncertainty in their conquerors; few were ready to follow the line of Churchill's urgings to the British in 1940 to "take one with you." In

1942, and the best part of 1943, the manufacturing industry worked to the best of its ability, held up here and there by scattered RAF bombing and lesser SOE sabotage. The entertainment industry thrived, too, while horse-race meetings were held as if the war was over—which, in the Vichy zone, it technically was. Intercourse between the people and the Germans may have been covert but it went on—by night if not by day. Some Frenchmen maintain that their country was the only one which, as a nation, collaborated; there are others who reckon that to be a member of the Resistance you had to be mentally warped.

In comparing those conquered nations whose governments escaped with France one has to remember that French life was controlled by decree and to bear in mind that ministers and officials had unavoidable direct contact with the German authorities. It was much easier for governments sheltering in Britain to adopt an aggressive stance—though even those were careful to restrain the wildest excesses of their compatriots and allies. Restraint was not only imposed on French rebels by the German curb. The Communists, eager to take action, were held back by sheer lack of resources. Attempts by the British to fly Russian NKVD agents from Britain into France and Central Europe broke down in 1942. No matter how strong the French Communist ties were with Moscow (and the evidence of direct radio links is conflicting) they were almost entirely dependent upon SOE for supplies and support. They were therefore anxious to please while fostering their own interests as best they might under differing types of political surveillance—from the Germans, the British agents and the patriots under Moulin.

Then there were the French Security Forces—the police whose loyalties were to their employers and whose sympathies to any SOE agents were by no means wholehearted and in ten per cent of cases quite hostile—and the *Milice*—that organization of thugs under J. Darnand which was the counterpart of every other pro-Nazi police force in occupied territories: a militia which played a deadly part in hunting down agents because they more easily assimilated the atmosphere and working of the SOE circuits and, in self-protection, had need to demonstrate zeal to their German masters. Men such as these also joined the French SS.

In this mire of intrigue the threat of double agents was omnipresent. Perhaps the most celebrated was Madame Mathilde Carré who began work as a radio operator for a Polish-oriented group called Interallié. She was caught and compelled to change sides and, incidentally, live with an Abwehr sergeant called Bleicher. At one stroke she betrayed Interallié and, in addition, continued to work her radio to

London—doing under duress what Lauwers had done by miscalculation. But a French agent called Pierre de Vomécourt, discovering
Carré's game early in 1942, persuaded her to turn coat again and once
more become a double agent. They were actually able to sell an idea to
the Abwehr (through the unwitting Bleicher) that Carré should go to
London with Vomécourt, he supposedly in blithe ignorance of her role
with the Germans, she to seek out all the inner workings of SOE in
London and report them to the Abwehr—to "play back" the
"playback." In addition the Germans were to be permitted to watch
the pair being picked up—an offer that turned into farce after the
Germans accepted it and became eager watchers of, first, an abortive
pickup by a Lysander and then a tragicomedy fiasco on a storm-swept
beach where boats from a British MTB could not outride the surf. On a
later occasion they at last got away by MTB and carried their story to
London where Carré made a full confession of her activities. Subsequently, however, the attempt at "playback" failed and de Vomécourt was captured on his return to France.

The Carré defection was but one incident in the disruption of the
early SOE penetrations of France. By early 1942 more than half the
agents sent in had been eliminated while those who survived were hard
put to recruit supporters. Throughout 1942, however, the number of
airlifts increased by a factor of four as Moulin's mission and other
Gaullist agents began to inspire potential partisans. Fatalities among
SOE agents got no less and the toll of hostages rose, but a revived
patriotism burgeoned as disenchantment grew against the Vichy
government and anti-German propaganda became widely circulated—and believed. Always, too, there was the background noise of
the BBC broadcasts, interspersed with coded instructions to SOE
agents to give a menacing impression.

Suddenly, every Frenchman was driven to an urgent reappraisal.
On November 8, 1942, an Anglo-American task force landed in French
Northwest Africa, bringing Frenchmen momentarily into conflict with
the invaders, until Pétain's deputy, Admiral Darlan, put an end to
opposition and cast his lot with the Allies. At this moment of climax
and maximum confusion, when every past loyalty was upturned, came
the crunch for Western European resistance. Pétain was forced to
dance in public to Hitler's tune because Hitler no longer felt able to
trust the Vichy government. Hitler was compelled to occupy the
Unoccupied Zone, ending forever his show of friendship for France,
disarming the armed forces (thus striking a heavy blow at the cadre of
the Secret Army) but simultaneously still further dissipating Ger-

many's strength with the commitment to guard the newly acquired provinces.

Thus, as the Allies' long-term military prospects were improved in North Africa they were reduced somewhat in France. Furthermore Darlan's swing to the Allied side forced them into political disarray since his presence in power conflicted with Allied support for General Giraud (whom they had "extracted" from France as a prospective leader of the French in North Africa) just as the Americans' anti–de Gaulle line conflicted with British sponsorship of the Free French. Even though Darlan was soon to be removed by an assassin's bullet, Giraud and de Gaulle were to be bones of contention among the Allies as well as irreconcilable rivals for future power in France. The former, however, was totally out of his depth both in modern orthodox warfare and in politics and clandestine affairs, while the latter, somewhat unwillingly at first, walked a diplomatic and political tightrope—but with progressive assurance. Already de Gaulle was an intransigent match for statesmen of world class—a leader whose cause was propagated in France by the indefatigable Moulin.

The tug-of-war among the French leaders transmitted itself to the nation's interior via the British SOE and their American colleagues from the Office of Strategic Services (OSS),[3] which, in September 1942, had more or less merged with SOE to become a joint organization known as SOE/SO—in London, that is, though nowhere else. The British persisted in giving help to almost anybody who offered resistance. But the Americans hedged, in response to State Department distaste for de Gaulle, favoring almost any agent other than a Gaullist one; indeed they were on much better terms with the Russian NKVD. In France itself the original, external links via the American diplomatic corps in Vichy were cut and so, even though the Americans preferred Giraud, they could but hamper and not prevent Gaullist penetration. There actually came a delicate moment when Gaullists and Communists tended to club together against interference in French politics by Americans working through pro-Vichy channels.

Paradoxically that winter, as the Allies at last ended their long run of defeats and started on the road to final victory, tempers among their statesmen frayed. But diplomatic tension in London, Washington and Algiers was nothing so terrible as the strain upon those within France who tried to generate clandestine resistance and guerrilla warfare. In permanent danger, the heart and brain of the Resistance for over a

---

[3] Dealt with in more detail in Chapter Fourteen.

year, stood Moulin. Overwrought, he was brought back to England for a brief rest in February 1943. But at the end of March he returned, unshakably loyal to de Gaulle and content in the knowledge that the Allies were positively committed to the support of French Resistance even when qualifying their views with doubts about the higher French leadership. Though the rival claims of Giraud and de Gaulle were unreconciled by Roosevelt and Churchill at the Casablanca Conference in January, they had confirmed the strategy of total war against Germany. The air offensive was to be prosecuted with relentless fury, day and night; Sicily was to be invaded in July and, later, at a place to be decided, the mainland of Europe. As the Allied statesmen progressively discarded their humanitarian restraint, war was brought closer to the populace: one step towards terror led to another. Sabotage, said the Chiefs of Staff directive, issued at the end of March, "should be pursued with the utmost vigour," but attacks against communications and other targets must be "regulated and integrated with our operational plans." Concerning partisan warfare, by formed bands, they stated nothing definitive—and hardly surprisingly. Allied thoughts on the subject remained as vague as Churchill's notions of how an invasion of Europe might be prosecuted: at this time he talked rather airily of throwing ashore twenty armored divisions to join a cloud of partisans (the early Fuller theme, be it noted), but he was unconvinced and unconvincing. In any case it was only in Yugoslavia that the Western Allies detected the activities of a pugnacious, viable partisan army and even there the situation was clouded by contradictions and misrepresentations—as will later be described.

In reality the weightiest British military intervention in Europe until well into 1943 came from commando coastal raids and the deeper penetration of a highly sophisticated raiding force which began life in the Middle East under the auspices of General Wavell. In the summer of 1940 Wavell had formed a special desert reconnaissance and raiding force called the Long Range Desert Patrol (raised to a Group known as LRDG). A year later, at the goading of Second-Lieutenant David Stirling, L Section, soon to be called the Special Air Service (SAS), was formed with the specific object of attacking enemy communications and airfields by surprise, using parties of four men as opposed to the large commando troops. Approach might be overland by jeep, from the sea by canoe (by members of the Special Boat Squadron [SBS], which later became part of the SAS), or from the air by parachute. They were an élite, carefully selected from men of determination and intelligence, and trained to superlative infantry standards to operate any type of weapon in the world as well as being expert in the handling of explosives. SAS was the equivalent, in fact, of the German Brandenburg Regiment, aiming for the *coup de main*, daring reconnaissance and deep raiding, acquiring the habit of appearing by surprise to strike at weakness while avoiding strength. The unit cut its teeth in the desert with an initial raid by fifty-five SAS parachutists intended to demolish Luftwaffe fighters on their bases in the Tobruk area as precursor to a major offensive—Operation Crusader—which was about to be launched by the Eighth Army in November 1941. The raid was a disaster because a high wind scattered the parties across the desert. In the end only twenty-two men returned with not one fighter to their credit. But, gaining experience, the SAS began to achieve results out of all proportion to its manpower. Soon it was striking further afield, its first incursions into Europe beginning in 1942 with SBS raids on the Greek islands, where airfields were attacked—though with dubious success and punitive losses. Often, however, the achievements of a few highly trained and uniformed raiders were proportionally more economic than the work of large, indigenous bands—with the possible exception of those in Russia and Yugoslavia. They underlined the advantage of cool professionalism over hotheaded enthusiasm when working in the enemy rear areas. For the remainder of the war there would hardly be a theater of war where small parties of the SAS type were not mingling with the partisan groups, executing the trickiest jobs by sleight of hand rather than brute force, hitting targets which were beyond the reach of air power, too, and winning Hitler's accolade: "These men are very dangerous. They will be hunted down and destroyed at all costs."

In April 1943 Moulin set the seal on fifteen months' negotiation by establishing the Conseil National de la Résistance (CNR) and thus combining the principal insurgent parties in France. It brought Frenchmen into closer accord than for many decades. But it was short-lived. On June 9 Delestraint, the head of the embryo Secret Army, and his chief of staff, were arrested, and on June 21 the Gestapo, exploiting information that stemmed from suicidal breaches of French security, captured Moulin and the core of CNR at Caluire. This was the greatest coup ever achieved by the Gestapo. Yet once more they were to demonstrate their total incompetence in fighting the partisan struggle, for instead of working systematically and patiently to break down Moulin's resistance, they indulged in the only form of interrogation that ever seems to have occurred to them. They beat the man to pulp and so ruptured his internal organs that, within a fortnight, he died

—with his secrets intact. More than one sufferer at the hands of the Gestapo has testified that a beating merely raised anger and determination to resist; the greatest betrayals came from the untouched.

Moulin's death stunned CNR since, in creating unification, he had centered everything upon himself; on June 21 he, not de Gaulle, had been the man of France in every sense. Now there was another vacuum dangerously coinciding with a furious row between de Gaulle and SOE, over the future direction of French clandestine affairs, and between Churchill and Roosevelt over French sovereignty. Churchill thought de Gaulle posed a threat of serious estrangement between Britain and the USA "and that none would like this better than de Gaulle"; at the same time he could not ignore the fact that de Gaulle's man, Moulin, had welded Frenchmen together. The growth of European resistance raised some strange political paradoxes. While every Allied government sought the formulation of long-term national policies, the indigenous partisans of Western Europe crawled like white ants within the rotten structures of discredited regimes, looking almost as intently to the East for guidance as to the West. And though the Germans were at last awakening to the importance of the partisan threat, in practice they were on the verge of losing their preeminent role in Europe's development. There were more powerful political forces at work within the partisan movements than those represented by sheer force of arms.

CHAPTER EIGHT

Alles ist verloren

After the defeat of the German Army at Stalingrad and the eviction of Axis forces from North Africa in the spring of 1943, the battle against Germany had been decided though two years were to elapse before the Allies consummated victory. In May Hitler was far from ready to concede defeat, but even those of his entourage who recognized the truth also realized that the struggle for Europe was only beginning. In 1942 the partisans had contributed little of vital importance to the victories of the Red Army; nothing at all to the delaying action of the Western powers whose plans were conditioned by Russian survival; and in Yugoslavia they had merely pinned down a few Axis divisions which might have been useful elsewhere. Partisans had a nuisance value —that was all. It continued to be argued among soldiers and airmen that aid to partisans was a waste, deflecting vital supplies from more effective projects.

Consider the partisans' part in the Russian defense of the Caucasus. Their activities in the vicinity of Bryansk had tied German troops to antipartisan operations when they might have been better engaged in rest and recuperation, but had not delayed the start of the offensive. In fact, the German penetration of the open Caucasian steppes met with scant partisan resistance and entered a land whose inhabitants—Cossacks, Georgians and all sorts who resented the Bolshevik regime—were eager to join them. It was a repetition of the old story of passive support for the side that appeared to be winning. It was a fundamental of Russian strategy that they concentrated on strengthening the partisans behind those fronts where forest cover was thickest but where the German tide was receding. The Caucasian steppes they wrote off as territory that was unsuitable either for immediate political or partisan activity.

One might have expected, therefore, that when the Russians drove westward from Stalingrad towards the River Dnieper, in the winter of

1943, they would have been aided by an overwhelming uprising of partisan bands. German intelligence (probably over-pessimistic in the shadow of defeat) recorded what looked like a wall of partisan bands stretching northward from Bryansk past Vitebsk to Nevel, bands which traveled in blocks of some five hundred each and descended, when the opportunity offered, to break railways, wreck trains and demolish isolated depots. While the battlefront was in ferment there was little the ground forces could do to check this activity. In the area of Army Group Center alone the Germans sometimes counted anything up to one hundred and fifty flights a night by aircraft which dropped supplies or actually landed within the partisan zones. The depth of partisan operations also increased. Aircraft penetrated anything up to eight hundred miles behind the lines to supply partisans located west of the Dnieper. Against this massive effort the Germans' resources were spread far too thin. On the ground they were reduced to the minimal forms of passive defense and in the air they were at a nadir since aircraft of all kinds were being drawn increasingly to the defense of Germany and the Mediterranean front.

Not that the Russians found life easy. There are reports of partisans being dropped in bags from low-flying aircraft into deep snow, their sole additional protection a thick wrapping of hay: there was a parachute shortage. Most difficult of all in the cold winter was food supply. Everybody preyed on the unfortunate peasants; the Germans, who took what they wanted for themselves as well as in an effort to deprive the partisans of sustenance; the partisans, who were compelled to live off the peasants because airlifts rarely delivered food—only agents, arms and ammunition, and propaganda material. Thus partisans frequently became distracted from their primary rôle to go foraging in the interest of personal survival. This plundering of the countryside antagonized thousands of would-be recruits. Nor was famine confined to the irregular armies alone. As the main Red Army approached the Dnieper it too began to run out of supplies and its spearhead units became faint with losses.

Here they were thrown back by a German counterstroke under Field-Marshal Eric von Manstein which, in concept, resembled the partisan technique. For, as the Russians advanced, the German mechanized army melted away, deluding the Russian General Staff into imagining a total enemy collapse—a belief made more credible by the habitual propaganda overstatement of enemy losses. But all the time the Germans had been concentrating a strong counterattack force, beyond reach of the Russian forces, that went practically unnoticed by the partisans who, if legend is to be believed, infested the area. Suddenly, on February 20, the Germans struck hard and rolled the Russians back in the direction of Kursk. It was the old kind of rout, the sort which partisans habitually failed to mitigate. This time they gave neither clear warning nor significant combat assistance. The issue was decided, as usual, by regular forces—a few hundred tanks, guns and aircraft with the trained infantry who had always been more than a match for irregular forces and whose lines of communication, though sometimes cut, were never so disrupted by partisans as to be incapable of maintaining adequate stocks for the front line soldiers. Only when the thaw came with mired fields and choked roads did a German logistic failure occur. The irrefutable evidence of conventional success by regular forces is the plainest denial of partisans' claims to have killed countless thousands of Germans and to have destroyed almost as much material as could possibly be transported to the front.

In the aftermath of Stalingrad Hitler has been depicted as a leader deprived of self-assurance. For one short spell he gave his generals a freer hand, perhaps because his intuition failed, possibly because he had run out of constructive ideas. But the brutal facet of his policy persisted. Genocide multiplied, Himmler's SS went berserk—despite the piously expressed thoughts of the Reichsführer on the desirability of abstaining from encouraging partisans by acts of violence. The immense project of exterminating the Jews, which had begun tentatively and inefficiently in 1939, had been boosted by Heydrich, under Hitler's instructions, in January 1942 and brought to a frenetic peak by Heydrich's successor, Adolf Eichmann. It was working at full pressure by the end of 1942. In July a report to SS Gruppenführer Wolff told Eichmann, "From July 22 onward a train will leave daily with five thousand Warsaw Jews for Treblinka via Malkinia. Furthermore a train will leave twice a week with five thousand Jews from Przemysl to Belzetz"—and this was but part of a vast traffic throughout the Continent. It did not go unnoticed, even though the true purpose of this migration was known but to a few. But it largely went unresisted. Scattered opposition in the occupied countries was hardly ever prompted by pro-Jewish sympathy. Very occasionally Jews took up arms to defend themselves but mostly they behaved as normal individuals everywhere in that, faced with a terrible threat, they tended to persuade themselves that "it couldn't happen to them." Was this not at the heart of every man's reluctance to resist? Indeed the simplest acts of sporadic resistance by Jews and Poles were sufficient inducement for the SS to accelerate the program of liquidation. A letter of December

10 from Dr. Hummel, the deputy governor of Warsaw, provided one good excuse:

> On October 7 and 8 in many of the railway junctions around Warsaw outrages have taken place resulting in the derailment of service trains. Hand grenades were thrown at the Café Club and the station restaurant. . . . As regards the Resistance Movement it can be stated that in recent months it has been reinforced from outside and that the internal divisions of this movement are receiving weapons. Our reprisals have consisted of imprisoning fifty Communists, the imposition of a fine of 1,000 zlotys on the city of Warsaw and the inauguration of a curfew from 7:30 P.M. . . . In October there were 256 cases of outlawry and 286 in November. In general they were not crimes of a political nature but perpetrated by criminal gangs which have grown stronger as a result of the evacuation of the Jews. Jews on the run have joined these gangs, in particular young Jewish girls. We are waging a pitiless war against these gangs but so far we have been unable to liquidate them.

Both sides were pitiless. Rival Polish guerrilla bands occasionally fought among themselves, burning the villages of those who showed partiality for one political faction or another, or where German sympathizers were suspected of dwelling. Sometimes the relatives of a German killed by partisans in Poland received his genitals by post as a way of bringing the war home to the Fatherland.

In the second week of January 1943 Himmler visited the Warsaw ghetto and ordered the arrest of "all the proletarian elements suspected of outlawry," an order which was first implemented by armed SS on January 18. And then the unexpected happened—a few inhabitants took up arms and shot back. For the rest of the week, as deportation was stepped up, it was to the accompaniment of intermittent grenade explosions and fighting. The participants were mostly Jewish Communists driven to desperation by the knowledge that eighty-five per cent of their fellows had already gone to the gas ovens and that the rest must soon follow. But the inferiority of the combatants' armament was deplorable. For the sixty thousand Jews who remained in Warsaw in January, there were just a few revolvers and a handful of grenades; many more arms and explosives were in the hands of Poland's Home Army but an appeal by the Jews for their supply in March went unanswered. The leaders of the Home Army felt they must conserve their force for a more propitious moment—and they were probably right in thinking that this was not the time.

In the meantime Himmler had ordered the destruction of the ghetto and its total elimination as "a dangerous center in a continual state of ferment and rebellion." But with only fifty SS men in support of two sections of Ukrainian and Lithuanian police the SS leader, von Sammern-Frankenegg, was quite unable, during March and early April, to penetrate the ghetto and extract the belligerent Jews. German fears of a wholesale uprising spreading from the ghetto into Warsaw and throughout Poland drove them to plan the final elimination of the area by brute force in place of the previous "persuasion." A major operation, scheduled for completion in three days, was arranged to begin on April 18 and a new SS leader, Jurgen Stroop, was sent to assist along with reinforcements of just over a thousand men—mostly Waffen SS.

At dawn on the 18th they moved and at once met resistance of such dimensions that, despite a mere handful of casualties, the Germans withdrew in confusion. At this von Sammern-Frankenegg is said to have cried, "All is lost"—and promptly was replaced in command by Stroop. Next day the Germans returned to the assault in earnest and the fighting intensified. Their losses that day were 12 men out of the 1,293 engaged. The nature of the fighting was meticulously described by Stroop in day-by-day reports which were devoid of all compassion. Flatly he wrote: "The tank used in this action and the two heavy armored cars were struck by Molotov cocktails. The tank was set on fire twice. . . . We caused the enemy to retire from the roofs and elevated positions into the cellars, bunkers and sewers. During this mopping up we caught only about two hundred Jews. . . . The Jews hid in the sewers; we ordered them completely inundated. . . . The Jews and criminals resisted from base to base and escaped at the last moment across lofts or through subterranean passages."

Jewish reports are fervently passionate and, in the nature of all such first-hand descriptions of close-quarter fighting, wildly exaggerated in connection with German losses. One wrote, "Somewhere near the wall stands a group of SS men surrounded by gaping Poles. A woman appears on the wall waving a small red flag and shouting at the Poles to duck out of the line of fire. Suddenly a group of Jews appears from below ground. . . . They pelt the SS men with hand-grenades. . . . There are even rumors that the revolt in the ghetto will be helped from the outside . . . there are all kinds of rumors. For example that the Germans will bomb the ghetto tonight from the air."

It is easy to lose sight of the actual balance of forces involved amid the emotional stresses unleashed by a guerrilla action which was to last throughout two months' systematic mopping up of a highly intricate built-up area; this was the first protracted urban guerrilla action attempted by greatly inferior forces and is of importance when considering all subsequent actions of its kind. The fact remains that the diversion of German effort by over sixty thousand Jews never amounted to more than the first thousand or so men committed. Apart from minor forays by Polish Home Army detachments in helping a handful of Jews to escape from the city, there was no outside aid given to the Jews, and the Jews survived so long mainly by evasion of the enemy in the maze of hiding places provided by wrecked buildings and underground passages. The German figures speak for themselves and stand practically unchallenged. On April 19 they deployed 1,238 SS and police plus 55 Wehrmacht soldiers of whom the latter provided crews for a single 100-mm howitzer and a manpack flame-thrower. The Waffen SS manned three heavy antiaircraft guns, two heavy armored cars and a single old French tank. This force was not strong by any means, but by May 16, when the operation closed, the Germans reckoned they had accounted for 56,065 Jews of whom nearly 14,000 had been liquidated during the operation: in addition they thought some 5,000–6,000 had died in the explosions and fires which had been created by dynamiting bunkers and houses and in smoking people out of the cellars. Bodies were frequently seen floating down the sewers. German losses seem to have been about 70 killed and wounded.

Cold statistics conceal the bitterness of the struggle as the Jews were hauled into the open to be shot or cremated in the ruins—or transported. They omit the disgust of the Jews that only a few of the Polish Home Army came to their help, and they leave out the spectacle of Jewish women detonating grenades among themselves and the Germans as they were captured, or of Jews who fought until the flames reached them and then threw themselves from the roofs rather than surrender. How hopeless was this fight can be assessed from the tally of arms captured by the Germans (some of them actually belonging to the Home Army and seized outside the Ghetto)—in all fifteen rifles and fifty pistols. Afterwards the Ghetto was completely destroyed or, as Stroop put it, "The ruins contain only enormous amount of bricks and sand which could be utilized." He spoke his own epitaph at his trial in 1951 (when he was found guilty and executed): "A revolt can only be quelled by terror."

Fighting of a random kind continued to flare up for weeks afterwards in the Ghetto, but the heart of the resistance had been crushed in the one Jewish locality where it had occurred. Elsewhere the Jews mostly allowed themselves to be herded to their doom with a strange apathy that defeats description. Yet the martial performance of this most harassed of all people is truly remarkable taken in proportion to overt resistance to modern police states. What other minority, unaided and grossly outnumbered, fought back with the ferocity of the people of the Warsaw Ghetto?

Remarkably, as Himmler was giving his order to destroy the ghetto, resistance of another sort was made manifest much closer home. Within Germany itself the docility that had prevailed since 1933 found relief only in secret plottings by a few soldiers and civilians who never contrived to bring their schemes to fruition. The German people's goodwill towards Hitler had been undermined when, on April 26, he announced, "I possess the legal right to compel everyone to do his duty. . . ," appointing himself "Supreme Law Lord" in addition to all his other powers as Chancellor and Supreme Commander. Underground there were mutterings by all and sundry—and not just among the old Communists awaiting their chance, though their very existence angered the Nazi leaders. A Communistic group called Rote Kapelle within the Air Ministry, that was signaling information to the Red Army, was a spy ring and not a spontaneous element of popular illwill; it might lower Göring's prestige but it could also be snuffed out with thorough SS ferocity. The affair of the anti-Hitler White Rose Letters circulated by a group of Munich University students shortly after the disaster at Stalingrad was, however, something unique, especially at a moment when German confidence in their leader was distinctly shaken.

A classic piece of Nazi ineptitude was all the situation needed to throw the university into a rage. Paul Giesler, the Gauleiter of Bavaria, tried to quell disaffection when he spoke to the entire student body to instruct them where their duty to the Fatherland lay. In the same speech he managed to introduce lewd references to the "proper" function of the female students. Now, it has to be realized that the majority of the male students were experienced soldiers whose good fortune in being at the university was simply that they had been made unfit by war service to continue in uniform. They had seen what was wrong at the front and they were insulted when Giesler attacked them as "useless academics." In a body the students roared their disapproval and swept into the streets to demonstrate in a manner which had been forsaken in Germany for a decade. The impulsive rising caught on in much the same way as had the uprising in Amsterdam in 1941. All sorts of acts of sabotage took place: the telephone exchange went out of action for three days and Radio Munich for seven, though this did not prevent news of the revolt spreading as far afield as Vienna and the Ruhr, where there were demonstrations which provoked the SS into opening fire. Meantime two young student leaders, Hans and Sophie Scholl, threw leaflets from a university balcony calling on the people to

"Fight the Party" and asking youth to rise up in revenge upon those who had dishonored Germany.

This rebellion was, of course, magnificent and the finest ever expression of all that was good and liberal in the German character. It gave long-term hope for the future, but for the leaders it was a death warrant. The Scholls were immediately grabbed by the Gestapo and beaten up with practiced thoroughness. Facing Roland Geisler as he presided over a Senate of the People's Court in Munich, the twenty-one-year-old Sophie Scholl, one leg in splints, displayed the same courage as had impelled her to act as flea against elephant. When she went to the scaffold, along with her brother, it is said that she smiled.

If the German soldiers at the front heard of the White Rose uprising it is possible they would have disapproved. They were engaged in a fight for life to stem the Russian advance and then drive it back past Kharkov. The notion of the political "stab in the back" of 1918, which had been put around after defeat in the First World War, was easily resurrected to stiffen the officers' resolve. First-hand experience of Russian relentlessness was a strong antiseptic against those who may have dreamed of a conciliatory approach to the Bolsheviks. In any case, the average German soldier, heavily outnumbered and short of modern equipment which the home industry was only just beginning to manufacture in anything approaching sufficient volume, had very little opportunity for political reflection. When he was disengaged from the enemy at the front he was back helping to clean out partisan nests in the rear. Even when traveling on leave he had to stand constant guard in case the train was ambushed.

When the spring thaw brought Manstein's counteroffensive to a halt at the end of March, it left a great Russian salient flanked in the south by a German one centered in open country surrounding Kharkov and in the north by the guerrilla-infested Bryansk-Orel bulge. The opportunity was thus presented to Manstein of cutting off the Kursk salient as soon as the ground had dried at the beginning of May. With justification the attention of military historians has focused upon what was to be a ponderous battle of giants, one that was so slow and self-evident in its preparation by the Germans that the Russians had ample warning of its coming. The Lucy Spy Ring, providing the Russians with incontrovertible information about the impending blow, guided the other intelligence agencies in the search for detailed information of German arrangements between Kharkov and Orel. Thus an unusually long period was granted to the defense and for the partisan bands, tired after the winter campaign, to reorganize.

Hitler and his generals had many reasons for delaying the offensive—the need to rebuild their tank force with the latest machines, to train and assemble reinforcements, to give the soldiers at the front a rest and to acquire bigger stocks of supplies. Yet it was better that they should act swiftly by surprise. During the first half of April, when the Germans were on the crest of victory, there was barely a smattering of guerrilla activity even in the dreaded Bryansk forests. But on the night of April 15, shortly after the Germans halted, every railway line out of Bryansk was cut to announce the start of a period in which it was a certainty that something would go bang after sunset.

The Germans could have operated much as they chose had they tried. A supreme example of their omnipotence was Operation Buffalo, the evacuation, in May, of the Rzhev salient to the northwest of Moscow in an area said to be thick with partisans. Dumps, equipment and soldiers were withdrawn practically unhindered. Even the civil populace was wholly removed.

Though the railway might be interrupted for extended periods, it is equally true that the movement of supplies and replacements to the front kept pace with the staffs' flexible schedules, which could always compensate for hostile actions. It was found possible to give a fair proportion of the German soldiers rest and retraining even when extracting special parties for short, sharp raids against partisan bands whenever information pinpointed a worthwhile target. But as time passed the German radio intercept teams became deeply impressed by the mounting volume of radio traffic between the partisan groups and the nearby Red Army regular formations to the eastward, and the intelligence staffs were constantly adding to the number of identified bands gathering in the sectors which soon would act as launching pads for the Manstein offensive. They recorded an increase of air supply traffic in May which amounted to one thousand per cent over February. Even if the bands failed to interrupt the logistic buildup they were sure to provide precise information of the German movements—as undoubtedly they did.

The delaying of the offensive beyond early May to some undisclosed date in the future was an invitation to disaster. The Russians had more time in which to organize the partisans, to say when and where to strike when the German offensive began and, above all, to plan the course of operations once the Germans had been quelled and the major Russian counteroffensive launched against the exhausted Germans. The underlying irony of the Kursk offensive—called Operation Citadel by the Germans—was that it sacrificed every element of surprise and that the German General Staff, convinced of its vulnerability, perfectly foresaw the likely aftermath of a repulse. They correctly envisaged a major Russian assault hitting them simultaneously with a partisan descent upon the lines of communication and the sudden uprising of an insurgent army in their rear. For the Germans there loomed an awful dilemma. If they kept complete faith with Citadel they were compelled to move vast supply dumps and nearly all their reserves close to the front; this the partisans would be unable to prevent. If, on the other hand, the Germans recognized the inevitability of defeat there was a danger that men and matériel at the front would be cut off when the partisans rose. Nothing would then remain as rearguard against the principal Russian advance after it started. Their only reasonable insurance schemes were complete withdrawal (as at Rzhev) and the cancelling of Citadel, or the elimination or neutralization of the partisan bands before Citadel began.

Hitler would not cancel Citadel, neither would he name a date. Antipartisan operations had to be carefully coordinated with the start of Citadel. Delay them too long and the troops involved would be lost to the offensive, perhaps even as reserves if they became deadlocked in a clinch with partisans. Start them too soon and the advantages won by destroying or dispersing the bands might be nullified by a few days of recuperation and reorganization by the Russians. It was eventually decided to compromise—to do as much as possible in selected sectors in an order of priority. Five large antipartisan operations were projected in the forests surrounding Bryansk.

They fell upon partisan forces which were tougher than those of the year before. Effective command was exercised by a former NKVD officer called Yemlyutin through a staff and an elaborate radio network and courier service operating in safety from east of the line. Orders were formulated on instructions from the HQ of the Red Army Front and could be transmitted rapidly into action by a military organization of brigades subdivided downwards, in the conventional military manner, to platoons. The leaders and key executives in the field were well-trained men sent in by the Red Army; the massed rank and file, on the other hand, were not necessarily trained at all. In fact the partisan army was a weak dilution of a typical mass-produced Russian infantry force. It had light artillery and mortars, horses, occasionally a few vehicles, and the units fought with the mobility and tactical inhibitions of infantry the world over—avoiding enemy strong points in order to strike at his weak ones. But when they themselves were attacked in strength, they had no option but to disperse because the superior firepower and better training of the German formations were almost bound to prevail.

Not that life was easy for those German soldiers. Weighed down by equipment the fighting man advanced to coordinating orders which inevitably restricted his initiative. He was advised to carry as many submachine guns as possible as well as a mortar or grenade launcher for high-angle fire; yet it was also felt better to carry more ammunition than weapons. For supplies he was recommended to carry rations for one day more than seemed necessary, and for communications a walkie-talkie radio (with its batteries) and great quantities of signal cartridges to keep touch between subunits. Every additional item reduced the agility of the unfortunate marching man and gave an added advantage to the guerrilla, who nipped back from cover to cover, sniping, ambushing and forcing one redeployment after another on the sweat- or rain-soaked German infantry. This was jungle fighting, quite different from the cut and thrust of armored warfare in that the combatants were protected by skill alone—plus luck.

The five German antiguerrilla operations prior to Citadel represent a turning point in the campaign on the East Front. First to take place was Ziegeunerbaron, an operation lasting from May 16 to June 6, which absorbed no less than the equivalent of four infantry and two panzer divisions, plus ancillary police, to comb out a reported force of six thousand partisans scattered through a triangle that was seventy-five miles long and about fifty miles wide at the base. The Germans claim to have eliminated about four thousand of the enemy, destroyed 207 camps and captured 1,128 small arms, but these figures can no more be substantiated than can the effects of the operation as a whole. During the period of the sweep (in which it was complained that the density of troops to such a vast area of woodland and swamp was quite inadequate) partisan activity practically ceased. But within a few weeks there were said to be three thousand back at work again, threatening the lines of communication. Naturally, in the course of the operation, the railways and roads became safer, so supplies moved more freely and the essential stocking up at the front proceeded apace.

Two operations launched to the north of Bryansk on May 19 and 21 were more specific in their objective than Ziegeunerbaron. They aimed at located bands and were of the cordon and search variety with the object of total annihilation. But Osterei used lower-grade security troops and managed only to disperse the band while Freischütz, though employing the best parts of a corps and moving through thick country in almost constant rainfall, succeeded only in catching a part of the enemy force; the rest slipped away as so often before. Nachbar-hilfe, also launched on May 19, but to the west of Bryansk, used two divisions but suffered the same difficulties as all the others when committed to wooded terrain. Short-range ambushes by partisan rear-guards delayed the German advance; local firefights broke out and disorganized the orderly German progress; subunits began to fall out of touch and opened up gaps through which the partisans could infiltrate to safety. In due course the central camp was discovered—with its stores and airfields mostly demolished by the Russians before they retreated—but the core of the band survived, its losses but a tithe of the wastage that was taken as normal in this pitiless theater of war. Of the fifth operation, Tannhäuser, one can only record a hollow German victory: forewarned, the gang of seven hundred had shifted.

Tannhäuser ended the sequence of antipartisan operations on June 23, yet by the end of the month there were so many bands in evidence again that it and its predecessors might never have taken place. Once more the railway lines were being shattered and road convoys ambushed; again the Germans dared move only in large parties. And still Operation Citadel awaited the order to start. Not until July 2, in fact, was it issued—for the 5th—but by then it went in against an enemy whose regular forces were perfectly poised and whose partisan army had so far recovered as to pose a most serious threat to the Germans, no matter how successful they might be in the approaches to Kursk. Yet for all their numbers, new organization and durability, the partisans had utterly failed to prevent the Germans attacking. Indeed the German Army advanced on July 5 with a strong sense of its old invincibility, even if at headquarters there were feelings of disquiet at what might loom ahead and what might strike in the rear. If this sense of insecurity is interpreted as a serious inhibition it was the one important partisan achievement prior to Citadel.

As the Germans attacked, the balance of strategic power lurched hard against them. Until then the other battle fronts had absorbed minor proportions of their effort. But on July 10 the Western Allies invaded Sicily at the moment when it became clear that the attack at Kursk was abortive. On the 12th Hitler called off Citadel. A vast Russian offensive threatened its flank in the Orel sector and absorbed all remaining German reserves, and the partisans were fiendishly busy in the German rear—the harbingers of far deadlier threats to come. But principally reinforcements were needed in Italy and could be found mainly from the Russian front. The air battle over Germany also rose to a new crescendo: July 24 marked the beginning of a series of four air attacks on the city of Hamburg in which 3,095 sorties carried 9,000

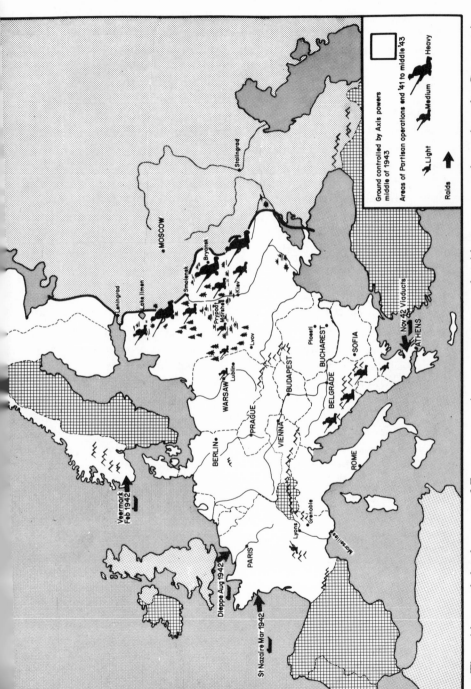

The widespread development of European partisan movements as the tide turns strongly against the Germans in mid-1943, shortly before the Italian capitulation.

tons of bombs in an orgy of destruction which killed 50,000 and wounded 40,000 people, sending over a million scurrying for safety in the countryside and destroying more than half the buildings. On August 16, the night after the last Axis troops had left Sicily, RAF bombers struck at a new target the contents of which would one day usher in a new phase in the art of mass destruction: they attacked the rocket experimental station at Peenemunde and in so doing delayed the development of long-range strategic weapons which, had they not been checked, might have enabled the Germans to devastate British cities with impunity. Thus air power attacked the very sort of technical target which, had it been possible to tackle it with partisans, might have justified immense losses in manpower. But it was simply impossible to introduce partisan forces of sufficient size into a hostile country to destroy major targets. The Germans, for example, could not have assaulted a radar factory in England nor the Japanese an atomic plant in the USA. Air power might *just* have got them into the vicinity, but the reaction by defenders and local populace would have been fatal.

Bad news filtered through to the German people in the summer of 1943, but it reached the Italians with unrelieved force. As Sicily fell into Allied hands Benito Mussolini was deposed on July 25 without bloodshed in the nearest approach to constitutional methods that could be expected of so rare an event. The deposition of Mussolini, and his incarceration by those who had taken over, was one thing; it was another to reckon upon the imminent withdrawal of Italy from the war. A study of the map showed Italian troops fighting feebly at the German side on nearly every front—filling gaps if nothing better, for the Italian soldiery never had much heart for the fight. Yet at any moment the halfhearted friend of today might become the determined foe of tomorrow and it was an undeniable fact that the bulk of Italian formations were in either Italy or Yugoslavia. What would be the outcome if they were allowed to change sides, to fight an organized or guerrilla war on home ground against the Germans or in Yugoslavia along with the most deadly partisan army of all—Tito's?

CHAPTER NINE

Balkan Toils

"Militia and armed civilians," wrote Clausewitz, "cannot and should not be employed against the main force of the enemy, or even against sizable units. . . . They should rise in provinces lying to one side of the main theater of war, which the invader does not enter in force, in order to draw these areas entirely from his grasp." Tito's Yugoslavian Partisans somehow or other managed to contradict that dictum. During the so-called First Axis Offensive of 1941 and early 1942 they had been engaged against sizable enemy units and it was arguable whether or not they had risen to one side of the main theater of war. To the Germans the Balkans were important in that they provided vital materials and lay on the flank of the Russian front, acting partly as a base for supply of their armies in North Africa and offering a springboard for further penetrations into the Middle East should these prove desirable. Tito's rising also broke Lawrence's rule which demanded sympathy from a friendly population. Great segments, on the contrary, were hostile to the Partisans: racial differences supervened, regardless of party or creed, and the adherents of Nedic and Mihailovic bent to the German will and were pliable to the Italians.

Fancy the irony of a situation in which Tito, the Communist, found himself opposed by Mihailovic's Cetniks, who in turn were aligned with the Royalist émigré government, which received official recognition from Moscow. He still had radio contact with Moscow but apparently little prestige, for, despite promises, they had yet to fly in a mission, let alone supplies, and totally omitted to speak of his Partisans. Imagine too his misgivings about British intentions. For after their first emissary, Hudson, had shown favor to the Partisans there came that long silence broken only by BBC news and local intelligence that the British were actively supporting the Cetniks. With practically every hand against them Tito and his followers were chivied from one end of the country to another.

Between January 15 and 26, 1942, the Germans stepped up their offensive in the Balkans, though the divisions diverted from all over Europe were wanted badly in Russia. Their 342nd Division fought to the last moment before being transferred to the Eastern Front and, in a stiff little operation, which the Partisans call the Second Offensive, lost 150 dead and wounded, plus 300 from frostbite, in exchange for 521 partisans dead, 1,331 captured plus numerous rifles, machine guns and a few pieces of artillery. To the Partisans this was a harrowing and yet creative period. Dragging their wounded they arrived at Foca in eastern Bosnia on January 25. Here, in due course, they were to be attacked again, but this time only by an enemy force depleted by the need for their redeployment to Russia. Hence the Partisans were able to hold their own and, moreover, expand their strength. At the same time their anger was advantageously inflamed by Cetnik intransigence and cruelty. At this moment the pattern of future conduct in the Balkan campaign was sealed. Quarter would be neither asked nor given for the rest of the war; the whirlwind of cruelty would swirl up, destroying everything in its path and obliterating the slightest tendency to mercy or chivalry. Now, too, the Germans crystallized their antipartisan strategy. If troops could be spared from the main battle front they could be deployed against Partisans; but the battle front came first. This is in marked contrast to suggestions that Partisans deflected men from the main battle to fight Partisans. They rarely did. What might seem a major operation to the Partisans was, frequently, just a minor incident to the Germans.

For weeks on end Tito's Partisans were able to withstand the Second Axis Offensive, keeping a hold on the Foca region and inflicting losses on their enemies. In the same period they enhanced their prowess, learning lessons swiftly from mistakes in battle which might never have been learned any other way. Sometimes, in the political confusion of the times, the Cetniks fought at their side, shifting allegiance at the whims of leaders whose aim was a short-term military rearguard action as insurance against some vague, long-term scheme for restoring the old political order. Perhaps the greatest partisan feat in this period was their solution of logistic problems. Deprived of regular sources of supply they could only live off the country and arm themselves from the enemy. In this connection the Cetniks and the Italians were the best providers, the latter the more likely to collapse in an ambush and drop their arms in the ensuing flight. The Partisan order of combat priorities thus became empirically established as the Second Offensive rose to a climax throughout April and May: avoid the dangerous Germans if possible, attack the Cetniks and Italians,

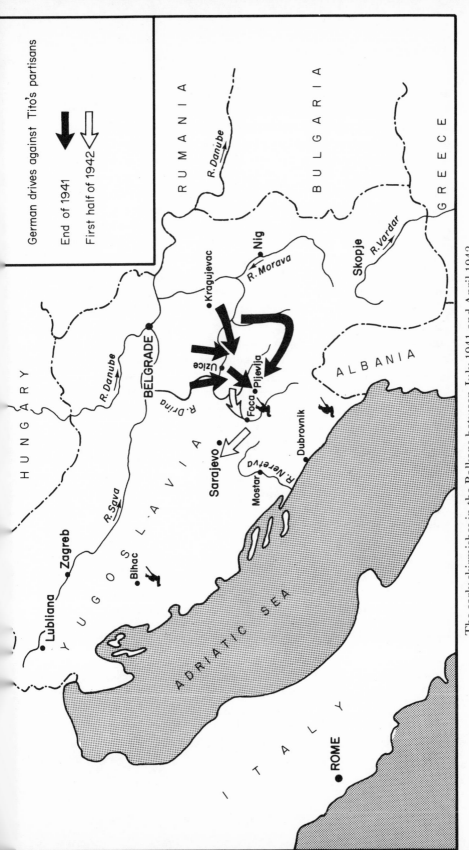

The early skirmishes in the Balkans between July 1941 and April 1942.

German drives against Tito's partisans

End of 1941

First half of 1942

reinforce ideological faith, and recruit manpower. Tactics throughout remained those of the pure guerrilla—ambush followed by quick disengagement; fluid defense by rearguard actions and the shifting of effort from one part of an infiltrated region to another—the entire process utterly dependent upon sound intelligence of enemy intentions gleaned from those of the populace who supported the cause and from agents (whose identity is undisclosed) within the German command. And overall lay the cloud of brutality and the ritual slaughter of innocents, the wounded and the politically abhorrent.

At the summit, however, stood the Partisans' greatest asset—Tito himself. F.W.D. Deakin, who, in 1943, was to head a British mission to Tito, has portrayed him as of "deceptively quiet personality, used to imposing his authority with few words or gestures, commanding an instinctive and total respect from those around him, sure in judgment and deeply self-controlled." This was no Makhno of wild excesses, nor yet a Trotsky even though he recognized the vital necessity of building a formal political unity and military organization to further his aims. Certainly he was to be compared neither to Lawrence nor to any of the Russian guerrilla leaders after 1941, for each of these had depended upon extensive help from external government and army agencies. Nor can Tito be measured against Moulin, whose political problems and environmental circumstances were so very different, although they shared the indefinable characteristics of command by sheer force of "quiet" personality as opposed to extrovert filibuster. Perhaps the closest resemblance to Tito of any other twentieth-century great political and guerrilla captain is to be found with the Irish leader Michael Collins, for both strove to reform a national political structure while directing an intensive armed struggle and did so by thoughtful dexterity rather than emotional histrionics. It is likely, however, that Tito was the most imperturbable of them all, a virtue that counted for much in the desperate situations in which these vital leaders found themselves.

By mid-April the Partisans had won a temporary breathing space in that they had prevented their multifarious opponents from driving them from Foca. There was a lull until May 4 when every anti-Communist force within striking distance began to converge, under German direction, upon the Foca position—the Third Offensive according to the Partisan calendar, but just a series of minor operations in the German rating. The Germans planned to drive the Partisans westward towards a stop line established along the River Neretva. With air support they made careful progress into the Partisan-infested areas, doggedly trying to forge an impenetrable strategic ring backed by heavy weapons, but fatally hampered by the Italians, who chose this moment to reduce their forces in the areas to which the Partisans were retreating.

Shortages of food and ammunition supplies were spurs to the Partisans' strategy. They were eating watery soup and sour plum pulp while improvising armament and expending enormous energy clambering up and down mountain slopes to engage the enemy from tactically superior positions. On May 10 Foca had to be abandoned. Once more Tito and his men were compelled to shift in order to break through the Neretva barrier and so retire into a fresh and safer mountain fastness in western Bosnia.

The guerrilla army crossed the Neretva and trudged past Jajce, which it reached on September 25, and then on to Bihac, which it captured in November. It was almost unique in that it imbibed a discipline that far excelled that of any other force of similar nature. Looting was forbidden and the ban was enforced by execution of those who broke it; all stores had to be bought from the civil populace; coercion of noncombatants was frowned upon, though inevitably innocents who were taken as Cetniks must have suffered. Relations between the sexes within the movement were elevated to a high moral standard; there is little evidence of petticoat government, nor was the part the women played undervalued, since it was considerable in all fields of activity. By the end of November this unique army, in the final stages of a long fighting retreat through tortuous country, was still growing and not dissolving as a regular army might have done. By then it stood at twenty-eight brigades, each between three thousand and four thousand men and women—and the movement controlled something like three quarters of the entire country, not only where its main concentration ruled in Bosnia and parts of Croatia but also throughout the land where scattered parties lurked aggressively among the enemy. Nevertheless, the main communication centers and arteries still functioned quite smoothly in Axis hands. Minerals were shifted to the north (for Germany) and supplies to the south and onwards to Greece, if not through Yugoslavia then by sea along the Adriatic or by the longer route through Bulgaria.

The Axis had now to recognize the presence of what amounted to a hostile army in their midst since Tito's forces had nearly outgrown the pure guerrilla concept even though their basic tactics remained in the guerrilla mode due to lack of heavy weapons. Moreover they knew that Tito was something exceptional, not just a warlord. He was strong enough to summon safely an "Anti-Fascist Council for the National Liberation of Yugoslavia" in Bihac on November 26, to which representatives came from all over the country. Here the aims of the movement were stated in public. It was a demonstration of independ-ence—a plea to the Allies to recognize the influence and power of the Partisan movement, as well as a gesture of defiance to the Axis, who were unable to intervene. On December 28, 1942, Hitler raised the strength of his forces in the Balkans to that of an Army Group, com-manded by General Loehr as commander-in-chief, Southeast.

In yet another way the Bihac meeting marked a watershed in Tito's campaign. It foreshadowed a series of renewed attempts by the Allies to disentangle the cat's cradle of conflicting opinions regulating sup-port for the various factions within Yugoslavia and, moreover, focused attention on the only secret army within the Western orbit which was doing something more constructive than plan and wait for easier days.

After the Hudson mission collapsed in the turmoil of the First Offensive and the unfortunate Hudson was forced to take to the hills, where he endured the life of a destitute refugee, Tito's attempts to make permanent contact with the Russians also foundered. But Mihailovic had restored radio contact with the Royalist government in London (and thus indirectly with Moscow) so that, for all practical purposes, his was the solitary organization recognized by the Allies as offering positive resistance to the Axis. Unchallenged, he fed them false information which bore no relation to the real nature of his collabora-tion with the Axis.

Not until April 1942 did Hudson emerge from the wilderness and rejoin Mihailovic in his Montenegrin stronghold. And it was June before he was able to report to London that he had proof of Cetnik collaboration with the Axis, such were the delays in communication which hampered the primitive guerrilla movements. In the months that followed, through a new radio set brought in by British operators, Hudson was able gradually to paint pictures of Cetnik insincerity (contradicted by Mihailovic's slander of Hudson) which were at total variance with what Mihailovic was telling his own government and which, to Tito's disgust as he struggled towards Jajce, were being broadcast by the BBC. The tone of news sent out by the BBC and, from July, by the Russian-sponsored radio program "Free Yugoslavia," helped to polarize the factions, the former mentioning only the Cet-niks, the latter at last drawing official Allied attention to the existence of the Partisans as a viable force. Nevertheless Hudson doggedly believed that the Cetniks in Montenegro might just be turned to Allied account. As a result SOE Cairo continued to lend currency to British and American government policy by supporting the Cetniks, whose leader, after all, was Minister of War in the recognized Yugoslavian government.

Throughout the summer of 1942, when the Germans seemed on the verge of overrunning the Russians, Hudson wrestled with a mass of conflicting evidence—unable it seems to form a coherent opinion of his own, and thereby confusing SOE and his political masters. It is hardly surprising: he was isolated and had suffered grievously. At one moment he was asking for a substantial arms drop to the Montenegrin Cetniks; at another unwittingly underwriting a deal diverting Allied money to purchase arms from the Italians (!), for use against the German-run rail link through Serbia; and at yet a third moment he was signaling (in September), "The Partisan organization is miles ahead of Mihailovic's." The last opinion, at any rate, was accurate. Mihailovic consistently declined to sabotage the Axis on the pretext that to do so would merely invite the Germans to take over from the Italians in Montenegro and disrupt his plans for personally taking over the government in Belgrade "when the Italians collapsed."

At the end of December a fresh agent (who was more experienced in Yugoslavian politics), Lieutenant-Colonel S. W. Bailey, was dropped in safety to Mihailovic with orders to make an independent reassessment of the Cetnik organization. Quickly it became as plain to him, as it had to Hudson, that the Cetniks were keener to have the Italians for allies than anybody else and that their dedicated enemies were the Partisans. Bailey began his report as Churchill and Roosevelt were meeting at Casablanca in January, as the campaign for 1943 was being planned and as the Russians rolled forward after their victory at Stalingrad. To the Allied Chiefs of Staff it now became important for the Axis in Yugoslavia to be harassed as a diversion from their other schemes even though no actual Allied landing in the Balkans was planned.

The Allies thus demonstrated their ignorance of events. General Loehr, at Hitler's instigation, was throwing in a larger and better force than ever before assembled against the Partisans in what he called Operation Weiss and what was known by the Partisans as the Fourth Offensive. There was a drive from the north by four German divisions, including SS (Eugen) and the Third Brandenburg Regiment—thieves hunting thieves—and Nedic's Ustas Divisions towards Bihac with the intention of seizing the bauxite-producing regions that were once under Italian protection. This had the incidental effect of driving Tito's forces towards the River Neretva, which once more did service as a stop line, held by Italians and Cetniks—the Third Offensive in reverse in fact.

At this moment the Allies realized another fundamental point. Unless they supported the Partisans, who, day by day, looked the more likely to govern the country in future, Tito would turn irrevocably to the Russians, who, in due course, would reach the Eastern Yugoslavian frontier. The British were much more afraid of a Communist-dominated Balkans that the Americans. Moreover the subject could not be debated since public morale was stiffened by pro-Russian slogans. But the fear was securely implanted in the British diplomatic mind and never again forgotten.

Thus the Fourth Offensive contained a deeper political implication than the Axis can have dreamed of when they started this routine, large-scale, antiguerrilla action. True, they had been stung by the realization that the emergence of a new state within the German sphere of hegemony could not be tolerated, but the herding of Tito's main force towards the Neretva, and thus in the direction of Montenegro, did more than reclaim bauxite and instigate a battle. Besides bringing the Partisans into collision with the Cetniks it also thrust them towards Albania and Greece, two countries whose guerrilla forces were nothing so vigorous as those in Yugoslavia, but where, nonetheless, strong Communist-inspired movements existed, ostensibly backed by SOE.

The uneasy peace which permeated most of Greece throughout 1941 was extended into 1942 despite an urgent need, on the Allied side, for the Axis line of communication to the Piraeus, and thus through Crete to North Africa, to be attacked. Confidence as well as latent strength had been shattered when a British party, landed by submarine on the island of Antiperos in the spring of 1942, had been captured in possession of its list of contacts in Athens; many Greeks paid with their lives for that indiscretion. But in any case the Greeks were split among themselves. The proroyalist party of National Union, the prorepublican EDES and EKKA and the Communist EAM regarded each other with hostile suspicion as each endeavored to create dominant strength. There also emerged a wide mental gulf between the guerrillas who lurked in the hills and the bulk of the populace who subsisted in the towns. Those in the mountains were the natural fighters, bred into a world of brigandage and inured to a life of abject poverty. The townsmen were perhaps more sophisticated but just as gullible to propaganda by the rival parties as their tougher neighbors in the open country. Each political wing possessed its own secret army—the weak EKKA's under Colonel Psaros, EDES's under Colonel Zervas and EAM's (the best organized of all) called ELAS. SOE had the political task (laid down by the Foreign Office) of coordinating them. It also had the military role of attacking logistic targets, regardless of which party happened to be strong in a particular strategic locality. SOE, for military reasons, hoped to unify; inevitably it played politics that were disruptive. Thus the British party of twelve, led by Colonel Myers, which, after an earlier cancellation, landed near Mont Giona on September 30, had two quite different aims. Myers was told primarily to engage in an act of sabotage against railway targets and then withdraw by submarine while Colonel Woodhouse, his deputy (who, unlike Myers, was bilingual), was to stay behind as liaison officer with Zervas of EDES.

There ensued terrible confusion amid "blind" drops, corrupt communications, tenuous contact with rival guerrilla bands—and only a tentative convergence in the direction of the viaducts and bridges which were marked down for demolition. The guerrillas they met were a poorly equipped, sparsely clad and armed bunch, though it was found possible to get ELAS and Zervas to work in harness. The Zervas group was the better if only because, on October 23, they had conducted a successful ambush against an Italian convoy in the Louros Gorge. This in its way was a classic, small guerrilla operation initiated by the mining of the leading tank in the gorge, followed by the engagement of the nineteen trucks and their occupants by fire from the hundred guerrillas in the peaks above, the blowing up of a bridge behind the column after the last vehicle, another tank, had passed across it, and then the systematic killing of the panicking Italians as they scattered in search of cover beneath the crags from which rifles and machine guns rattled. Lastly came a charge by the triumphant Greeks to slay the remaining Italians before stripping the convoy of its contents, loading them onto mules and vanishing into the hills.

Myers finally settled on the Gorgopotamos viaduct as his target —an Italian-garrisoned river crossing just to the south of Lamia on the main Salonika-to-Athens railway. The operation itself had to be postponed by stages, partly because of the time needed to collect sufficient men and stores, and partly because the ELAS were slow to make up their minds due to their politically motivated fears of Axis reprisals. When at last the garrison was assaulted and the bridge blown on the night of November 26 (note how it took nearly two months to arrange this single operation) it was a complete success. The line was stopped for thirty-nine days just when Axis fortunes in North Africa were at their nadir and those in Russia on the brink of doom. Any suggestion that this operation affected Rommel's operations in North Africa is, of course, false: the battle was decided long before the bridge was blown. But the happy conclusion of one successful operation encouraged SOE Cairo to assume that, in Greece, they had found at last a happy hunting ground where sabotage missions could operate in an environment so much more politically welcoming than the Yugoslavian one. SOE, still suspect in the consideration of GHQ and desperately anxious to prove its worth after two years' mediocrity, at once decided to create a network of missions in Greece under Myers (who was promoted to brigadier and told to stay in Greece despite the fact that he could not speak the language). Almost simultaneously both Myers and Woodhouse drew the conclusion that EAM and ELAS were Communist controlled and bent upon taking over the country.

Thus, rather suddenly there appeared in Greece the threat of internal feuding which existed among every other guerrilla movement. SOE teams, composed mostly of young men of action rather than elders with diplomatic wisdom, were plunged into negotiations to disentangle complex political intrigues which could mold Europe's future, instead of pursuing military operations designed to harm the Axis. From difficulties such as these the Axis largely stayed happily aloof, content to guard the essential communications, reacting only when provoked, and stirring up different factions regardless of future damage to social relations.

The quest by the guerrillas for arms went on relentlessly—the Axis armies or the more gullible British liaison officers acting as the agents of supply for emergent political factions. During the winter of 1943 it was EAM/ELAS who began to take charge, their improved organization, better propaganda machine and greater ruthlessness in pursuit of their objectives putting them ahead of Zervas. With spring came the first direct EAM/ELAS political challenge and, from then on, mounting chaos in a country engaged in civil war within the framework of the anti-Axis struggle. In the forefront stood the British—doing all they could to placate both sides in the interests of their own war effort and their obligation to the original exiled government. Well aside waited the Americans. Sabotage of Axis rail links would continue, mainly at the hands of British agents and only rarely by the Greeks, who were far too busy rearming and pursuing political quarrels, while fending off British requests with fair words and excuses in the manner of Mihailovic.

Albania, too, was kept in a ferment as much by factional disputes and political maneuvers as by hostilities against the Italian occupation. When Italy first invaded the country, in 1939, only local resistance had occurred, though since then the customary triumvirate of rival parties had appeared. These were the Royalists, run by Abas Kupi, who from 1941 was aided by the British, the Republicans under Bal Kombetar who were as anti-Communist as anti-Royalist, and the Communist National Liberation Front (FNC) run by Enver Hoxa.

Guerrilla warfare was made easier in Albania by the nature of the mountainous country, the natural brigandage of the populace and the ineptitude of the Italian garrison, which, like most Italian garrisons, preferred to live and let live, to dwell convivially in the towns instead of looking for trouble in the country. Thus there was ample opportunity for the guerrillas to recruit their strength and measure it against each other. However it was not until Mussolini was deposed in July 1943 that a seriously coordinated rebellion took place—and drew upon itself fearsome reprisals from the five Italian divisions stationed in the country.

A cynical outsider reviewing the Balkan situation in mid-1943 might have concluded that nothing much had changed in local politics for several decades. And yet there *was* something new and potentially sinister—the widespread growth of Communist movements to a standard pattern. The danger was that, without a democratic test of public opinion, these independently minded nations might find themselves taken over by governments against which there could be no appeal. There is no evidence to prove that Russia, the principal Communist country, laid down uniform guidelines for local parties. Indeed we have seen how the Russians tended to ignore Tito. Likewise the Albanian Communist movement not only grew strong with SOE help but determined to run the country itself, without Russian supervision. The Balkans at that moment were outside the Russian sphere of influence and the Allies preferred to get as little involved as possible. Everything they projected there was viewed militarily—merely in the nature of a distraction from the coming Allied invasion of Sicily (due to take place in July). The series of rail-cutting expeditions brilliantly undertaken by the British and a handful of Greeks throughout June, embarrassing as they were to the Axis by severing the main lines in forty-four places and putting the Asopos viaduct out of action for three months, did little to help win the war. Instead it improved the local guerrilla bands' prowess and trained them all the better for the internecine combat upon which they were bent. Likewise attempts to create secret armies of indeterminate political persuasion merely recruited the future contenders in a civil war.

It was Mihailovic who guessed and suggested in February 1943 that the movement of Communist Yugoslav Partisans towards Greece (a movement early detected by British eavesdropping on German radio traffic connected with the Fourth Offensive) could be the first step in a plan to link all the Balkan Communist movements, but this was largely discounted in the Allied camp. It must be remembered that, at that moment, neither the full strength of Tito's Partisans nor the degree of

Communist infiltration of Greece and Albania was understood. The earlier ineptitude of GHQ and SOE Cairo had partly seen to that. As the summer passed; as fresh missions to Yugoslavia (notably that led by Deakin to Tito in May 1943) came to close quarters with the Partisans; as Bailey reported unfavorably on Mihailovic, and Myers and Woodhouse evaluated the Grecian imbroglio, and a mission to Albania assessed the situation there, insight would deepen. But the overriding suspicion of postwar Russian intentions had not yet been formulated.

Tito, of course, held the key to the Balkan situation, and largely because his withdrawal before the German-Ustasi Weiss Offensive actually served as the impulse to bring about a decisive encounter with the Cetniks. Tito's execution of this campaign within a campaign was masterly. Using his 7th Division to act as rearguard to hold off the enemy sweep from the north (while the wounded were evacuated) he threw the bulk of his army eastward to attack the Cetniks on the Neretva with the aim of opening a way back into Montenegro. His strategy, in essence, was the refusal of intensive action against enemy strength, as represented by the Germans, and concentration against weakness—the Cetniks. Closely attended by incessant bombing, by food shortage and the ravages of typhus the Partisans were compelled to fight their way past Italians and Ustasi outposts before they could even reach the combined Italian Cetnik line on the Neretva. This was a slow-moving, inexorable battle whose development, though dictated by the complexity of the country, was made easier than the previous winter's campaign in that the weather was milder.

Mountain warfare for peaks and defiles swallows army formations like ants in a hayfield. The initiative passes swiftly from attacker to defender and back. Yet true mobility can best be practiced through the byways of such tortuous terrain, and the element which moved faster than any other in this battle was the corps of two Partisan divisions which Tito sent by forced marches to cross the Neretva near Jablanica. At Prozor they launched an attack on the Italians supported by "seven field guns and thirteen field pieces," to quote Dedijer, who goes on to quote an officer called Terzic who speaks as if this puny artillery force could fire a grand barrage. "First we shall give them 150 howitzer shells, then suggest they surrender. If they refuse, they will be wiped out." But the Italians and Cetniks did not at once surrender and battle raged long on the Neretva as a race developed between the German attempt to break Tito's rearguard, and thus crush the Partisan flank from the north, and the Partisan effort to escape through a passage driven into the mountain stronghold of Montenegro. Fortunately for the Partisans the primary rebuff at Prozor was attended by local success further south near Mostar where their 2nd Division routed the Italian Murge Division, capturing its tanks, guns and equipment and scattering the men. Meanwhile the column of wounded was painfully dragging its way nearer the Neretva, praying for the breakthrough that would ensure its safety, hoping the typhus would abate and desperate not to fall into German hands, which meant death. Perhaps it was Tito's insistence on protecting the wounded from almost inevitable execution if captured which was the key factor in maintaining Partisan morale at a consistently high level. "We shall give all we have to save our wounded men," he said to Dedijer. Perhaps also it was the satis-faction of attacking even when in direst peril which raised morale to unprecedented heights during the crisis of the Fourth Offensive—but the euphoria created by good propaganda linked to a fervent political motivation must never be ignored in an evaluation of this kind.

Steadily the protagonists became compressed between Prozor and Mostar, the Partisans squeezing the weaker Italian units and the desperate Cetniks, yet simultaneously trying to escape the German trap by infiltrating their way through ravines and across mountain passes. At last, at the beginning of March, the Neretva line began to crumble while the German assaults were stalled by exhaustion in ideal defensive country. By the middle of the month, the Partisans were safely over the Neretva, pressing the Cetniks hard. But lacking the steadfastness and purpose of the Partisans, the Cetniks broke and were pursued into Montenegro, dispersed and discredited. Here was Tito's perfectly timed valediction, for now the Bailey mission was able to confirm the inherent brittleness of the Cetniks in action and watch them dissolve into an undisciplined rabble which lost faith in its aim as its leader continued to procrastinate. It was the very strain of defeat in the field that made Mihailovic, in an outburst to Bailey, publicly reveal his duplicity when he angrily declared that he found the Italians better friends than the Allies. Indeed, Mihailovic by now could count only on the Italians for help—and even they were being discouraged when German protests to Mussolini brought orders forbidding the supply of arms. The Germans, ever wary of Mihailovic, launched Operation Schwarz against his Cetniks in May as insurance against their interference if an Allied invasion came—an operation which also hit Tito's Partisans in their new refuge in Montenegro.

Clearly fighting during the Fourth Offensive in Yugoslavia ex-ceeded the limits of irregular warfare. Formation grappled with for-mation, fronts were formed and assailed, formal rearguard actions held off long prepared offensives, and the Partisan formations fought to retain their cohesion, dispersing in the guerrilla fashion ever less willingly as time passed. When Deakin joined Tito at the end of May 1943 he found the Partisans again under pressure, this time from the Fifth Offensive (Schwarz), which had rapidly succeeded the Fourth in pursuing Tito into Montenegro and hemming him in close by the slopes of Mount Durmitor. Indeed Deakin's arrival coincided with a critical phase of Tito's rearguard action, causing Tito to delay his own retreat to the last moment in order to meet the new mission—and putting himself in peril. But by this time the Partisans were firmly in control, more heavily armed and better able to dictate the course of battle through their ability to stand and fight instead of automatically giving way. They did not possess the ability to make a protracted stand but, using the intricate terrain, could delay the enemy to the point of distraction. Not that the Germans themselves considered Partisans better in quality than brigands: on May 5, for example, orders to the 118th Jäger Division laid down that anyone who participated openly in the fight against the Wehrmacht and was taken prisoner was to be shot after interrogation.

Tito could now arrange diplomatic exchanges in the knowledge that the Western Allies were at last becoming convinced of his military value and political significance—even though the irksome BBC reports still gave as much credit to the Cetniks as to the Partisans. The British Foreign Office braced itself for a break with the Royal Yugoslav Government if it continued to support Mihailovic. The hesitation over recognizing Tito was caused by an instinctive distaste for any Communist régime, and by worries about the effect of reversing the policy of only supporting *de jure* émigré governments, which might lead to involvement in the ramifications of Balkan diplomacy.

In the end it was Churchill who broke the deadlock after reports from Yugoslavia had clearly defined, to his satisfaction, who was fighting for the Allied cause and who against. On June 22 he had told the British Chiefs of Staff that extra air transport should be made available to the Partisans with "priority even over the bombing of Germany"—an intervention which went far deeper than the mere resolution of the Yugoslavian impasse. Churchill was demonstrating his support for partisans everywhere in their battle to obtain more aircraft from Portal and Harris of the RAF, who, throughout the preceding months (and those to follow), did all in their power to starve SOE. On July 26 the Chiefs of Staff agreed to support SOE in the Balkans "if necessary at the expense of supply to the resistance groups in Western Europe"—a procrastination which led Lord Selborne (now head of SOE) to take the matter to the Defense Committee on August

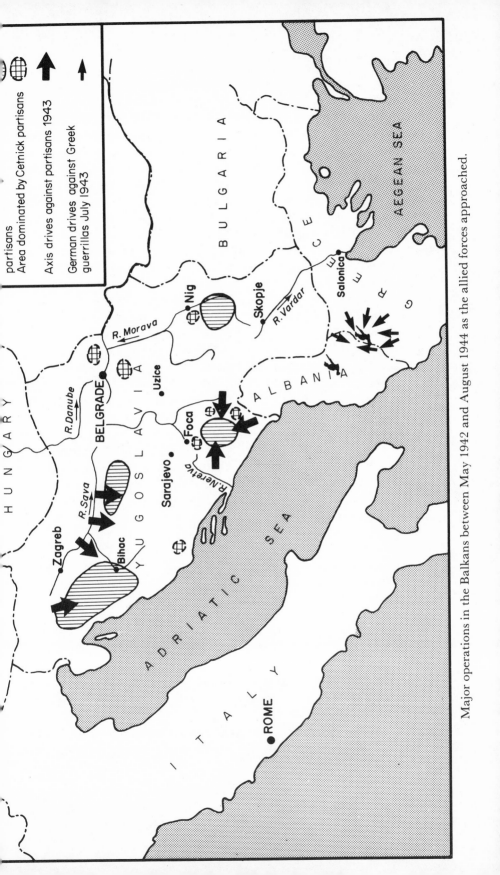

Legend:
- ⊕ partisans
- ⊖ Area dominated by Cetnick partisans
- ⬆ Axis drives against partisans 1943
- ↑ German drives against Greek guerrillas July 1943

Major operations in the Balkans between May 1942 and August 1944 as the allied forces approached.

2 "since resistance was booming." Again the Prime Minister sided with SOE by emphasizing the need to stimulate resistance among the people of Europe brushing aside the fear of reprisals with a resounding quotation from Tertullian: "The blood of the martyrs was the seed of the church."

On July 7, as the invasion of Sicily began, Churchill had written to General Alexander, the Commander-in-Chief, drawing his attention to the Partisans' achievements and adding: "If we can get hold of the mouth of the Adriatic so as to be able to run even a few ships into Dalmatian or Greek ports, the whole of the Western Balkans might flare up, with far-reaching results." This reflected the military approach by SOE Cairo—though not by SOE London. A fortnight later he reinforced his case from the political angle when he wrote of the marvelous resistance of the Partisans besides that of the guerrillas in Albania and Greece, extolling the advantages of drawing more and better German formations into the Balkans as the Russian offensive intensified to the east and pressure fell on the Italians. "The enemy cannot spare these forces, and if Italy collapses the Germans could not bear the weight themselves. Great prizes lie in the Balkan direction."

The real significance of the passage was related to Churchill's dogged attempts to persuade the Americans to value the dividends offered by striking at the Axis underbelly—a theme he was to return to over and again in dispute with the Americans over their fixation upon military objectives—above all upon an invasion of Western Europe. "No objective can compete with the capture of Rome," he wrote to Alexander on July 22, "which in its turn gives a stage later all the advantages hoped for from the Balkan liberation. . . . The fall of Italy, the effect upon the other German satellites, and the subsequent utter loneliness of Germany may conceivably produce decisive results in Europe." Success by Balkan partisans, real or imaginary, was fuel for Churchill's arguments.

Before convincing results could be obtained, SOE Cairo had once more to be dusted down. Sweet-Escott was to conclude, after visiting the headquarters in July, that it was dominated by the Chief of Staff, Brigadier Keeble, of whom "nearly everyone went in almost mortal terror." Keeble was inclined to bully and "could tell GHQ that he was not responsible to them but to London. . . . There was no coherent planning." Woodhouse was to write of SOE Cairo that "the gap between it and those serving under it in the field was wider than is normally the case in military formations." He goes on to quote the case of the first party of four British parachutists dropped into Greece and how, four months later, SOE had no trace of their names, adding, however, "the gulf was caused not by the individuals but the system." In September, nevertheless, when Gubbins took charge of SOE London, Lord Glenconner, who was head of SOE Cairo, almost simultaneously resigned, his withdrawal shortly followed by the replacement of Keeble in November. Thus at a critical moment in the development of the Mediterranean war, with the Balkans on fire, Italy invaded and knocked out of the war, SOE, whose role was bound to be of the greatest importance, was in upheaval.

Ten months would elapse before British liaison officers were withdrawn from Mihailovic. The Americans, because they attempted to fight battles separately from involvement in European politics, would take even longer to recognize the *fait accompli*. The Americans were novices in the European political field, ill adjusted, above all, to the deviousness of Balkan politics. They would not or could not recognize that Tito had won the diplomatic battle as a result of success in the field. Victory, however, would not be complete until the guerrilla armies became regularized with heavy weapons, or the enemy withdrew of his own accord.

In June the first indications appeared that a vacuum might occur in the Balkans. The Italians, fearfully aware that an Allied invasion of their homeland was imminent, began the withdrawal of troops from the Balkans without, in every area, allowing the Germans time to fill the gaps. With thoroughgoing urgency the Germans searched high and low for reinforcements without reducing their offensive at Kursk—bringing in 1st Panzer Division from France, where it had been reequipping, scratching together a dozen local formations (some of them newly formed) and persuading the Bulgarians to contribute a greater share of occupying forces. On July 26 the Germans centralized command under Field-Marshal von Weichs, who replaced Loehr as Commander-in-Chief Southeast. Yet the emphasis of Weichs's task was put conventionally upon defense of the coastline against invasion. A strategic reserve of six divisions, including two panzer, was placed at his disposal for mobile counterattack while the securing of the lines of communication to ensure this formation's freedom of movement to threatened places was given priority. Therefore antiguerrilla policy perfectly emulated that practiced on the Russian Front—whence von Weichs had come. Nodal points and supply lines were given local protection while a whole series of small, preemptive raids were launched against partisans of all persuasions in order to keep them on the move and distract them from their offensive intentions.

The excuse to inject fresh and, above all, mobile forces into Yugoslavia was doubly welcome to the Germans, for they perfectly understood that a major shift in balance of power throughout Southern Europe was impending. While sparing a glance for the Partisans and concentrating their gaze upon the Allied armies poised in North Africa, they looked most keenly upon the reaction of their trembling Italian ally, Mussolini, and upon the minions who jostled for power at his elbow.

CHAPTER TEN

The Pulsating Underbelly

On July 25, 1943, the Italian political and military hierarchy in Rome deposed Mussolini, his removal from power coinciding with a series of shocks to German composure. Sicily was being conquered, Yugoslavia was in flames, the Russian Front was giving way and even in Western Europe there was evidence of chronic saturation by guerrillas raised by infiltration of Anglo-American agents. Nightly too, and increasingly by day, heavy bombers crossed the frontiers and pounded the German cities. Behind the scenes the Germans waited, mistrustful of assurances that the new Badoglio government intended to continue the fight on the Axis side, suspicious that its peace feelers were reaching the Allies, dreading the moment when the Italian Army might suddenly change sides and thus isolate those German forces scattered throughout Italy and the Balkans. Stealthily the Germans, too, laid their plans to preempt an Italian *volte-face*.

The method in which the armistice was negotiated by the Badoglio government with the Allies was inevitably devious. Not only was the essential need for secrecy a bedeviling factor but the sincerity of the signatories—particularly the Italians—was unauthenticated. The Allies dared not publicize the armistice until their troops made their principal landing in Italy (the landing on Italy's toe on September 3 was but a weak diversion), if for no more realistic a reason than that this would have given the Germans ample time to disarm the Italians before turning to face the invaders. Some Italians would have preferred to conceal their intentions until the Allies had won an assured military success. Badoglio desired the Allies to land close to Rome and thus cut in two the German forces which had entered the country in strength after Mussolini had fallen. General Eisenhower, the Allied Commander-in-Chief, while contemplating the concept of flying an airborne division into Rome, eventually decided against it, for fear of German air power, and placed his main landing at Salerno—well to the south of Naples. The Chiefs of Staff in London merely directed SOE to sabotage the railway lines from Southern France into Northern Italy, a scheme linked tenuously to the main landing and one which had only slight effect even though commendable efforts were made.

The announcement of the armistice came as a thunder clap, particularly to the Italians, catching both their civil and military authorities completely unprepared. One day propaganda said they were winning, the next it conceded defeat. Badoglio might prescribe cessation of hostilities with the Allies and defense "against attacks of any other origin" (meaning the Germans, of course) but on September 8 those were words unsupported by a plan. The effect on the Italian Army was devastating. In a great many cases the men, most of whom were peasants, heard the news prior to their officers and at once demobilized themselves, closely followed by the less dedicated portion of the officer corps.

The Germans, on the other hand, worked to a longstanding plan, dating from 1941, which they executed with their customary efficiency, disarming those of the Italians who showed the slightest sign of joining forces with the Allies, deftly suppressing riots which, like those in Naples, were caused by hunger. Apart from a few random incidents the neutralization of the Italian Army in Italy was an accomplished fact within a matter of hours and without any serious impediment to defensive action against the British landing at Salerno. But the netting of the Italian Army was by no means entirely accomplished; of those who did not vanish into civilian life or who avoided capture, the majority dispersed into the hills, where, with stolen equipment, they formed small, amateurish gangs. To their ranks were added the prisoners of war who had been held in camps throughout Italy—British, Albanians, Greeks and Yugoslavs—indeed in the weeks that followed the armistice the countryside was crawling with itinerants; exprisoners feeling their way south in the hope of regaining their freedom among the Allied Armies advancing northward; SAS patrols probing inland; the Balkan peoples trying to find their way home; the Italians endeavoring to determine their future loyalties; the Germans occupying nodal points, seizing the vital lines of communication, rescuing Mussolini by a dramatic kidnapping executed by the SS commando leader, the Austrian born Otto Skorzeny,[1] scheming to reestablish the shattered Fascist organization as a viable political force and hunting down those who looked like putting up opposition. Every endemic germ of

---

[1] Skorzeny, an officer of the Waffen SS, in July had formed his Friedenthal Special Formation which was intended as the SS equivalent of the Brandenburg Regiment. Among the operations then under consideration was a raid against Allied lines of supply to Russia through Persia.

guerrilla warfare permeated the land even though little had been done to prepare for it.

In the Balkans, of course, it was different since there guerrilla warfare was the established way of life. A race took place between Germans and guerrillas to see who could be the first to ransack the Italian armories—and the Germans had a start since they were informed of the armistice before the guerrillas. This was yet another penalty the Allies paid for the tight secrecy of the armistice negotiations. Even had SOE made a plan it would have been impossible to brief its agents in the field in time for them to take comprehensive action. So Tito and all the Allied representatives throughout the Balkans were as inhibited from intervention as the Italian command was prevented from making timely arrangements to shift its troops to places of comparative defensive safety. General Roatta, in response to General Gambara's request for instructions, could only reply, "Do what you can." It was already too late when, on September 9, the British commander in the Levant instructed the Italians "to oppose by force of arms any attempt made by the Germans or their vassals to disarm or disband the Italian military forces . . ."; and pitiful when the same British commander later told the Italians in Greece to lay down their arms and peacefully return to their homes.

In the Peloponnesos the Italians were confronted by a German corps (including 1st Panzer Division), and outmaneuvered in the political field by the German General Gyldenfeldt. He persuaded General Vecchiarelli to let the Germans occupy positions abandoned by the Italians, give up all their heavy artillery and issue an order to the troops not to make common cause with the guerrillas on the understanding that they would all be safely transported to Italy. In Crete there was another total surrender, though among the smaller islands there was a show of resistance amid a maze of negotiations with the Germans and a flurry of SAS interventions. There was fighting for Cephalonia and Corfu which ended when the Italians, divided as to their real duty and unaided by the Allies, laid down their arms before the end of the month. This pattern was repeated among the Aegean Islands: the Germans maneuvering the Italians out of the key position, the Italians wavering from indecision and the British capable only of promising help in a fortnight's time. Rhodes fell placidly by September 14 and the garrison, in common with many Italian garrisons, was taken timidly into captivity and transported to Germany. Only on Leros was there prolonged resistance, but this strongly fortified naval base had been left till last by the Germans and in the meantime had been heavily reinforced by the British. Isolated from air and sea assistance by the surrounding ring of German-held islands, the island eventually succumbed in November, emulating the fate of a smaller garrison which had been implanted on Cos. Thus a golden opportunity to reinforce the Grecian guerrillas with trained men and an abundance of weapons had been snuffed out by a masterly display of counterinsurgency warfare on the German part.

The evaporation of the Italian presence acted as a signal, as might be expected, for increased guerrilla activity in Greece—though not with such conclusive effects as the Allies would have hoped. Only in Thessaly had British liaison officers managed to persuade a sizable contingent of Italians—the Pinerolo Division and Aosta Cavalry Regiment —to join the partisans in the Pindus Mountains; here ELAS helped itself to the artillery and dissolved the division when it abjectly failed in its initial guerrilla attacks on German airfields. Elsewhere the negotiations which, throughout the summer, had been going on in an attempt to unify the political factions into one consolidated resistance movement, broke down when the Communist EAM took the opportunity to gain control regardless of the German presence. Once more SOE was caught in the crossfire of political warfare. Instead of attacking German airfields in order to prevent air attacks on the Aegean Islands, the guerrillas turned upon each other and began a civil war. Communist EAM/ELAS attacked the Republican EDES of Zervas in October. A ding-dong, though somewhat indeterminate, struggle took place. In this the Germans now participated, savagely attacking the populace, taking hostages, burning and massacring on a gigantic scale, regardless of whether guerrillas were present or not. One estimate puts the number of villages, with populations of between five hundred and one thousand, burned and destroyed in partisan territory as high as sixteen hundred out of six thousand five hundred.

Ironically the fury of the German punitive offensive (and a timely arms drop by the British) saved Zervas, whose fortunes against EAM/ ELAS had fallen so low by December 1943 that the Allied military mission (now under Woodhouse and joined by an American staff officer) was recommending he be abandoned in favor of the more successful Communists. For the Germans hit EAM/ELAS harder than Zervas and forced the former to seek an end to the civil war—an opportunity too tempting for Zervas to resist. Now he counterattacked the Communists, too, and with considerable profit. One thing was evident: a unified Greek secret army was an impracticability.

Since a German withdrawal from Greece seemed imminent, the British laid plans to harass it in order to divert attention from civil war. By attempting to involve the factions in what was known as Operation

Noah's Ark in 1944 they used, as bait, a conference to draw the two sides together. But the truce in February was broken in April when ELAS attacked the weaker Republican EKKA and wiped it out. So, throughout spring and summer, uneasy relations made the task of the allied military mission almost ridiculous, despite their efforts to keep Noah's Ark to the fore.

In Albania, meanwhile, the Germans had suffered far less trouble with the Italians than in Greece. Here their cleansing operations were a model of piercing efficiency and a demonstration of consummate mastery of antiguerrilla techniques. In the capital, Tirana, the Italian commander, General Rosi, was denied help by the Allies and engaged in talks with a German liaison officer. Forced to surrender his artillery, because it was immobile due to lack of prime movers, he was next refused consultations with the German General Rendulic just as that officer's columns were moving simultaneously to capture both corps headquarters at Dubrovnik and Podgorica. With all the higher command posts in their hands the Germans could turn at leisure on the leaderless units, informing them, "The war for the Italians is over, you will be transferred to civilian life." With swift precision telephone exchanges were occupied, weapons seized and men rounded up while, here and there, officers were shot just to discourage the others.

Now it was the guerrillas' turn to take advantage of Italian defenselessness and, with it, revenge. While the Germans fixed a firm grip with some forty thousand men on the coastal plain to fend off the expected Allied invasion, the Albanians hunted the surviving Italian soldiery amid the peaks and gorges. Those who were not slaughtered became lackeys to the guerrillas, forced to live in misery among a savage people who at once turned to settle differences of their own (egged on by divisive German propaganda) between Communists, Republicans and Royalists in the inevitable struggle for political survival. It was the Greek situation all over again except that, in Albania, the British military mission openly favored the Communist FNC since it alone demonstrated the will to tackle the Germans in addition to its other opponents. Then the Communists began to voice a desire to affiliate with their compatriots in Yugoslavia and Greece, thereby redoubling the suggestions by German propaganda that Tito and EAM aimed to seize sections of Albania for themselves.

Nevertheless the anti-German guerrilla war in Albania was prosecuted with something approaching the same dedication as in Yugoslavia. Thoroughgoing Allied support brought its own reward in the shape of an army of twenty thousand guerrillas which preyed ceaselessly on the lines of communication with Greece. At first the

Germans were merely driven to diverting convoy escorts from the two low-grade divisions allotted to holding the coast, but gradually, as their intelligence service plotted the growth of larger partisan formations in the hills, the demands for punitive expeditions increased. By August 1944 they were to be compelled to divert the excellent 1st Mountain Division from Yugoslavia to help reopen communications with Greece—a vital defensive move since, by then, the entire Balkan situation had deteriorated into a seething caldron of battling irregulars among which regulars only dared to move in overwhelming strength.

A foretaste of what was to become widespread in 1944 could be observed in parts of Bosnia and Montenegro as early as September 1943, when Tito and his Partisans began their attempts to digest the surrendering Italian Army. Here a land grab was as important as the seizure of arms. The Yugoslavs were staking claims for territory in the postwar era—for the long disrupted frontier province which had fallen into Italian hands after the First World War. But for the most part Italian formations fell captive to the biggest battalions which happened to be adjacent to wherever the Italians were located. And since the Italians were usually located close to the main communication centers, which were already in German possession, it was to the Germans that the Italians mainly surrendered. Italian officers were in a frightful dilemma, of course, torn between the desire to return home in safety, a feeling that they must do something to save their honor, and revulsion at coming to terms with Communist Partisans even though this might offer them the chance to fight on the Allied side—and therefore follow the official path to honor.

The Germans began to enter Italian occupied territory with brusque efficiency on September 9 aided by the Ustas, who declared war on Italy. Already strong in Montenegro, because of their current commitment to the fight against the Partisans, the Germans were able rapidly to overcome the bulk of formations with only the minimum of fighting, though some of the Alpini and random parts of different divisions took to the hills and joined the Partisans, while coastal detachments made token resistance at the ports. In Dalmatia, too, there was skirmishing followed by mass surrenders. Occupation of the port of Split, however, which was furthest distant from strong German forces but closer to the Partisan main body, provided exciting competition in a race between Germans and Partisans. Deakin describes, to perfection, the sort of disciplined, open warfare which pervaded this sector as the 1st Division marched from Buggno to Split. "The Yugoslav units . . . moved in ordered columns, day and night, pausing only at intervals for a few minutes' rest at a time. There were no camps or bivouacs and sleep was confined to such brief halts." Nevertheless it was a close-run thing, for the Partisans, as they neared Split, became embroiled with the Ustas, who were converging upon the same objective. Surprise contacts and ambushes broke out across a wide expanse of country. Yet apart from brushes between main forces the local Partisans in Split had acted independently and made the Italian commander (General Becurzzi of the Bergamo Division) prisoner. Therefore it was among an enemy in confusion that the Partisans arrived, unopposed, to accept a formal surrender and gather as much of the spoils as possible before the Germans arrived in strength to stiffen the lurking Ustas.

The Italians were in a fearful scrape, commanded to join the Partisans, whom they abhorred as "bandits," dreading the moment when the Partisans must evacuate the town and leave them defenseless against the oncoming SS (Prinz Eugen) Division, and thrown into terror by heavy dive-bomber attacks which developed against their barracks, killing several hundred of their number. A few were evacuated by sea, though several anti-Fascist officers expressed readiness to fight the Germans provided they remained separate from the Partisans—something the latter would not stomach. When at last the Germans arrived on the twenty-seventh it was to find the cupboard bare of Partisans and Italian equipment, but in time to mop up a belligerent battalion of light tanks and summarily execute those officers who had tried to join the Partisan side.

One must conclude that the Italians' metropolitan conscript formations possessed neither the urge nor the skill to convert themselves suddenly to highly mobile warfare, a conclusion which is reinforced by the knowledge that the more flexible and select Alpini, the Bersaglieri and the Carabinieri, were ready to take to the hills and give a better account of themselves. For all that the heart of Yugoslavia became German-controlled while the Partisans, still weak even if better armed with the scrapings of Italian equipment, took charge of the more irrelevant extremities.

In case an impression is given that the Italians alone were shirkers in guerrilla warfare let it be said that many conventional soldiers of the Allied nations were also loath to indulge in the practice—and nowhere more noticeably so than in Italy. Of the several thousand Allied sailors, soldiers and airmen held prisoner in Italy at the time of the armistice, the greater proportion were set at liberty and began roaming the countryside. Had they taken up arms *en masse* from the surrendering Italians they might well have constituted a formidable threat to the

German rear, as the Germans well understood. But lack of direction from SOE or the War Office (which, in fact, deprecated such a policy) added to years in captivity sapped the morale of men whose devout wish was to return home with the same alacrity as their late jailers. The vast majority made for obvious places of safety—the places first searched by the Germans and Italian Fascist supporters. Several hundred entered the neutral state of San Marino and were retaken by the Germans, who rarely paid respect to protocol when their security was in danger. Quite a number did, in fact, regain their freedom but far more went back into the cages. The smallest portion turned aside to join the first guerrilla bands that were tentatively being formed in the hills and cities from among the more pugnacious members of the Italian Army. The number of British who stayed to fight is sometimes put as low as fifty—an underestimate, perhaps, but not so very far from the truth. Inescapably an impression is imparted by those who did stay that qualities of leadership among several ex-prisoner-of-war officers fell below the standard required. Stuart Hood, a rebel at heart, records the arrival of a British major, accompanied by a batman, in their hideout. "He said we were under his command. We did not get up from the fire. We didn't think much of senior officers. . . . We had seen our elders bungle their trade of war, surrender, and then in the camps use their rank to obtain privilege, jumping—or trying to jump—the hungry queues." Trooper Douglas Davidson recalls the arrival of a British brigadier whose first order was for a bed and second for a woman.

Davidson's experiences with the Italian partisans were fairly representative of the movement in its formative stages. He joined a band of fifty which included seven Montenegrins, led by an Italian officer, near Matelica. They had rifles but were quite inactive. Because the Germans were employing *agents provocateurs* disguised as escaped prisoners of war, Davidson was compelled by the band to prove his fidelity by cutting the throat of a German guard during a raid on a local armory. This he did with the aplomb of the true guerrilla fighter and thus raised his status to that of band leader. Generally the time was spent in evading cordon and search operations, trying to rescue some Yugoslavs from a nearby prison camp and stealing arms and money. They engaged in bank raids but had no contact with SOE agents or neighboring bands. Indeed, that winter Davidson walked from Matelica past Rimini to Ljubliana without meeting any Italian partisans. In March, holever, long after the Allied advance had stalled at Cassino and the Anzio beachhead had been contained, Davidson tried to merge his band with a nearby Communist organization and together, using explosives which seem to have been airdropped "blind," [2] undertook the sabotage of the Ancona–Rome railway line. The merger was fruitless because, as Davidson immediately discovered, the sole Communist aim was domination and, when that failed, resolution of the problem by an ambush as he retired from the meeting. This he successfully foiled with the help of his seven Montenegrins.

In May, as the Allied Armies prepared their assault towards Rome and, in Britain, a vast armada got ready to land in northern France, a parachuted SOE agent arrived with the Communist band and began to arrange a series of arms deliveries by air. It was agreed that the arms should be divided between the bands, but Davidson had enormous difficulty in obtaining his share and became aware that, though the Communists claimed every drop for themselves, they had no intention of using the contents against the Germans. Instead they were hiding them for future use in the struggle for postwar power. To them the specter of Fascism loomed large, for possibly fifty per cent of the population still supported Mussolini.

Davidson was witnessing the automatic ranging of political factions and depravity under the guise of anti-German guerrilla warfare, which replaced the euphoria that followed the fall of Mussolini. No sooner had anti-Fascists tired of ousting Fascism than the forces of the future—Communists, Church, Christian Democrats, Liberals, Socialists and all manner of splinter groups—began to press their claims for recognition and power. Of these the Communists were by far the strongest since they contained within their hierarchy experienced ideological guerrilla fighters, men who had escaped Fascism abroad or in concentration camps, many of whom were experienced saboteurs from the Spanish Civil War. They assumed the evocative name of "Garibaldi" and formed action groups both in the mountains (mostly in the north) and in factories. To preserve the form of central government and prevent civil war such as had already begun in Greece, the Badoglio government in the Allied-occupied south created a National Resistance Movement with control vested in a Committee of National Liberation of Northern Italy (CLNAI) and a military wing called the Corps of Volunteers of Liberty (CVL). Ostensibly all parties, sabotage groups and guerrilla bands took their instructions from these sources, though it can hardly be claimed that control was very effective. Each group was compelled to drift because of the almost total lack of a coordinating communication system. Factions burgeoned as the Allies

[2] SOE/OSS arranged deliveries by the RAF (and, in a minor capacity, the U.S. Army Air Force) but, due to inadequate precautions, many agents and supplies fell into enemy hands.

jumped onto the bandwagon by according partisans the status of regular forces belonging to the Italian state and supporting them with a monthly subsidy of one hundred million lire and a generous supply of arms brought in by SOE agents.

In the meantime Kesselring had actually arranged a mutually acceptable truce throughout the winter of 1943–44 with selected partisans. So, for a period, it was Allied special forces which mainly sustained the underground war, sending in expert sabotage parties by sea and air. SOE, OSS and army troops worked in harmony even though the Americans tended to skate round the diplomatic snags. They all suffered in common. No. 2677 Special Recce Battalion of the U.S. Army, which landed fifteen uniformed men from the sea near Stazionne di Framura on March 22 with the task of demolishing the railway tunnel between La Spezia and Genoa, was captured complete on the twenty-fourth. On March 26 they were all shot by order of General Anton Dostler commanding the 75th Infantry Corps—be it noted, a Wehrmacht formation. The British SAS also made its contribution with widespread raids by individual parties. One officer, Philip Pinkney, landed by parachute in the north and demolished a railway tunnel near the Brenner Pass; he too was caught and shot, having achieved a small advantage for his side.

The first large-scale task for the Italian partisans, as they emerged from the truce, was support of the May 1944 offensive towards Rome and, later, of Operation Anvil, which was the landing due to take place in southern France in August as a complement to the main landing on June 6 in the north. CVL was asked to dislocate lines of communication, but this was more in the nature of a pious hope than a planned operation, for the only directives likely to reach the partisans came as a general appeal over the civilian radio to do all possible damage and to rise against the enemy—without specifying which targets were to be attacked. And so an uncoordinated series of demolitions, raids and random ambushes took place. Sometimes the partisans moved freely and dominated great areas. Gordon Lett suggests the paucity of armament belonging to his band in the Rossano Valley. "We would have sold our souls to the Devil for just one British machine-gun and some gelignite." Lett, who commanded a nonpolitical force of some fifty men called the International Battalion, was a master of small ambushes but these, as he wrote, petered out as soon as the Germans took local defensive precautions. When he indulged in larger operations in August, armed with air-dropped weapons, it was tragically different. Retribution occurred instantly when a dangerous situation was presented to the enemy. "Below us spreading as far as the horizon of dark mountains that marked the coastline was a myriad of lights—lights that wavered, and changed colour intermittently from bright orange to dull red. Hundreds and hundreds of fires were burning, each of them representing the house of some unfortunate peasant." Stung rather than paralyzed, the Germans, aided by Italian Fascists, were reacting in the routine manner; deterring the creation of a massive secret army, they drove even the most militant bands back into their shells.

The haphazard launching of a major partisan effort is described by Davidson. On June 5 they heard of the radio broadcast message calling for action by Italian partisans everywhere. "Attack the Germans, rise up and kill, wreck their railways and roads," it demanded—without being too specific as to time and place. That night they trekked through familiar hills and valleys avoiding hostile localities, carrying explosives towards a target of their own choice. One hair-raising moment they encountered another band going in the opposite direction but similarly engaged—a typical example of the chaotic lack of central control. To the southward the formal battle by regular armies for Cassino and Rome rumbled louder and drew closer.

The railway tunnel lay black before them, hollow and forbidding yet highly vulnerable. Carefully and deep within its interior they placed the charges, inserted detonators and paid back the cable through the tunnel's mouth to a safe distance beyond—and waited. At last, from the opposite end, they detected a train approaching. They completed the circuit, watched dust and smoke belch from the tunnel's mouth, heard the bang, the rumble of falling masonry, and a moment later, from within, an awful, thunderous crash as the locomotive tore among fallen stone, and the coaches, full of Germans on their way to the front, telescoped among each other.

Davidson remembers his satisfaction at his partisan work. "I was doing the job of a real soldier, which is to fight the enemy—even if guerrilla warfare had not been part of the tank driver's curriculum! When we blocked that tunnel for a fortnight, killed those Germans and blew up some pylons, I felt I had paid my way." But, he added, "In partisan warfare it is better to do a really big job or none at all. The small ones make for more backlash than they're worth."

Lack of closely associated high command in the field was a crippling handicap and one that persisted until August, when a field commander, General Cadorna, was at last parachuted into Northern Italy to take charge, assisted by two Chiefs of Staff—a Communist called Longo and a member of the Action Party named Ferrucio Parri, who, in June 1945, would become prime minister. By late summer CVL had a strength of eighty-five thousand, an influx of untrained men, encouraged to take up arms by news of the Allied victory at Cassino and the fall of Rome. It enjoyed local successes but none of significance, as can be judged by the German opinion that it was the guerrilla battle in Yugoslavia which caused a damaging drain on their limited resources. There were futile sacrifices. In Rome, in March 1944, for example, where the Committee of National Liberation (CLN) tried to combine the activities of all local parties and keep belligerence under control in accordance with Kesselring's appeals addressed to them through the Church, the Communist Action Group blew up thirty-two German police. In reprisal 335 hostages were taken and executed in the Ardeatine Caves. It was one of many atrocities, unilaterally perpetrated by the SS under Reichsführer Wolff, but also largely condoned by Kesselring, who, with his eyes fixed on the conventional battle in the approaches to Rome and in constant acrimonious debate with Hitler and OKW, had little time for minor incidents. Only much later in August did Kesselring clamp down on massacres and then for a purely military reason—that unlimited license to kill would lead to the collapse of his soldiers' discipline.

In calmer moments, after the war, Kesselring was to write and say much about his philosophy of antiguerrilla warfare, taking the line that prompt action by disciplined troops against specified targets was best. But by then he was on trial for his life in connection with the Ardeatine incident (and another) before a tribunal which found him guilty and sentenced him to death (later commuted to imprisonment). He adopted the conventional German viewpoint that guerrilla warfare was contrary to international law and, in Italy, converted the old Axis comradeship into a murderous holocaust. At first the partisans caused only slight annoyance to the Germans, who rather welcomed their emergence into the open in summer 1944, since it identified them for counteraction. But successes against the partisans were of the Pyrrhic kind, which Kesselring reckoned to have cost him not less than five thousand or probably seven to eight thousand dead between June and August 1944, when his army was in full retreat and deprived of the initiative against the guerrillas. The schism between the SS and the Wehrmacht, whereby the former took full and separate responsibility for rear-area security, was a subject for constant recrimination on Kesselring's part; he considered the battle against regular forces and partisan bands as one, but it was not until May 1944 that OKW agreed and Kesselring was allowed to take full responsibility for the entire Italian theater of operations with the SS directly under his command. Nevertheless the SS retained almost exclusive responsibility for anti-partisan operations, their special Guerrilla Warfare Operations Staff given a zone of responsibility that was kept flexible within the demands of the battle at the front. Thus no sooner was pressure at the front relaxed than greater effort could be applied instantly against the partisans by the troops made available. In practice this implied the conventional securing of vital lines of communication supplemented by specific operations against located partisan bands—the same system as in Russia, where it worked as well as the limited quantity and quality of resources allowed.

The SS predominated in all guerrilla matters and achieved an unrivaled and infectious reputation for brutality. Davidson remembers an SS raid on his village. A wounded SS man they had held prisoner and nursed (against their better judgment) was liberated. He at once identified everybody who had given the slightest aid to the partisans during the period of his captivity. As a result nearly every inhabitant was killed (including the priest, who, rather than escape, shot it out from the belfry of his church). "Our band never took another SS man prisoner after that," states Davidson.

Italian suffering throughout the premature uprising in the summer of 1944 was wholesale. The Germans attempted to cut both roots and branches besides trying to arrange truces with individual bands and so split the movement into antagonistic segments. An overall truce of convenience had been arranged in the winter of 1943–44 but collapsed after the execution of General Perotti and seven members of his command on April 5, and the shooting of one hundred young men of Benedicta on the seventh. There were similar occurrences at San Giovanni, Figline and many other villages in the vicinity of Florence at the end of August as the Allied armies drew near. Kesselring admits that the partisans in this district were very troublesome. Paradoxically, Allied reports give them less credit, though they handed over the government of the city to the CVL after it had fallen. Politics were, of course, at the root of Allied ambivalence; they had no desire to underwrite a civil war like that raging in the Balkans. They played down the activities of the partisans both then and later in order to keep the lid on a caldron coming to the boil. And this the Italians resented, though not simply because they wanted credit to be paid when it was due. Among the nations involved in the Second World War they acquired a miserable record of military failure; their arms did badly against almost every opponent. It was hoped that honor might be restored under the partisan flag besides leading to the acquisition of party political prestige and a stronger diplomatic voice at future peace talks.

By the end of September, however, the Italian partisans were exhausted and discouraged by their losses after the Germans had vigorously attacked them in all their northern strongholds as the battle front stabilized near Florence. Resistance collapsed, notably in the valleys; the casualties were immense and refugees either retired, chastened, to their homes, or fled across the Alps into Switzerland. Then, in December, what seemed like a stab in the back was administered by the Allied Commander-in-Chief Field-Marshal Alexander—an invitation asking the partisans to disband, giving as his reason the difficulties of supplying them during the winter months, but in reality trying to check the growth of the Communist element. Even in the summer months SOE supplies had been carefully channelled to political parties (though the U.S. OSS disseminated them with generous abandon, regardless of diplomatic consequences). Now all fell in line. Yet to sugar the pill with an invitation to continue the struggle in the spring was insufficient compromise and, in any case, impractical. A guerrilla movement thrives on enthusiasm which cannot be switched on and off like electricity. Eventually a political agreement had to be reached between the Allies, the new Bonomi government and the CLNAI by which 260 million lire a month were given in support along with promises of help by more Allied missions and air supply. But the process which had doubled recruiting in the warm spring now went into reverse; penal losses, deadlock at the battlefront and the onset of a hard winter prompted partisan desertions on an enormous scale. Entire units disbanded themselves and the Germans were able to take their ease even though the war was lost and entering its culminating stages.

As 1944 approached antipartisan operations had, from the German point of view in the Balkans, entered their last cumulative phase. The Sixth Offensive, which opened against the Yugoslavs in mid-October 1943, had been the last attempt to subjugate the country as a whole—a vast outlay of effort by twelve German, one Bulgarian and five Ustas Divisions in what amounted to an extension of the drive to subjugate the Italians. This immense force, which might have been so much better employed in Russia to halt the Red Army as it flooded through the Ukrainian plain to lap the eastern frontiers of Poland, was launched by Field-Marshal von Weichs in a valedictory attempt to expel the Partisans from the length of the intricate Dalmatian coast and clear the mountains of Slovenia, Bosnia and Macedonia, thus reestablishing land communications between Greece and Italy. Attempts to clear the towns of guerrillas failed in November. Nevertheless, by the end of January 1944, the Germans had achieved their territorial aims and more, for, in addition to holding the coast and all the principal communication centers, they had dealt a heavy blow to the Macedonian Partisans and snapped the links with their Albanian neighbors. But by then, too, they had increased the number of their own divisions to twenty in addition to the seven Bulgarian divisions and the mass of indigenous police and Ustas—and still von Weichs was complaining, correctly as it happens, that his resources were inadequate to the task. His pure German formations were of good enough quality but comprised far less than half the total regular forces engaged. Equipment was invariably second grade, desertions were rife, particularly among the Bulgarian divisions which had become infiltrated by Communists. In November the 24th Bulgarian Division refused to obey German orders and had to be extracted from the order of battle.

Terrible as was the destruction and loss of life in almost every Partisan zone, it nevertheless did nothing to quell Tito's expansion. As the Sixth Offensive faded away in exhaustion he could count on an enlarged army of three hundred thousand organized into eight corps of twenty-six divisions—one which admittedly lacked the strength to withstand an all-out assault by opponents with heavy weapons, but a quite indestructible force which was limited in size only by logistic restrictions—a force, moreover, which had dug its roots deeply into firm political soil, consolidated by an undisturbed meeting of the second wartime parliament (this time at Jajce) on November 29. Then Tito was elected President and Commissioner for Defense as well as commander-in-chief. Encouraged by Churchill's recognition of their diplomatic existence, and their right to decide for themselves the fate of King Peter in the light of the breakdown of confidence in the London government with its links with Mihailovic, they slowly broadened diplomatic exchanges in the winter and spring of 1944. In April the British finally withdrew support for the Cetniks, and in August the Americans copied them. But British aid was committed to the Partisans long before that. Their military mission under Brigadier Fitzroy MacLean, an able, cosmopolitan Member of Parliament and friend of Winston Churchill, now functioned at ambassadorial level with Tito. Late in the day though it was, Allied air transport on a large scale was being provided to lift in all manner of supplies, from ammunition to boots, and on the return trip was evacuating the wounded and saving them from the perils of survival under the enemy threat of execution. By April 1944 five British squadrons of Halifax and U.S. Army Air Force Dakotas, helped out by a Polish Halifax flight and two squadrons of Italian aircraft, under SOE and OSS direction, were flying nearly nine hundred sorties a month to Yugoslavia and Albania, and in June were to lift in 1,674 tons and evacuate 2,237 casualties—which became the monthly average. Sea transport was also employed whenever possible, but at first only to the island of Vis, which alone of coastal points remained in Allied hands after the Sixth Offensive. This became a formidable supply bridgehead defended by Partisans, British commandos and special forces.

One last offensive—the Seventh (Roesselsprung to the Germans) —was left in the German locker—a desperate but beautifully planned attempt by Brandenburgers, SS and mountain troops with tanks, in mid-May, to capture Tito and his entire staff along with the Allied military missions. It represented pure opportunism made possible by Tito and his staff's becoming so overconfident that they relaxed that constant vigilance which had preserved them during three years' hounding. The Partisans—or Yugoslav government as it now really was—had established an elaborate military and diplomatic capital at Drvar in Bosnia and left it virtually unguarded. Allied aircraft landed on Drvar's airstrip—the first U.S. Dakotas coming in on April 2 by night. The Germans were precisely informed of the nature and strength of the Drvar capital and for once were able to conceal their preparations from the Partisans. A single air reconnaissance mission was noticed by the British mission on May 24, but complete surprise was achieved when, at dawn on the twenty-fifth, a heavy air raid, aimed against Tito's personal cave, was followed by the landing of forty gliders gently touching down on the plateau to disgorge heavily armed infantry along with their support weapons. This was swiftly followed by SS parachutists to build up the assault force to 600. Distant mechanized units drove concentrically to their relief, intending to complete the envelopment. A furious fight developed between the Germans and Tito's small personal escort, which was greatly outnumbered. A nearby Partisan brigade ran ten miles to the rescue and was in action by 9:30 A.M. But by then the Germans had fastened a strong grip and were on the point of taking Tito. Had he not escaped through the hole in the floor of his hut near the cave, into the valley below, the course of modern Balkan history might easily have been changed. As it was the Partisans lost nearly six thousand of their number in some of the most ruthless fighting of the war; the Germans lost but a fraction of that.

Still the Partisans' war went on, for, of course, this was only a local affair, while the Allies prepared massive blows on and behind every front, timed to burst forth in June. Eventually the Balkans would have to be evacuated as the Russians pressed in from the north and Allied pressure built up throughout southern Europe and amid the hedge-rows and plains of northern France. Now, while Tito consolidated his hold upon those parts of Yugoslavia which lay apart from the route centers and lines of communication, was the time to take the offen-sive—to attack the railways and industrial plants which, since 1942, had provided immense quantities of valuable minerals for the German economy. At first Tito (who in June had been flown in a Russian aircraft for consultations in Italy) was most willing to lend help to special SOE demolition teams engaged in Operation Bearskin—a series of rail-cutting forays in the north to prevent the Germans rein-forcing Italy from Yugoslavia, timed to coincide on June 7 with the Italian uprising and the great Allied landing in northern France. But the attack on Drvar dislocated Tito's control system at the crucial moment (as the Germans hoped it would do). German precautions and bad weather intervened and the operation went off at half cock with the result that only scattered cuts were made which hindered instead of crippling the Germans. In August a similar operation, called Ratweek,[3] was attempted and this time with better results. The whole network of railway lines was cut and, in addition, barge traffic on the Danube attacked. But by then the Germans were in no state to resist in any but the most essential places. The Russians were closing in through Rumania and on September 8 the Bulgarians changed sides and began to attack their old allies. The tide of war throughout Europe was driving the Germans from their conquests.

As the Germans departed, the people of the liberated countries, in despair at a fresh wave of destruction, began to resist sabotage and bombing, which could only delay their postwar recovery. Partially because the Yugoslavian industrial plants and mines were located close to communication centers they had escaped sabotage. Now a ban was placed upon attacking them. It was a symbol of victory: the war was shifting into Germany, where the bomber attacks held sway as the Allies got closer.

[3] Not to be confused with SOE's Europe-wide operation in February which had as its aim the slaying of senior Gestapo men.

CHAPTER ELEVEN

Prelude to Overlord

As the Germany Army reeled back in Russia and fought desperate rearguard actions in Southern Europe, an invasion of Western Europe in 1943 entered the realms of conjecture—a possibility carefully implanted by Allied diplomatic and propaganda rumors as a distraction for the Germans' imagination. But the Germans were undeceived for, as their Commander-in-Chief, Field-Marshal von Rundstedt was to tell Liddell Hart, "The movements you made at that time were too obvious—it was evident that they were a bluff." If there had been an invasion little could have been contributed by the resistance in any of the occupied western countries. The French were in disarray following the disruption of the CNR at Caluire, the Belgians unready for combat and the Dutch impotent in the aftermath of North Pole.

French resistance in July 1943 was represented by some skillfully managed escape lines, well-directed propaganda,[1] the feebly armed Maquis to the south and a number of SOE sabotage circuits and missions—some in the process of building, while others collapsed under persistent Abwehr and SS countermeasures. To the Germans they were merely a source of anxiety due to the increase in quantity. Inadequate supply to SOE parties in the field curtailed their expansion, the RAF making but a token effort to improve it, as we have seen in Chapter Ten. Command and control were also in dire need of repair if resistance and guerrilla groups were to make a unified challenge. CNR had to be re-formed—but this took time and suffered from false starts. Although a mission, comprising Pierre Brossolette and Edward Yeo-Thomas, was proposed in July as an agency to reassemble CNR, it was September 19 before it landed in France—the delay a product of squabbles within SOE, when RF did all in its power to circumvent a demand that the Gaullists must decentralize in order to prevent an-

[1] The BBC was one of the most effective agents of resistance in Europe, its credibility giving it the power to instruct.

other Caluire. It was November before CNR was at last reconstituted, this time under the presidency of a future prime minister of France, Georges Bidault. An intellectual who stood closer to the middle of the political road than Moulin, Bidault was also blessed with the same magnetism and honesty of purpose as his predecessor. He could be trusted to bridge the gaps between the Communist and the Center and Right parties while guiding them into one channel of resistance without, however, surrendering to extremism.

Bidault's task was quite as difficult as Moulin's, for he took charge under an obligation to avoid central meetings at a time when Operation Overlord (the plan for the invasion of France) was only six months away, when the struggle for preeminence between de Gaulle and Giraud remained unresolved, as the two jockeyed for power at Algiers; and when the military structure of French resistance was practically in ruins.

Not that CNR was indispensable. On August 30, 1943, SOE, with its American colleagues in OSS (now jointly called SOE/SO) had defined its own role in Operation Neptune—the actual assault plan within Overlord. Its objectives were predictable—sabotage, attacks upon command and control installations, the hampering of German demolition measures and then an accumulation of raids against logistic targets in conjunction with air attacks. But genuine guerrilla warfare continued to be regarded by the planners as a "bonus rather than an essential part of the plans" because of the recurrent fear of excessive cost to the populace. In view of the known inferiority of the guerrillas, the realization that CNR was in disarray and the possibility that their activities might reveal the basis of the strategic plan, SOE preferred to play a strict military role and curtail the political parts.

The Gaullists, who largely controlled the Secret Army and its adjunct maquis, were isolated deliberately from the Overlord planners by the demands of security—a backlash from Dakar and Caluire and something the Gaullists bitterly resented. Yet this isolation in no way prevented them from formulating flexible schemes of their own—above all the Color Plans which might be adapted to any circumstances in collaboration with SHAEF when the time was appropriate. The Secret Army's plan "Vidal" was the French trump, an original idea of the late Delestraint—the suggestion of amateur bands attempting orthodox battle for bastions on dominating ground. The obverse of guerrilla warfare, it blatantly challenged the better-trained and armed Germans to a trial of strength for the honor of France. The Color Plans proposed the dropping of colored containers related to specified operations in the implementation of phased tasks behind the enemy lines. For example,

Plan Vert was aimed against railways and Plan Tortue against reinforcements. But the plans were very complicated and symptomatic of a schism between the professionals, who devised them, and the amateurs in the field.

The French orthodox military leadership, strongly entrenched in Algiers and under strengthening Gaullist leadership, called for the institution of the formal military chain of command comparable to the earlier clandestine operational system which had been based on the political and administrative structure within France. Two *délégués militaires de zone* (DMZs) had been appointed in 1943—one in the north and the other in the south—and over these had been placed a *délégué militaire national* (DMN), the latter eventually filled by the thirty-year-old Jacques Chaban-Delmas—another future prime minister. Beneath appeared an increasing number of *délégués militaires régionaux* (DMRs), of about one to every two Departments, aided by operational staff officers who prepared and executed the actual operations, thus leaving their seniors free to delve mainly in higher liaison and politics. Thus, while the DMNs and DMZs prepared the way for de Gaulle's preeminence, the DMRs (some twenty-five in existence in 1943, and thirty-eight by May 1944) guided the battle, albeit because any higher implementation of direct control was impossible due to inadequate communications. Inevitably each DMR enjoyed considerable autonomy, though helped in a specialized way by additional missions sent in by de Gaulle to contact the trade unions (notably those of the railways) against the day when industrial action could be converted into an instrument of war.

SOE's F Section, meantime, persevered unilaterally with its "circuits," which, like most types of mission, acted as coordinating and rallying agencies. They recruited those who desired to resist, trained and equipped them, paid the bills with vast sums flown in to prevent coercion of the populace, and directed each task on directions from London or Algiers—seeking to apply steady pressure on the Germans instead of saving up for one, maximum effort. Though members of F Section, at times for prestige purposes, laid claim to owning a vast secret army, in practice there was no such thing. Their circuits, small and isolated from each other, were relatively secure, but highly dependent upon the prowess of the circuit leader, whose success could be measured by the size of support he received from abroad. For example, the "Pimento" circuit, which operated with consummate efficiency under A.M. Brooks, on either side of the River Rhône, received more of the good Bren light machine guns than it could use, while less favored groups felt lucky if they got the poor-quality Sten submachine guns.

The tightest brake upon rapid development by SOE in Western Europe stemmed as much from its own mistakes and inexperience as from the prowess of enemy counterintelligence. The failure to detect the awful chain reaction from North Pole, outwards from Holland, has already been described, and, towards the end of 1943, was being felt within certain key French circuits (above all the one called "Prosper"). This led to their elimination at the very moment when rapid expansion was essential. Disruption of the original CNR at Caluire had been followed by an intensive Abwehr and SS sweep resulting in the capture or killing of many key agents. The penetration of Prosper became connected with other circuits (whose leaders were acquainted with each other). The defection of an important agent (under the mildest threat of torture) led, in turn, to the disclosure of arms caches, particularly in Brittany, where a promising build-up of a local maquis was smashed. Something like four hundred people seem to have been arrested by the Germans from among Prosper's adherents alone, and that was by no means the grand total. Might it not have been better to arm individuals rather than cache the arms?

Nor did the run of indiscretions end with the demise of a circuit, for even when the Germans failed in their attempts to play back a captured radio, there was always the possibility that a dangerously long time would elapse before news of a collapse became known (or believed) in London—and in that period new agents, arms and money went on being flown straight into enemy hands. The whole tragic (and frequently sordid) story is admirably told in *SOE in France*—a tale that sometimes fails to redound to the credit of SOE's directors in London, very occasionally throws up desertions by individual agents under barbarous treatment, but nearly always records courage of the coolest and highest order. On the other hand, it is the story of an enormous experiment in which nearly all the participants were playing with elements and situations of which they could have had no previous experience. The system was constantly evolving with few precedents to guide it. Costly mistakes, therefore, were inevitable.

SOE lived in close proximity to anarchy at every level. There dwelt in the Auvergnes—renowned for its inaccessibility—a maquis band said to be three thousand strong led by an ex–French Army NCO called Coulaudon (Gaspard). In April 1944 an F Section circuit called "Farmer" discovered not only that its appetite for arms and murder was insatiable, but that its intentions with regard to the Germans were far from clear. Coulaudon has been described by Russell Braddon in his book *Nancy Wake* as exuding arrogance, self-satisfaction and energy, perhaps a bluffer and certainly a bully, who is reputed to have tortured captured SS men by burning. As an historian of RF Section has noted, burning, even by the Germans, was somewhat unusual, "but anything might happen in the provinces where brutality was general." Captain F. Cardozo, an RF Section Officer of right-wing tendencies (who reached the Auvergnes May 8) appreciated that Coulaudon was a product of the Popular Front, whose political inclinations barely stopped short of Communism and whose ambitions were like those of a feudal baron. Cardozo scotched Coulaudon's ambitions by importing French regular officers from the original Vichy Army (ORA) who now were merged with the Secret Army and vested with the authority to make Coulaudon develop this private army into a good fighting unit. Farmer then moved further south, speeding about the country roads in fast motor cars, its red-scarved Spanish adherents causing a certain amount of offense to the local populace by their flamboyance. The French, not unnaturally, wanted to be liberated by Frenchmen and some critics have claimed that it might have been better if SOE could have spoken and acted with the voice of France instead of confusing a complex situation with the unilateral initiatives of the two sections in London in addition to the "Massingham" branch in Algiers.

This is not to say that SOE was a grand fiasco or that politics were all-consuming. Like Lett's Rossano group in Italy there were tough, nonpolitical bands in France. F Section's "Spiritualist," run by René Dumont-Guillemet in the suburbs of Paris, was distinguished for its successful mixing of political factions along with the strict discipline which enabled it to survive in an urban setting. It was fifteen hundred strong, with five thousand unarmed in reserve, and its fidelity sprang from a leader who despised "cafe-conversationalist resisters" and who made each man swear, "I pledge myself to reveal to no one that our organization exists. I swear I will hold myself, night and day, at the disposition of the allied armies. I swear loyalty and obedience to the leaders I have freely chosen. I know any backsliding will be punishable by death." This, as Foot points out, was no idle threat. No doubt a certain young Russian diarist would have approved. The system was by no means uncommon among the best disciplined armies in history.

Western European resistance suffered severely until 1944 from a chronic supply shortage because, in 1943, France lay third in order of priority of air support. The Italian islands came first, then Corsica and Crete and the Balkans, while Poland and Czechoslovakia came after France, taking precedence over Norway and the Low Countries. In November the Balkans moved to the top of the list while France remained third after enemy-occupied Italy (Corsica having been taken by French troops in a Giraudist invasion from North Africa, in which the local maquis worked closely with an SOE-trained French battalion in driving the Germans out). Not until the first quarter of 1944 did France come top in priority, and then only in consequence of yet another confrontation before Churchill between SOE and the RAF—the Prime Minister abandoning his reservations about guerrillas in the atmosphere of total war's uninhibited violence.

A persuasive report by Michel Brault (Carré's lawyer, who, since 1942, had worked with the maquis in the Rhône Valley) emphasized the poverty of arms supply to the maquis, as matters stood towards the end of 1943, and reduced to size the popular exaggerations regarding the strength of these forces. It led to a meeting under Churchill, on January 27, at which the availability of aircraft was again thrashed out between the airmen, the Foreign Office, SOE and the Gaullists. It was agreed that, while the RAF would continue to give first priority to the attack on Germany, SOE's operations would come next in order of precedence. Yet the change in policy was immediately noticeable only because, towards the end of 1943, two U.S. Army Air Force four-engined Liberator (B-24) squadrons (amounting, in fact, to only fourteen aircraft available) had been allotted to special operations (Operation Carpetbagger). Not until March was the British complement doubled to four squadrons. This raised the 107 sorties, which delivered 139 tons to France between October and December 1943, to 759 sorties and 938 tons in the next quarter and 1,969 sorties carrying 2,689 tons, in that following, as more and more aircraft were put onto the job. Yet though arms delivery between February and May may have looked impressive, including as it did 76,290 Sten guns, 3,441 Brens, 304 Piats (antitank launchers) and 160 mortars—a slight majority reaching the F Section circuits instead of RF's organization—quite a number invariably fell into German hands due to penetration of circuits. To the waiting partisans, however, the magnitude of each attempted delivery was a vital source of encouragement besides an expression of Anglo-American intent. H.H.A. Thackthwaite (a bilingual English schoolteacher) calling in March for three aircraft loads of arms and ammunition to be dropped to a maquis band in the Tarantaise, and working on the assumption that he would be lucky to get just one, was astonished to receive the promise of twelve, of which eleven arrived safely.

Something more devious than an altruistic desire to brace the partisans lay behind the increase in air resources. In 1944 the Americans at last recognized the fundamental political forces behind Resistance. In February it had struck the men of SHAEF that, since the British supplied and delivered most of the clandestine goods, the Western Europeans would draw a conclusion that the British alone favored their cause—with objectionable repercussions upon postwar relationships; the U.S.A.'s apparent indifference might even be judged as reflecting an anti-Gaullist line! At this time, however, the Deputy Supreme Commander at SHAEF, Air-Marshal Tedder, was still peddling the old RAF deprecations about "the merits of SOE/SO requests [for aircraft] and efficacy of the organization." Nevertheless, at the end of May, it was reckoned that only some ten thousand Frenchmen were yet sufficiently armed for more than a single day's serious fighting with another forty thousand armed in some degree—in other words that the Secret Army was not a viable force.

Minor sabotage was widespread, of course, though the assault on the Neptune-related targets was deferred until May—and even then kept in as low a key as possible for fear the maquis should rise prematurely and undermine its own security in addition to disclosing Overlord's strategy. There were frequent outbreaks of daring and locally effective sabotage, the best circuit leaders accepting risks as part of essential, practical training for the recruits; the bulk of Frenchmen regarding them as a useful way of keeping the Germans in a state of tense uncertainty, though well knowing that nothing decisive would come of isolated raids. In France the idea of "taking one with you" was stronger in 1944 than it had been in 1940, however. Even the vast majority, who had not the remotest connection with any official resistance organization, nurtured a thorough detestation of the Germans.

Waterways (the specialty of a brilliant circuit called "Armada") came in for a lot of destruction in 1943 as locks and barrages were blown up, stranding hundreds of the barges which carried a high proportion of inland traffic and acted as links with coastal trade. These attacks could be compared, in some respects, with the highly successful RAF breaching of the Ruhr dams in May—the comparison between repeated and coordinated disruptions of concrete by a few well-trained saboteurs, employing an unsophisticated technology, and the one-time-only assault on a single target by a handful of well-trained airmen using highly sophisticated technology. The first had long-term effects and maintained a persistent threat; the second, with the higher capital outlay, caused greater shock but soon lost its impact.

Many sabotage campaigns failed, as frequently did RAF raids. Attacks on the railways sometimes misfired and never caused prolonged stoppages. Penetration by agents of vital target areas—such as the U-boat bases, Atlantic Wall fortifications, the newly built rocket weapon sites aligned against England and, indeed, the entire coastal belt—was almost impossible due to the density of German troops and the watchfulness of their guards. The extraction of intelligence from these areas was already difficult enough without being made harder by SOE stirring up the authorities with trivial aggressions. In the heavily defended zones airpower was best suited to the immensity of destruction required—as it proved, with widespread and often indiscriminate violence throughout the months prior to Neptune.[2]

Only occasionally was industrial sabotage attempted, partly because, for quite obvious reasons, factory owners were opposed to the destruction of their plants. Indeed, the workers themselves, no matter how patriotic, preferred to keep their jobs. It was clearly preferable, if the Allies were absolutely determined to eliminate a key factory, to limit the job to the inside kind rather than have recourse to total destruction by bombing, which almost invariably caused damage off-target and the indiscriminate killing of civilians. (By the same token railway destruction would have been preferable by sabotage instead of bombing if only the saboteurs could have inflicted lasting damage.) Some factory owners, such as the Peugeots, were happy to cooperate with SOE in response to a promise that the RAF would make no further attempt to bomb their factory at Sochaux. A word with a director (who had helped already to finance an F circuit against a British Treasury promise of repayment after the war) and the factory was kept out of action by selective internal sabotage for the rest of the war, without disrupting its fabric or causing widespread damage. The Michelin family were less flexible, however, and, for refusing to sabotage their tire factory at Clermont-Ferrand, had the mortification of seeing it ripped apart by the RAF.

Undoubtedly the most effective single act of accumulated sabotage was that perpetrated by the Gaullist "Armada" team, which, beginning in 1942 with dynamite stolen from mines and quarries, expanded its activities at the end of 1943 and in early 1944 by waging a protracted campaign against electricity transformers and pylons to such an extent that one part of France was reduced to "a pylon graveyard." Whole blocks of French industry went temporarily out of production, while the export of electricity to Germany was also curtailed. It was a moment of truth when the Germans had to bring in coal to replace hydroelectric power—an additional load upon the already overstrained transport system. Of course the populace suffered too: the French had a cold winter in 1944.

In *SOE in France*, Foot reproduces a list enumerating 150 separate

---

[2] German intelligence reports of May and June 1944, while relating the feeling of expectant tension among the population of France, also refer to resentment against the bombing—a sentiment which Allied soldiers were also to encounter when, later, they moved into Europe.

acts of industrial sabotage in France alone, caused, he says, by a mere three thousand pounds of explosive. Of these incidents only 4 occurred during 1942, before the turning point in the war, and 22 after the landing in Normandy. But by then liberation was imminent and the plant better left for the future prosperity of France. Moreover the bulk of sabotage which took place subsequent to mid-1943 was insignificant against a background of soaring German home production, which increased despite the depredations of the bomber offensive. Except for loss of power, stoppages in industry were largely unimportant, because they were only of a few days' duration.

Disagreements between the principal French political parties persisted, as might be expected, to the end, though the flag of resistance attracted closer national unity as the invasion drew near. In March 1944 de Gaulle proclaimed the intended amalgamation of all Resistance forces under one head, introducing the Forces Françaises de l'Intérieur (FFI), and placing them under the command of Major-General P.J. Koenig. But the FFI never achieved unity. Secret Army, OAS and political private armies merged when it suited them, while the Communist FTP stood apart, trusting nobody but itself and emphasizing its rivalry with the Gaullists.[3] Shortly before the invasion, however, de Gaulle achieved one recognizably important unification. By becoming the head of the Provisional Government in Exile he at last managed to rid himself of Giraud. Only in Algiers was de Gaulle supreme, however, for in London the British and Americans declined to tell his followers Neptune's date—let alone the details of French participation, and refused separate cipher facilities to the French for fear of a security breach. Not until June 4, two days before the assault, was de Gaulle brought to London, where Churchill let him in on the plan. But on the third, de Gaulle had taken the precaution of proclaiming himself head of a provisional government of France and so the meeting between the two leaders was stormy. While de Gaulle bitterly resented his exclusion from a military operation which employed French soldiers, Churchill was unwilling to accept de Gaulle as a head of state, reflecting Roosevelt's view that "I am not able to recognize any government of France until the people of France have an opportunity to make a free choice." Thus Fighting French Forces and FFI were, for the moment, deprived of a formal joint command with

[3] The position of FTP, like its parent Communist Party, was always precarious in France. Its leadership was split, its security so tight as often to prevent orders being passed in time for implementation; its composition only faintly Communist in practice—probably less than a quarter were "Red" and less than a third of all indigenous, combatant French actually members of FTP.

their allies at SHAEF in the forthcoming campaign, which, by its very nature, would test public support for de Gaulle and his rival contenders for political dominance.

The balance of main forces in Western Europe is outside the scope of this book, and is detailed in other books; the balance between guerrilla and antiguerrilla forces is almost impossible to establish. Leverkuehn describes the never-ending struggle against SOE and claims that eighty radio installations were put out of action between April 1942 and March 1943. Most German records, however, foretold a losing battle after 1943 as the special security services, but a few thousand strong, became saturated by the overwhelming arrival of innumerable hostile parties in their midst. Giskes realized the hopelessness of it all as, on the one hand, he battled to keep pace with the declared enemy and, on the other, tried to frustrate the SS's takeover bid for the Abwehr. Overall casualties to SOE agents seem to have been somewhere in the region of twenty-five per cent, which, in four years of war, is low by comparison with an infantry unit, which could suffer nearly one hundred per cent turnover in a few months' intensive combat, and of RAF bomber crews who lost ninety per cent in a tour of thirty missions.

A strict equation between the Allied forces which operated behind the German lines in Western Europe with those on the other fronts is impossible (even though there were many similarities) because they endured in totally different environments. Those in the West were given adequate support far too late to enable them to flourish, and throughout suffered from something of which the Russians had rid themselves within a matter of months—divided command plus a general misunderstanding and mistrust by the orthodox military leadership of their role and potential. Prior to D-Day the main contact between SOE and Supreme Headquarters Allied Expeditionary Forces (SHAEF), under General Eisenhower, Twenty-first Army Group, under General Montgomery, and the various army headquarters was through "cells" located within those headquarters. These cells tried to coordinate the military requirement with the myriad "circuits" and maquis ceaselessly shifting in the enemy rear, endeavoring to make common cause within the intrigues of the Gaullist FFI, F Section and any other special forces or transport agencies. If SHAEF and Twenty-first Army Group sometimes underestimated SOE's offerings it is hardly surprising, for the irregulars, in all their diversity, failed to engender unshakable faith while, in size, they were but a small proportion of the highly trained regular formations which were about to go into battle. It was natural that Eisenhower, his commanders and his staffs should place more faith in the parachute and commando formations of proven reliability which would spearhead the invasion; next giving preference to the highly trained élite raiding forces, such as the SAS; and only finally turning to the FFI—in effect putting their trust in cool, uniformed quality before hotheaded, plain-clothed quantity.

In readiness for D-Day SOE had formed two types of special mission, over and above the circuits, though instructed to work in conjunction with the circuits and the maquis when they came into contact. These were the inter-Allied missions, the first of which (Union) parachuted into the Rhône Valley on January 6, 1944, led at first by H.H.A. Thackthwaite, accompanied by a United States Marine officer, Peter Ortis, who had once served in the French Foreign Legion. Their allegiance was to RF, their task usually (though not always) to move among the maquis (in uniform) and direct their efforts towards guerrilla warfare as their primary contribution to the future —suggesting activities that fell somewhere between the sabotage demanded by F Section and the outright warfare inherent in Plan Vidal—organizing rather than leading. Twenty more inter-Allied missions would follow (all but five after D-Day); some two strong, like Asymtote, which contained the celebrated Yeo-Thomas, sent in to maintain politico-military links; others, like Cardozo's Benjoin (which consisted of six men of mixed nationality) instructed to identify an independent maquis group and link its activities to the threads of Allied strategy. Of these missions it would seem that only seven achieved worthwhile military results, though their psychological and political inspirations may well have been invaluable.

Then there were the uniformed Jedburgh teams—usually six strong, also inter-Allied in complement, employing many Frenchmen and about a hundred officers from the American OSS. Their job was to expand the existing circuits—acting as rallying points, providing instruction to the indigenous guerrillas and links with the Allied forces as they advanced. Eighty-three of these teams were subsequently sent in after D-Day, the delay of their dispatch prior to that date being justified on the usual grounds of guarding the security of the Overlord and Neptune plans, as well as sanctifying the policy of curbing an uprising until the enemy were virtually on their knees.

American participation was on a grand scale even though its influence was somewhat submerged under British and French domination. OSS had, after all, existed for only two years, though its birth, delayed for so long due to Roosevelt's reservations, State Department objections and FBI self-interest, had been followed by a rapid though painful growth. William (Wild Bill) Donovan may have been a legendary and inspiring organizer, but he also stirred up resentment by his empire building, while his flamboyant personality militated against secrecy. OSS, reflecting traditional American isolationism and Roosevelt's rather naive attempt to keep the action of war separate from politics was, in this case, confused by political events to an even greater extent than SOE had been in its early days. Between OSS and the State Department was the same clash of interests as between SOE and the British Foreign Office—neither party seeming capable of resolving their differences into a common policy. For example, though the United States had, in due course, to arrive at some sort of agreement with Russia over Poland's future, the State Department forbade OSS to become involved with Polish resistance—a ridiculous situation, since the Poles were inextricably bound up with action on so many fronts. Likewise, OSS intelligence agencies which operated into Scandinavia from neutral Sweden and into Central and Southern Europe from Switzerland simply could not run in blinkers. Its schemes were bound to lead to political involvement. Nevertheless, so far as partisan warfare was concerned, OSS tried to develop on strictly military lines of its own and formed its own operational groups (OG), which were the equivalent of the German Brandenburg Regiment and the British SAS. The original directive laid down, in fact, that OSS would "collect and analyze strategic information and plan and operate special services." [4] In size and scope the four OGs provided by OSS fell somewhere between a British commando troop and an SAS patrol. Lavishly equipped, these parties of thirty-four men contained a high percentage of French linguists. They were based in North Africa and operated in the South of France. Thus, in due course, they would be able to give more support to the Anvil landing in August than to Neptune in June.

The SAS found a place within the Allied Order of Battle by way of reward for its achievements in Southern Europe, though before anybody had carefully defined its rôle. Like the Brandenburg Regiment, it had won swift expansion out of success, but there the resemblance ended, since the German organization was more specialized and carefully adjusted to Abwehr-type operations. In June 1944 the SAS was twenty-five hundred strong, organized as a brigade of two British and two French battalions, plus a Belgian squadron. They were ready to fight anybody, including each other, since there was no love lost between the two British battalions, and the French battalions were also

---

[4] OSS thus resembled the French BCRA, with its separate departments for Renseignements and Action, rather than SOE, with its specialization in Action.

at daggers drawn. But unlike their nearest equivalent, the OGs, they were divorced from SOE/SO command and put directly under HQ Airborne Forces, which had little knowledge of or sympathy with these specialist bands operating independently in heavily armed jeeps. As SAS activities had to be cleared with all other interested operational departments it could hardly be expected they would be allowed free-ranging missions.

At first it was Airborne Forces' intention to integrate the tiny SAS jeep patrols with the main landing, dropping 1st SAS in the confined space between the German coastal defenses and armored formations—thus inserting them into the very places where SOE circuits had found it impossible to work because of the enemy's density of occupation. This led to the resignation of the battalion commander—an unusual event in time of war, though it was not, according to the SAS history, "so much that this was a near suicidal mission . . . but that it was an ineffective form of employment; there would be no time to organise proper damage to the enemy, and greater opportunities elsewhere would be missed." Perhaps the resignation by W.S. Stirling did some good, for, in due course, 1st SAS for the most part landed far from the front, only a few of its patrols being located in Normandy for raiding through the lines. The main body of the brigade was to establish bases in what were well-founded areas of resistance—in Brittany, where the local populace were traditionally independent of mind and action; to the south of the Loire, between the Vendée and Châteauroux; between Vierzon and Le Creusot; and in the Morvan Mountains to the north of Dijon. From these bases, in conjunction with the local maquis and their Jedburgh leaders, the highly trained, élite SAS were meant to set an example—to sharpen the teeth of the amateurish, maquis bands.

SAS patrols, like the Jedburghs, were to campaign in uniform behind the enemy lines, staying clear of those areas where heavy German concentrations lay. In effect this provided them with great scope, for the Germans were thin on the ground except in the coastal areas, the entire defense having been stretched to breaking point long before the invasion began. In May, when the intensive and systematic bombing of the railway system started, traffic began gradually to run down, though never to a complete halt. Increasingly, however, the railways demanded more maintenance than the Germans could afford and this forced them to depend ever more on road, air and water-borne traffic.

In the invasion area there was what amounted to an armed truce with the Resistance because the main SOE effort was reserved until

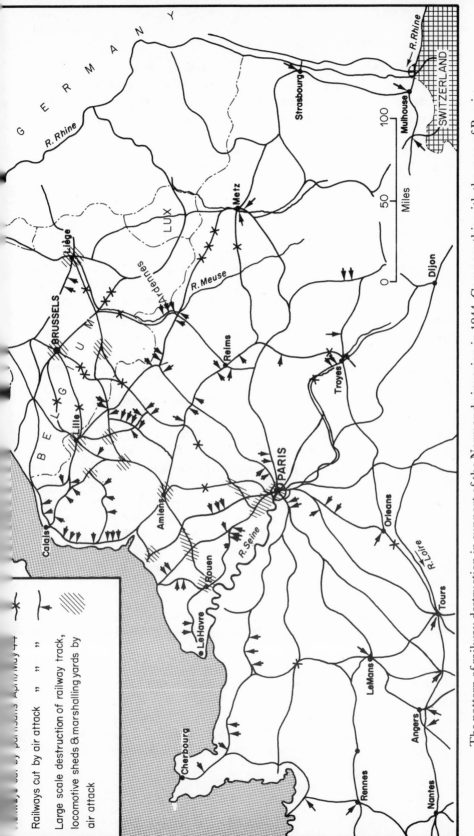

The pattern of railway destruction in support of the Normandy invasion in 1944. Compare this with the map of Russia on page 209.

close upon D-Day. This by no means relieved the Germans in Northern France and Belgium from tension. An inter-Allied mission (Citronelle) which landed in the Ardennes in April found small groups intermittently ambushing the Germans among the close and intricate hills and woodlands. But the heaviest activity of all, of course, centered upon the original maquis country to the south and here the pugnacity of the guerrillas at last awoke the Germans to their peril. Where Union (now under its commander designate, Fourcaud) operated, minor uprisings led to the sort of stand-up fight that Plan Vidal recommended and SOE deplored. In Ain and Haute Savoie seven hundred maquis tried conclusions with a vastly superior German/Milice force and, inevitably, received terrible punishment, collapsing when they ran out of ammunition. This, as Foot remarks, "was magnificent, unforgettable but tactically unsound." It was worse, for it led to the kind of retaliation which epitomized German behavior in all other parts of Europe—the mangling of people—the old, the women and children in their homes—along with extinction of the vital leaders upon whom the maquis depended if they were to have the slightest chance of making an impact when they at last received positive direction and sufficient armament.

Against this background of courage, losses, minor triumphs and rising SOE confidence, the Germans were all too well aware of the increasing influx of supplies to guerrilla bands they could no longer contain. They heard, nightly, the strings of BBC radio messages which meant much to the guerrillas but nothing to them except that events were mounting, out of control, to a climax. If, in the week before June 6, Wehrmacht intelligence reports discounted an imminent invasion due to inclement weather, the volume of clandestine radio traffic ought to have warned them that something unusual was afoot. On the night of June 1 hundreds of warning messages were heard, followed on the evening of the fifth by twice as many executive messages as usual. Next came the definitive order: "Today the Supreme Commander directs me to say this: In due course instructions of great importance will be given to you through this channel, but it will not be possible always to give these instructions at a previously announced time. Therefore you must get into the habit of listening at all hours."

Suddenly the phased program had been replaced by total call-out, without warning the alarmed members of SOE and FFI listening to the broadcasts. How did this come about?

The answer is to be discovered in the Supreme Commander's dread of failure and a last-minute attack of cold feet upon the part of his staff. Eisenhower is reputed to have prepared two broadcasts for the sixth—one for success and the other for failure. Moreover he transmitted his fears to his staff (or perhaps they communicated theirs to him) with the result that, shortly after June 1, requests were made to SOE for a maximum effort. On the third a senior staff officer from special forces briefed SHAEF's chief of staff, General Bedell Smith, about the implications of a change of plan, particularly the dangers of making it at the last moment, when nothing could be done in compensation. But Eisenhower's mind was made up. It was to be *toute le monde à la bataille*. Just in time to change the executive broadcast on the fifth, but far too late to arrange special help for those of the Resistance who were to be prematurely thrust into action, he authorized total call-out—an order to which Koenig, at FFI, raised no objection. Thus, to quote the American historian Charles Macdonald, "If the French were to contribute they would have to act everywhere at once, even if that exposed them to reprisals."

Orders for 1,050 rail cuts went out on the night of the fifth, as did instructions to the maquis of the Vercors to begin resistance on D-Day (without specifying whether it applied to Neptune on the sixth or to Anvil, which finally took place in August in the far south). Excitement was mounting at all levels of command and the threat of unnecessary mistakes created. The Germans appreciated the significance of the messages to the Resistance but still doubted the imminence of invasion. In England the first troop-carrying aircraft were taxiing out for takeoff.

CHAPTER TWELVE

Retribution in the West

Of the fifty-nine German divisions located in France and the Low Countries on June 6, 1944, few were far from the coast, where they presented a thin grey line against the expected invasion. Only in the Pas de Calais, where the threat seemed greatest and the infantry divisions lay two deep, and in Isere, where the maquis were highly active, did infantry stand back from the coast. The remaining inland formations represented the mobile reserve of panzer, panzer grenadier and parachute divisions whose task it would be to strike towards the coast once the heart of the invasion had been recognized. In essence, therefore, antiguerrilla measures did virtually nothing to bend the Germans from the classic defensive posture of shield and spear. War-limont comments that the only special measure Hitler ordered was the allocation of two or three low-grade divisions to the West, and Colonel Emmerich, who was the Operations Officer of First Army, confirms the weekly situation reports from Army Group B when he states there was little activity on the part of the Resistance "either in the zone of operations or in the dispersal area of First Army"—a comment of importance since Gascony was a zone reputedly well organized by SOE.

The coastal deployment of the German infantry did not, of course, rule out forays against the partisans. The pattern of opportunist anti-guerrilla raids was copied from Russia, the effectiveness of each operation a direct reflection of the quality of the units concerned—from the crushing successes earned by the highly professional Wehrmacht, to the bitter hatred stirred up by the brutish inhumanity of the SS departments and *milicien,* and the partial neutralizations achieved by the indifferent foreign formations composed of White Russian, Cossack and Mongol peasantry. Not that the latter were to be despised; they stuck doggedly to their German overlords, despite all efforts by SOE agents to wean them away—possibly because of an overriding fear of being sent back to the prison camps.

Until 1944 the Wehrmacht's task in controlling the Western occupied countries had been less ambiguous than in the East. The High
Command maintained its traditional influence and Canaris's Abwehr
operated with comparative freedom in the battle of wits with SOE and
the SS. Early in 1944, however, the defection of several Abwehr agents
to the British gave Himmler the opportunity to persuade Hitler to
combine the Abwehr and SS intelligence agencies into one German
intelligence service, placing the new organization under Ernst Kal-
tenbrunner and at last ensuring SS domination. Thus Canaris was
removed from the stage and made to concentrate still more on the rôle
of intriguer against Hitler along with the handful of army officers who
were conniving at Hitler's assassination and the destruction of the Nazi
regime. There is justice in Wheeler-Bennett's assertion that the Abwehr "displayed no very great efficiency either as intelligence officers or
as conspirators." It had, after all, signally failed in its primary role of
discovering the Allies' principal intentions. But Wheeler-Bennett is
perhaps a little hard on Canaris when he calls him "devious rather
than brilliant" and less than just if, by implication, he denigrates the
Abwehr's efforts in the anti-SOE field. Here it had been all too efficient
for comfort. One is led to ask, if the Abwehr had been given complete
control of all resources, including the misguided sections of the SS, how
much more disastrous the effects might have been on the nascent SOE
circuits? If, in the summer of 1943, the rivalry between the Abwehr and
SS had been so acute that the former was reputed to have been lenient
with SOE, how much easier might SOE's work have become a year
later, when the Abwehr was abolished and the inept SS took over in all
its bullying unsubtlety?

The raids against SOE circuits, principally in urban areas, went on.
Paris was kept firmly under control and the coastal zones stayed quiet;
shortly before the invasion, Army Group B reported the population in
the theater of operations as "friendly." Nevertheless the Germans were
fully aware that, although there was a lull in sabotage, they were
committed to two kinds of combat—the struggle between well-drilled
regular formations in the dense Normandy bocage and the guerrilla
warfare which spontaneously burst into flame, guttered, glowed, and
then flamed anew throughout the rest of the country.

It began in earnest when the participants in Plan Vert crept cautiously from their homes in the dusk of June 5, stealing through the
curfew heavily laden with charges to lay against rails, signal installations and rolling stock—a pattern of sabotage which merged with the
widespread destruction already caused by the aerial bombardment.
The night throbbed with aircraft engines, bomb bursts and gunfire

flickered over the coast. Close upon midnight, near Isigny, parachutists drifted down. First to arrive were a British officer and two men of 1st SAS, followed fifteen minutes later by a French SAS party, carrying Very pistols and gramophones to simulate the signs and sounds of a large-scale airborne landing. With them, too, came several hundred dummies with built-in firecrackers—all designed to confuse the German command as to the true center of Allied incursion. It was effective. The Isigny party drew away from the coast the reserve regiment of 352nd Division, which, had it remained, might have decisively counterattacked the Americans on Omaha Beach at the moment when their landing stood poised on the brink of failure.

The sudden overnight appearance of uniformed SAS units and Jedburghs on French soil, linked with euphoric propaganda messages on the BBC, intoxicated the French people. They fancied themselves on the eve of instant liberation. For the first time, as a nation, they threw off restraint to hoist their colors in battle and exorcise the stigma of 1940's disgrace. Hatred of the Germans overcame discretion. Regardless of whether they were already linked to a Resistance group, they became part of what several participants and historians describe as a vast, "spontaneous" uprising. Of course the action by Allied agents and propaganda inevitably modified the degree of spontaneity.

The net result of the call-out was an almost total neutralization of a railway system that was already in ruins from the bombing—but not all of it was from blatant destruction. Instructed by their unions, which were Resistance infiltrated, the railwaymen began a systematic "go-slow," throwing schedules into chaos and deferring repairs to damage. Yet in terms of supply the Germans suffered but a marginal initial embarrassment. Most battle zones were previously stocked for prolonged combat and the roads remained relatively free for motor convoys (even if the extra petrol expenditure could be ill afforded). More harmful was the difficulty of moving reserve formations quickly from inactive regions to the points of danger—that is, to Normandy from the South of France and, above all, from the Pas de Calais. But at the height of the rail interdiction period (throughout June), when the French were most enthusiastic about waging guerrilla warfare, and as yet undeterred by retribution, the Germans were loath to move more than a proportion of their reserves to Normandy. They feared the first landings there were but a distraction from the main invasion yet to come—fooled in fact by the Allied deception plan. And when, at last, the decision came to shift formations the redeployment was not nearly so difficult as some accounts suggest.

The protagonists of guerrilla warfare make much of the travails of the 2nd SS Panzer Division in its journey from Toulouse to Normandy. Warned to move on June 7, its tanks did not start until the eleventh because railway rolling stock was unavailable. The road convoys had passed Limoges by the eighth and were on schedule, but then entered a zone belonging to an efficient circuit called "Wrestler" in an area thickly populated by maquis, SAS and Jedburghs. A series of ambushes were sprung, minor casualties inflicted and the advancing columns slowed to a crawl. The SS men looked upon ambushes as slights upon their honor. The kidnapping of the colonel commanding the 3rd SS Panzer Grenadier Regiment led to an exhaustive search and further delay. Ahead, the Allied air forces wrecked every bridge across the Loire except one, which was so weakened that each truck needed to be towed across individually. Tempers within the SS division became frayed and betrayed failings in discipline which inevitably led to unchecked brutality. On thin evidence of *franc-tireurs,* they massacred the local populace at Oradour-sur-Glane—murdering something like seven hundred people as they burned the village to the ground.[1] The maquis and their adherents claim due credit for delaying this SS division, though rather more goes to the air forces who inflicted the longest delay at the Loire. One suspects, however, that the prime cause of delay lay within the division—for its bad initial movement plan, for allowing trivialities to hold it up and for losing its sense of composure under pressure. When at last it reached the front it rarely gave a good account of itself—perhaps it was shaken by its experiences, maybe it never was a very good division.

It is a fact that the 17th SS Panzer Grenadier Division, 276th Infantry and 708th Infantry Division, plus several more units stationed to the south of the Loire, moved to the battle zone with scarcely any difficulty. Emmerich writes: "The only precautionary measure which the [First] Army had to take was the reinforcement, by its own bicycle patrols, of the security details employed for the protection of the railroad lines. . . ." Where does the truth lie? Did the guerrillas and air power shatter the lines of communication or did they not? As usual in such cases there has undoubtedly been much exaggeration of the damage caused. Destruction was absolute in many areas, but nonexistent or patchy in others. Traffic continued to cross some rivers: there were areas where, due to the failure of an SOE circuit, the sabotage task was left undone; and others where the local maquis were either nonexistent or under such German pressure that they were

---

[1] Let it be remembered that the Oradour massacre was almost unique in Western European Resistance experience—one compared with hundreds of similar holocausts in the East, an index, perhaps, of Resistance performance.

defeated in detail or forced to disperse. Some circuits, of course, were almost too well organized and successful; Wrestler, run by a British WAAF officer, Pearl Witherington, cut eight hundred lines in June and just about every cable in sight. But it so devastated its zone that the German air reconnaissance was able to define Wrestler's boundaries with deadly accuracy and thus guide countermeasures in the right direction.

The unevenness of clandestine performance must largely be laid at the door of the Allied Higher Command, since not until July 1 was the direction of Resistance placed squarely under one headquarters. Only then, as the battle waxed fiercely, could de Gaulle be persuaded to put aside his indignation with the Allies in order to permit the creation of a joint headquarters under König. This would absorb the FFI, F and RF Sections and become known as Etat-major des Forces Françaises de l'Intérieur (EMFFI), falling under the provisional government, as well as SHAEF, to command the forces in the field and liaise direct with SOE and the SAS. Had this been implemented when FFI was formed in March all might have been well, since the new headquarters would have had time in which to shake down before being pitched into action. As it was a number of experienced staff officers from F and RF Sections suddenly found themselves working at a furious pace alongside inexperienced French regular officers, dealing with units in the field which had no recognizable organization and whose prowess was as variable as the men who led and served them. Besides those French officers who had emerged from cover in France and who were rather disparagingly called "les naphthalines" (because of the smell of mothballs from their uniforms), there were others on the staff in England who were out of their depth—the sort who arranged a complex airdrop to the maquis and forgot to ask the RAF for aircraft. Nor did the introduction of EMFFI achieve unity of operational command throughout Western Europe. There remained ample scope for misunderstanding within SOE/SO, with SOE's Massingham Headquarters in Algiers and with those branches of SOE which worked for Belgium and the Netherlands—Sections T and N, respectively. The dividing line between SHAEF's Overlord with EMFFI, and Allied Forces HQ Mediterranean's Anvil with Massingham was never fully defined. There were several ugly disagreements in France due to this. Likewise there were difficulties in coordinating operations in the Ardennes, where French operators crossed frequently into Belgium and Belgians sometimes took cover in France.

The partisan campaign in France is worth study because it produced contrasting examples of the art. Foremost in French memory is the saga of the Vercors, that looming plateau to the west of Grenoble where the conventionally minded French Army officers elected to fight a misconceived battle of the kind favored by Delestraint—attempting to hold a bastion with its perimeter resting strongly atop precipitous cliffs, its weak points the many narrow cols that provided access from the valley below. It was never SOE's original intention to initiate a major rising in the Vercors in June, though some such event appeared to be feasible in August after Anvil had made progress. But the Eucalyptus mission (manned by officers with scant knowledge of the French language), which became delayed in Algiers and did not finally set forth until June 28 arrived to find a *fait accompli*. The uprising had attracted several thousand Frenchmen to the plateau where they were being organized, in the time left over between factional disputes, by officers of the Secret Army under Colonel Huet, of the maquis, and SOE. These were soon joined by an American operational group—so there was certainly no shortage of cooks to spoil the broth.

It was a perilous situation even though the plateau had been cleared of Germans. The enthusiastic French Army, thrilled by the sight of the tricolor flying free after four years, possessed neither the strength, training nor weapons to hold so extensive a perimeter. Yet it engaged in flamboyant offensive operations, the OG springing a most fruitful ambush on July 7, which so shook the Germans that they assessed the fifteen man team at battalion strength. But those who sallied far from the plateau were often betrayed by German double agents who had joined the stream of new recruits, while the aftermath of the ambush on the seventh added to German knowledge telling them that, on the eleventh, still more maquis were being called up. This acted as a spur to the Germans. In the South, where they were not involved in fending off an invasion, they had time to strike at the partisans using two infantry divisions, part of a panzer division, a parachute company and an assortment of Russian troops and security men—a force more than ten thousand strong, well supported by artillery and aircraft.

The Vercors Plan was always an invitation to disaster. The original Union report by Thackthwaite had underlined this, pointing out that lack of heavy weapons was sure to be fatal, and that so long a perimeter, with many points of access, was by no means impregnable. Even had heavy weapons been supplied they would not have saved the day since their high ammunition expenditure could never have been satisfied by air supply alone. But on July 11 Koenig at EMFFI was sending laudatory messages to the Vercors and telling SHAEF that virtual control of nearly the whole of France was possible if only supplies could be delivered. On June 15, 75 of the big U.S. B-17 bombers had been allocated and on the eighteenth this was increased to between 180 and 300—a sizable diversion from their primary strategic bombing role. Massed daylight drops of supplies (Operation Zebra) were projected for June 22 (delayed by weather until the twenty-fifth) into all those areas where partisan fighting was known to be intense. One hundred seventy-six B-17s battled through, under strong fighter escort, to drop more than 2,000 containers to the maquis of the Haute Savoie, who were under heavy pressure. On July 14 it was the turn of the Vercors, where 72 B-17s unloaded 860 containers holding small arms, ammunition and clothing. That day 322 of the U.S. aircraft delivered 3,780 containers all told—the rest falling near Limoges and Chalons-sur-Saône. That day, too, the Germans began to concentrate against the Vercors.

The investment of the plateau by the Germans began on the seventeenth and on the eighteenth was tightened, pressing back the three thousand defenders to the cliff tops. On the twenty-first came the main assault—but not where the French expected it. At 9:30 A.M. under cover of an air bombardment (which overwhelming Allied air superiority might have prevented if they had attacked the German airfields) twenty gliders swept down upon the Vassieux air strip, which, just like the one in Yugoslavia at Drvar, had been prepared to receive Dakota aircraft, and disgorged 200 of the best Waffen SS. They set foot on ground that was barely defended and were safely dug in before Huet could transfer reserves for a counterattack. But the reserves in any case were already needed elsewhere, because the two-pronged German assault upon the top of the plateau from north and south had begun in earnest, timed to coincide with the glider assault, and backed by heavy fire from artillery and mortars. The attack was irresistible and would probably have been so even had Allied parachute formations been flown in as requested by the French. Frenchmen with small arms alone were forced to endure the shelling without the slightest chance of response. In less than two days they were beaten and forced to disperse from a concentration they should never have adopted. And in so doing they again betrayed their inexperience, for although so many fighting men were able to escape, they left behind their camp followers, whose treatment by the Germans was as pitiless as that meted out to partisans elsewhere in Europe. Over a thousand died.

Recriminations over the Vercors were to become legend, concealing the fundamental error of attempting conventional combat in a guerrilla setting. It is paradoxical that the less celebrated actions are those where the French best practiced the guerrilla art—a condemnation of the overriding journalistic approach which has distorted the writing of partisan history. On the French-Belgian frontier in the Ardennes, for example, Mission Citronelle found itself the center of the same carnival spirit which, in the halcyon June days, enthused the Vercors. Men arrived by the hundred, some carrying musical instruments but all too few with weapons. They hung around in groups while the mission tried to organize and acquire weapons and ammunition for them. George Whitehead recalls the extraordinary feeling of euphoria that existed, but to this day cannot quite explain how one parachuted load contained lampshades and nothing else. Like Eucalyptus, Citronelle met difficulties under heavy enemy pressure as a German-led Russian regiment pressed in upon them. But, unlike their colleagues in the Vercors, they were quick to disperse, after the first expensive brush at a cost of a hundred French dead. They took shelter on the Belgian side of the frontier and for the next two months or more waged a war of hit and run against an enemy who never quite got their measure. Perhaps it was the expertise of Citronelle's guides—a combined force of smugglers and customs men—which enabled them to evade their captors in the frontier's approaches for so long.

Cardozo's Benjoin Mission in the Auvergnes fought like true guerrillas, too, close by Mont Mouchet alongside the maquis under Coulaudon. "We withdrew to the plateau through phased positions until the moment arrived at which further withdrawal was impossible. Then we dispersed, reformed later and started again." Twice in June this maquis, along with Benjoin, survived heavy antipartisan attacks, and in August earned its reward by liberating Clermont Ferrand. By then they were staunch veterans, hardened in the combat which, initially, had weeded out the self-interested opportunists whose morale shattered before the first enemy stroke.

Citronelle and Benjoin survived in territory that was fairly remote from enemy troop concentrations. Far more hazardous was the task of those who took action in Brittany, where the enemy were thick on the ground both with coastal defense infantry divisions and the three parachute divisions which lay along the spine of the peninsula as a reserve against invasion. Breton resistance had taken a hard knock when the arms caches had been raided in the aftermath of the Prosper disaster. But the arrival of one hundred and fifty men from the 4th French SAS battalion on June 5, to the north east of Vannes, injected fresh impetus in an area which, as the Germans were fully aware, harbored a potentially aggressive group of Frenchmen. The tasks given to the one-armed SAS leader, Commandant Bourgoin, were "to sever as far as possible all communications between Brittany and the remainder of France" and also try to raise a full revolt. For this latter role Bourgoin had the assistance of an F Section circuit plus six Jedburghs while, as the days passed, more SAS were flown in with heavier equipment to spread their influence throughout the peninsula. Bases were set up which became magnets to the local secret army, which flocked in, as Bourgoin put it, "like a fair."

They caught the Germans on the horns of a dilemma, plumb in the act of redeployment. Third Parachute Division (which had been located adjacent to the SAS dropping zone) was already en route to Normandy on the eleventh (traveling by road because the railway had been made unusable, according to the Germans, by air attack). Thus the parachutists were unavailable for counterguerrilla actions, that task going to coastal defense infantry, of German-Russian derivation, who had to be sent inland at the very time when, in the German view, the possibility of further landings on the Brittany coast was by no means remote. On the twelfth the first German attack against an SAS base camp took place, the SAS reacting with an instant dispersal though not without loss to themselves and the local guerrillas. Six days later a far heavier attack struck the main SAS base near Rennes, although this time it was Bourgoin's good fortune to be in indirect contact with forty U.S. fighter-bombers which put in so sustained a series of attacks that, combined with the ground defense, he won the day.[2] Dealing with the general internal situation at this time, Army Group West at last appreciated the gravity of the situation building up in its rear. No longer were the population rated "friendly" or just "expectant":

> There has been a continuous increase during the last few days in the number of isolated young men on the roads or of small groups on foot or on bicycles, so that there appears to be suspicion that extensive recruiting is in progress for the Resistance Movements. . . . In Belgium and the Belgian Frontier Zone there are increasing signs of a Resistance Movement under energetic leadership . . . Sabotage acts on the increase. In Brittany steady reinforcement of well-trained, well-armed men and experienced leaders (partly French parachute troops trained in England) arriving by air . . . have led to the formation of powerful groups.

A week later the Germans were reporting, apropos Brittany, that "despite successful mopping-up operations and capture of weapon and ammunition dumps, recrudescence of sabotage activities towards end

---

[2] The staff officer who coordinated that attack was M.R.D. Foot, the official historian of *SOE in France*.

of week. Enemy's next objective presumably to equip terrorist groups. . . ." And as, throughout July, further withdrawal of their parachute formations continued and the battlefront in Normandy broke open to release American armored divisions in the direction of Brittany, the Germans recognized their fate: "Projects better planned, betray in nature and execution disciplined performance by trained forces." The reports then went on to list the communication targets that were being attacked and the number of enemy losses as "168 dead including 16 parachutists, 117 taken prisoner (including 4 parachutists)." The professional performance by Bourgoin's SAS shines through these German reports. Caught in a situation that was never of his wishing, he had loyally tried to foster a revolt but, with good sense, had abandoned it as soon as the danger was realized. There was to be no Vercors débâcle in Brittany. Henceforward he would fight dispersed, accepting such supplies as opportunity and his excellent radio communications made possible, restraining the enthusiasm of the maquisards, ambushing and harrying the enemy while building a force that was thirty thousand strong by the end of July—extending clandestine influence to all parts of the peninsula except where the Germans stood concentrated. More SAS from the 2nd Battalion came down to the north of Nantes on August 3, but by then the Germans were defeated. Faced with the improved effectiveness of SAS ambushes they had increased the size of their antiguerrilla patrols and thus reduced their overall cover of the peninsula. As the spearheads of Patton's Third Army reached Avranches on July 31, and turned westward towards Brest, the Germans abandoned hope of holding a line across the peninsula's base. Instead they turned tail for Brest, St. Nazaire and La Rochelle. Hot on their trail, and picking up discarded equipment and stores along the route, the SAS kept pace: they had suffered forty per cent casualties but were still full of fight.

Somewhat late in the day, EMFFI now decided to take a hand —one suspects for political rather more than military reasons. On August 1 they briefed a large inter-Allied mission called Aloes to land in Brittany on August 3 under a Colonel Eon, whose experience of guerrilla war was as nothing to that of his second-in-command, Dewaverin, who once ran de Gaulle's secret service. By then the tide of battle had moved rapidly westward with Bourgoin and his ancillary guerrillas in full cry of the beaten enemy. Aloes landed, in fact, *behind* the American spearheads, arriving just in time to take part in the mopping-up operations and, above all, to arrange the collection of German armaments which were essential to the FFI since it suffered badly from lack of heavy weapons. These captured weapons would now arm Frenchmen who laid siege, along with the Americans, to the Atlantic ports. Yet this, as Eon has pointed out, was contrary to SHAEF policy, which held that, as the armies made contact with the FFI, their arms should be collected "and put into safe custody, so formidable appeared the danger resulting from the presence of these 'armed civilians' at the rear of the Allied columns." The danger in fact was slight and if it existed at all lay mainly with the Communist FTP, described by Eon as "my best shock troops."

As earlier in Russia, so now in France as, throughout August, the Allied armies raced towards Germany through France, Belgium and Holland. Where German resistance weakened, the partisans gathered strength until the best of each nation left cover to fight in the open, turning partisan warfare into People's War. Sabotage now became a mixed blessing. One SOE operative blew a railway long after dispatch of the signal telling him to desist—the message simply failed to reach him in time. An OG in Quercy, after spending a week in hiding, ventured forth to demolish a viaduct with an overgenerous dose of explosive only to discover that the Germans had withdrawn four days previously. SAS patrols roamed the forest rides, ambushing German convoys that passed on the run. They did more damage than the indigenous partisans, but suffered heavier losses for their daring in addition to drawing retribution upon the populace. Hitler's vendetta against the SAS continued unabated: of the hundred who were captured all except four were executed.

The omnipotence of the SAS patrols came, in addition to their superior equipment and training, from supreme mobility. Sixty men, carried by twenty armed jeeps, drove two hundred miles behind the German lines from Rennes to the Vosges, bumping against the enemy, inflicting casualties and themselves losing twenty-eight men and eleven jeeps. As the fighting spread northwards, the Belgian SAS company was dropped into the Ardennes to link hands with Citronelle and the Belgian partisans who infested that intricate terrain. And, as usual, it was these professional patrols which acquired the soundest information about enemy dispositions and intentions, they who had educated military insight into the meaning of any particular activity and the first-class radio communications to report it. One SAS patrol, for example, was able to get a sight of a map showing German dispositions along the River Somme just as Allied armor was approaching.

As the German retreat continued it became, more than ever, the task of partisans to preserve rather than destroy. Every demolition charge laid by the Germans was a target for neutralization—and in this respect the FFI may have made its most useful contribution. Key

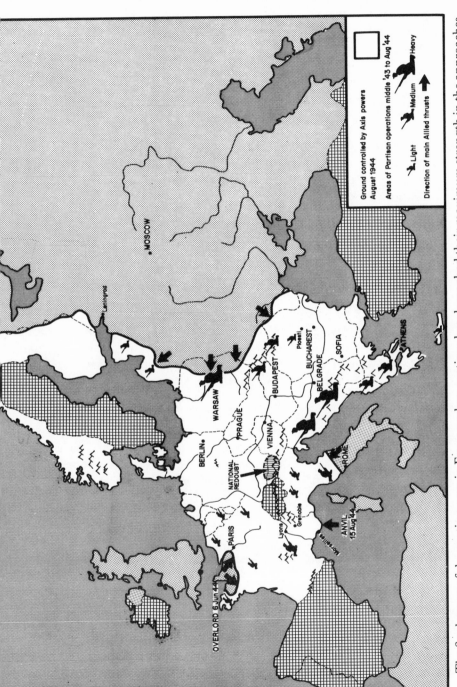

The final stages of the partisan war in Europe when partisan bands reached their maximum strength in the approaches to the German frontiers.

bridges across the Somme were saved from destruction by members of the FFI who removed the charges before they could be blown. Allied columns which were prevented from pushing on by the need to guard prisoners were relieved of the task by Frenchmen and Belgians only too pleased to see Germans at the wrong end of their guns. The vital port of Antwerp fell intact to the combined thrust of a British armored division aided by the Belgian Armée Secrète. But it was in Paris that the northern Resistance fought its major action, and here that the political future of France—and in certain respects, Europe—was settled.

By mid-August conditions in the French capital had become chaotic. Disruption of the railways by bombing and the go-slow was made absolute on the tenth when the railmen went on strike. Distribution of food broke down and there was famine. Paris's power supplies began to fail utterly, and then the police, by order of the Resistance, went on strike on the fifteenth as the result of being disarmed by the Germans—on the same day as the Allies landed in Southern France. At that moment, in the North, the nearest American spearhead was less than a hundred miles from the capital, though, paradoxically, the Americans were the only contenders who did not immediately want to possess the city. They planned to advance on either side and let it fall of its own accord when the Germans voluntarily withdrew or surrendered. But it was Hitler's will, at a time when forces at his order were fighting tooth and nail for another European capital city, Warsaw, that General von Choltitz, the commandant, should "defend Paris to the last, destroy all bridges over the Seine and devastate the city." Meantime, alongside the conventional military concept, there raged a fierce battle of intrigue between French political forces, whose military strength was derisory. The Communists jumped the gun on the eighteenth by publishing posters calling for military action. Since they themselves possessed only 800 weapons, their call was purely politically motivated. Morally, however, it was not unjustified since, till then, the CNR and Gaullists had made it a condition of armaments supply to the FTP that they must fight in the van of the battle—a sacrificial role that could not be rejected by the Communists if they were to preserve a stake in acquiring popular national control on the crest of the liberation wave. The essence of the Gaullist game—most ably played by Bidault in his finest hour as head of CNR—Parodi, the delegate general, and the DMN, Chaban-Delmas —was to preempt every Communist maneuver. They kept faithfully to the original Moulin philosophy of "collaboration . . . strictly within the limits of the struggle against Germany" but "definitely ranged against the Communists" in all else.

On the nineteenth, in quick response to the Communist challenge but in defiance of an order to refrain from an uprising, CNR took the initiative. Under their orders the gendarmes seized the Préfecture de Police, while FFI of all political shades raced to take possession of the Hôtel de Ville, the Palais de Justice and the Ministries of War and the Interior. Possession of key offices with their telephones meant real power in the political struggle. Tricolors appeared at strategic points, flying above the grim struggle for supremacy which raged as Gaullists, under Bidault's instructions, took charge of the vital centers of administration—those most closely connected with law and order, electricity and food. Bureaucrats and politicians argued fiercely to dominate the seats of power while the soldiers engaged in dangerous but less momentous physical combat.

Choltitz, meanwhile, was under many deadly pressures—fear of the SS, who, in the aftermath of an attempt by the army to take Hitler's life on July 20, could be relied upon blindly to support Hitler's demands; dread of a French revolt that it was beyond his power to contain; reluctance to commit an act of destruction that would forever brand the Germans as vandals—but at bottom an honest soldier who rejected amoral orders. Through intermediaries he made contact, on the twentieth, with the FFI and arranged an armistice that would give opportunity to withdraw the German troops by noon on the twenty-third. At the same time he allowed the French to take charge of the city and bring in food. But, despite this local armistice, scattered shooting continued—in part, no doubt, because of the impossibility of telling every partisan what was intended, but also because, to the Communists, an end to the fighting at that moment was politically unwelcome. Perforce the Germans turned once more to arms, attacking the ill-armed French, whose quest was as much for enemy weapons as strategic positions. In a fierce urban struggle the gloves were removed and Paris became seriously threatened by prolonged fighting.

That day the Americans were unexpectedly informed, through König at EMFFI, that the commander of the 2nd French Armored Division, General Leclerc, had been appointed interim governor of Paris by de Gaulle—an extraordinary state of affairs since Leclerc's division, at that moment, was sixty miles in rear of the leading American tanks. On the twenty-second the Americans found, once more, that soldiers are the servants of politicians. They could not prevent the French armored division from going to Paris, nor could they abandon the FFI. So they also committed one of their own infantry divisions to the relief of Paris so as to take part in its surrender.

The toughest operation, in fact, was to be found beyond the city boundaries and Leclerc's men sustained quite heavy losses in their approach. The Parisians, meantime, were engaged against five thousand Germans with fifty guns and a company of tanks—a disciplined force which might only have been overcome after a long fight even had it been unreinforced and if the French were prepared to suffer quite incommensurate casualties and damage to their city. Fortunately Choltitz had no intention of making a protracted defense, merely wishing to impart an impression of doing his duty while there was the remotest chance of Hitler's effective intervention, waiting for an appropriate moment to make an honorable surrender. The atmosphere in Paris was electric and yet far from chaotic. Firing was loud and long ("tiresome" as Choltitz described it) but casualties and damage light. The vanguard of Leclerc's division reached the prefecture on the evening of the twenty-fourth, though it was the following afternoon before Choltitz was captured and brought to sign an instrument of surrender with Leclerc. In this last act, too, the Gaullist French managed to assert the same independence as had their emissaries in every other important department. They excluded the local American commander from the ceremony, thus ensuring that the capitulation was signed in the name of the provisional government alone. For what else, they might have asked, had they been fighting?

During the liberation of Paris women took up arms more frequently than anywhere else in France—or, indeed, in Western Europe. French womenfolk have their roots in the home and play their essential part from the background. All along they had been deeply involved in undramatic but no less important Resistance tasks—as guides for escapers, couriers and radio operators, but rarely indulging in direct action. In Paris a higher percentage were to be seen bearing arms. I asked one Frenchwoman her reactions when she and her family as members of the FFI stood in almost perpetual danger. She replied, "When you are twenty and in love you do not fear death."

In the South of France seven of the eleven divisions which invaded after August 15 were French. Here, where the FFI was favored by the terrain, operations were simplified against an enemy whose density was low. The swift advance of the Allied forces, from Marseilles to Lyons on their way to join hands with the Overlord armies, was the product of an overwhelming superiority in conventional land and air forces working in conjunction with guerrillas who accelerated an invincible progress. The ambushing of escaping Germans took second priority to efforts aimed at preserving bridges and communications. Faced with overall collapse in Normandy, the Germans to the southward were compelled to begin an immediate withdrawal to their own frontiers, into the Atlantic coast ports or across the mountains into Italy. Plagued by outbreaks of street fighting at Marseilles, which rapidly spread to Grenoble, Lyons and nearly every major town, besides ceaseless harrying by the maquis as they descended from the hills, the Germans had but one aim—to preserve cohesion as they retired in haste. Yet, grossly outnumbered as they were, they extensively damaged the port of Marseilles and easily took possession of the Atlantic ports. Nor was the First German Army enveloped by the link-up on September 12 at Dijon between the northern and southern invasions—a failure which some historians blame on de Gaulle for keeping Leclerc's armored division in Paris as insurance against his political succession—just when the Americans needed it at the front. Nevertheless it seems likely that, of the one hundred thousand prisoners from First Army who fell into Allied hands, about one third can be credited to the FFI—above all the twenty thousand who were cornered near Limoges but who insisted upon surrendering to the Americans instead of suffering the indignity of laying down their arms to French irregulars.

The question of the future employment of the FFI, and the FTP, along with the arms they had been given or had captured, was a thorny one. Although the two factions had kept separate (except in the South, where quite often they had fought side by side) each was keenly aware of the threat from the other at a time when central government was almost nonexistent. A plethora of provincial deities seized local power, acting unilaterally though mostly pronouncing allegiance to de Gaulle. The Communists, still aiming at ultimate power, were loath to surrender what arms they had; the FFI, eager to justify itself as the personification of the French revival, was looking for new fields to conquer. But the Communists failed in their challenge and finally surrendered their arms without fuss, while the remainder of the Resistance forces were incorporated within the French Army to undertake the siege of Atlantic ports or to fight in the conventional battle along the eastern frontier. Almost imperceptibly an irregular army became merged with regulars.

Most of the émigré governments had accorded recognition to de Gaulle's provisional government in June 1944, but it had been withheld by the British and Americans. In mid-August, on the eve of a triumphal return to Paris, the Germans had helped de Gaulle by arresting Pétain, Laval and Herriot—the remnants of the old establishment and his only serious rivals. On the eighteenth Churchill was "deprecating taking any decisions about France till we can see more clearly what emerges from the smoke of battle"; in September he was of the opinion that, "The welcome which the maquis [by which, no doubt, he meant the entire Resistance] gave the [Algiers] Committee seemed to me a decisive point in favour of its more formal recognition." Not until October, however, was he recommending this step to Roosevelt and it was the end of that month, to a chorus of dissent from the U.S. State Department, before recognition was at last agreed. Thus the political impact of the FFI may well have been its greatest contribution to achieving recognition of a France ostensibly unified under de Gaulle.

Within Belgium and Holland the work of the secret forces and resistance took a rather milder and more ordered course than in France. Not only had lower priority been given to their forces, but, as we have already seen, the conditions were unsuitable for true guerrilla warfare. There was considerable passive resistance as well as sabotage, but outright fighting was largely avoided. Indeed, in Belgium, it was hardly needed (so swift was the reconquest) and, in any case, contrary to Eisenhower's policy to call for it prematurely. As he wrote on July 12, when the German lines in Normandy stood firm "the need for discretion and security is greater now than ever before. Only by the exercise of strictest discipline can the ranks of the Secret Army be maintained intact and capable of rendering the Allies that assistance on which I am counting." Eisenhower had learned his lesson. The Belgian resistance, unlike that of France, was not to be exposed to a blood bath and, in due course, its main purpose, along with that of the British, would be stabilization of its liberated territories to quell dissidents and ensure the safety of the Allied lines of communication.

Holland was only called upon for one major, overt act in aid of the advance—its resistance never having recovered from the early disasters of penetration. When the Allies landed by air at Arnhem on September 17, the railways were asked by SOE (on Eisenhower's request) to go on strike. It was a reasonable request, for the country was expected to be liberated within weeks. In the outcome Holland suffered because, after the Allied landing failed, there was no way of ending the strike. Food distribution broke down and famine followed.

In the wake of liberation and unification came the inevitable sludge of retribution—throughout France and all the Western occupied nations. Though internecine combat of a Balkan type was avoided, there were elements which had to be "cleansed" as part of an act of vengeance and contrition. Some fell in battle beside their German masters (above all the SS, who were hunted like vermin). The rest were eliminated in the prisons or during clandestine encounters. In France it was Darnand's reviled *milicien* who were boisterously hunted down in company with proclaimed Vichyites who had openly toed the German line. But in addition to people who had deliberately backed the Nazi side there were those who, by accident or design, had become associated with the Germans—people with contacts among the collaborators; men whose daily work in the public service had made it impossible to evade contamination; the politically inept who failed to recognize their peril; and the women who, for one reason or another, had consorted with Germans. Upon them a wrath that was often unjustified fell—the personification of fundamental bestiality which is the natural product of total, clandestine warfare. Vendettas were purged and class rivalries settled to leave a residue of long-lasting bitterness. With so many weapons available and the excuse "In the name of the Resistance" at hand, large-scale killing was easy. Law and order suffered. The toll in death and depravity is impossible to compute. In France the estimates of those who died vary between one hundred thousand and ten thousand; the most reliable figure seeming to be about forty thousand—a ratio of one per thousand of population as the price for four years' confusion and disgrace.

In Belgium and Holland, respectively, where the excesses may have been milder, Degrelle's Rexistes and Mussert's WA and Home Guard came in for the same sort of backlash as hit the *milicien*. Yet one must retain a sense of proportion in the European context. In the West the old order, dressed, perhaps, in slightly different clothing, reestablished itself and averted civil war. Hard words there might have been in France between de Gaulle and the Allies who had put him in power, but militarily the Allied armies were saved from concern about their lines of communication in a country which quickly proved its power to govern itself. Likewise, in Belgium, civilized government was reasserted despite the threat of a constitutional crisis with its origin in King Leopold's behavior during and after the 1940 campaign; that would take six years to settle but never disconcerted the Allies. In parts of southern Holland, too, when Queen Wilhelmina's popularity was in some doubt and where the local resistance had been anything but enthusiastic, the Allies had few governmental difficulties.

The contrast between West and East was indeed startling. As the one was returning to normality by ordered means that were ruffled only slightly at the edges, Germany's other neighbors were on the eve of a cataclysm. The tide of liberation which was sweeping through Poland towards Germany and the Central European states had the power and turbulence of a hurricane behind it.

CHAPTER THIRTEEN

Liberation Russian Style

For what remained of the war, once their offensive had spent itself at Kursk, the German Army was condemned to retire upon the Fatherland, leaving in its wake a desert of destruction. So long as it had gone forward or held firm and imparted an impression of incontestable supremacy, it had kept the populace and the partisans under control; but when hard pressed everywhere by enemy regular and irregular forces its grip relaxed and partisans prospered.

Not, as we have seen, that the Soviet partisan forces were entirely "irregular." Those which fought in the approaches to Kursk had been well organized by Red Army officers trained in the partisan schools. New types of demolition charges had come into use—one of them designed to be laid in chains to make 500 rail cuts at once. Nevertheless, shortages in supply were more crippling to the partisans than to their opponents. Each major operation against the railway system demanded a prior period of restraint while stocks of explosives were laboriously accumulated—mainly from air deliveries because the taking of German material was so often a hazardous and self-defeating operation. Poor communications continued to hamper tactical flexibility: in July 1943 for every 1,061 partisan bands there were only 300 radio sets, and as late as March 1944 many partisans remained unarmed.

There was an emotional chain reaction among the partisans as the Red Army moved steadily eastward. The individual citizen who lived within the zone of occupation was presented with the choice either of simulating a burning patriotism or of being liquidated when the Red Army and the NKVD arrived. For example, a White Russian called Gil, who in 1942 had formed what became known as the "First Russian National Brigade," to help protect the German lines of communication, came under duress in July 1943 as the Red Army drew close. He decided once more to change sides. Making contact with local partisans he shot those of his leaders who were steadfast to the Germans and then renamed his formation "First Anti-Fascist Partisan Brigade," continuing in command, despite the investigations of a commission flown in from Moscow to cleanse the brigade of disaffected men, until he himself was killed in action the year after.

Those Russians who assumed the worst decamped westward as members of the German Auxiliary Forces, Vlasov Army or Kaminski Brigade. The brutal story of the scouring of the old occupied zones by the victorious Soviet forces will never be told in full, but we may be sure that it was of unparalleled ferocity, far worse than anything meted out by local partisan bands to collaborators when the Germans were still in occupation—when village headmen, railway workers and police auxiliaries were threatened and killed with impunity. We catch a glimpse of what transpired from the comments of an ex-Russian officer upon the purge of the inhabitants of Orel after the town fell.

> Almost everyone who had stayed was deported for "collaboration," even workers in the community services and women who had had children by the Germans. In addition all men were mobilized into the army immediately. The Soviet Government could not provide uniforms and weapons for all these people and many were sent into battle in civilian clothes. The rifles of dead and wounded were collected on the battlefield and at once issued to the ununiformed and completely untrained men so that they could be sent into battle immediately.

Experienced Germans, though detesting the partisans for their "underhand" methods, were usually a match for them as individuals. Reinhold Drepper, young and unwary, was patrolling the Minsk-to-Smolensk railway one night in the autumn of 1943 with a well-seasoned NCO when he spotted movement behind the low hedge bounding the track. Rather to his surprise he was told to ignore it and they continued to walk towards the spot as if nothing was there. His leader, in fact, had seen the two saboteurs long before Drepper and was merely making sure of his enemy. At last, as they drew level, the NCO swung sideways, firing his submachine gun from the hip with a burst which apparently hit the mine's detonator and blew both Russians to shreds, hanging them from the overhead telegraph wires. Drepper's main impression was of the NCO's assurance that the partisans would allow them to pass without firing, a demonstration of complete knowledge of the enemy intention. Drepper, who is an educated, whimsical man, now living in England, adds that, though the German Army rank and file was respectful of partisans, they were never obsessed by them.

Sabotage against the Germans accumulated slowly throughout July 1943, as their initial withdrawal gathered pace. In the Pripyat area, for example, during the three weeks prior to Operation Citadel, about eighty cuts a week were attempted, but in the succeeding three weeks only ninety, of which more than half were abortive. But from then onward the number of cuts multiplied enormously as the Germans were compelled to concentrate upon the main battle and leave the partisans unmolested. Nevertheless the Germans successfully moved nearly eight thousand trains a month through the infected area.

In a way those partisans who were busy blowing up track and rolling stock were helping as much as hindering the Germans. The Germans, as they retired, instigated a vast demolition program, destroying everything that could not be removed and, if Russian evidence at the Nuremberg trials is to be believed, far outdid the partisans in the volume of matériel destroyed. Figures of 65,000 kilometers of rail, 13,000 rail bridges, 500,000 kilometers of signal cable, 36,000 post office and telephone centers, 91,000 kilometers of roadway and 90,000 road bridges were quoted in evidence. Much of this, in fact, must have been by partisans. For example, on August 3, 1943, they detonated 8,422 rail cuts out of 16,000 in the ensuing month (the falling off due to shortage of explosives), in September they damaged or destroyed 109 locomotives and in October cut down 1,472 telegraph poles. Who then created the logistic desert? One asks to what extent partisans contributed to the detriment of future advances by the Red Army and the rehabilitation of the countryside? Certainly the proportion of rail cuts credited to partisans, aircraft and artillery shows that it was the partisans who took the lion's share—aided, as they so often were, by special engineer detachments flown in for a task that went on interminably until the Germans had withdrawn.

In terms of performance in withdrawal and advance it can only be stated that the main difficulty in the way of German extrication from envelopment came as the result of Hitler's mania for hanging on too long to every bastion. It was not, at any rate, caused by partisans. Usually, when permitted to operate at their own discretion, the Germans broke free from the Russian embrace without much difficulty. At the same time the Russian rate of advance never matched that of the Germans' in 1941 and 1942, even though their numerical superiority was far larger in proportion. Moreover, when the Russians ran out of fuel in the logistic desert that was in part their own creation, it was for increasingly longer periods of time. For example, it had taken little more than two months for the Russians to rebuild an offensive capability after their 250-mile drive from Stalingrad ran out of sup-

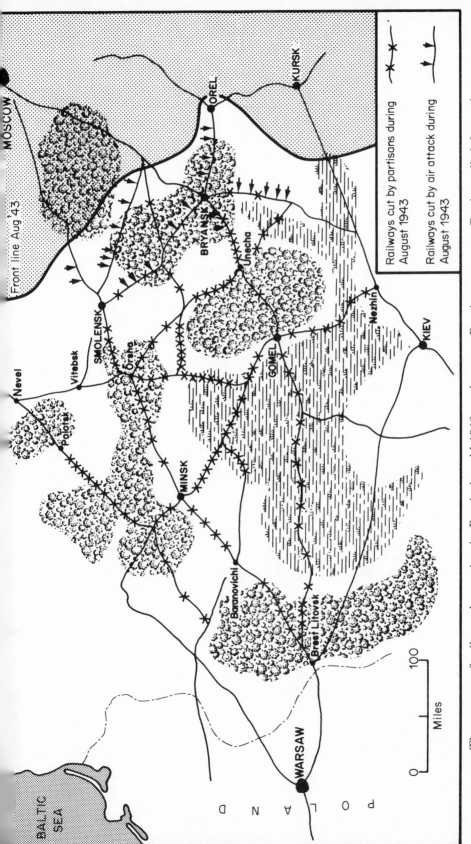

Front line Aug '43

Railways cut by partisans during
August 1943

Railways cut by air attack during
August 1943

The pattern of railway destruction in Russia in mid-1943 as the great Russian summer offensive rolled forward.
Compare this with the map of Western Europe on page 185.

plies near Kharkov at the end of March. But after their next step from Sumy to Kiev (a mere 150 miles) had been brought to a halt, it was again another seven weeks before they were ready to assault again, and this time the distance moved forward was even shorter than before. As the Red Army approached Poland and its regenerative powers were reduced, on the other side the Germans became more concentrated, which enabled them to recover more quickly and arrange effective antiguerrilla operations.

Contradictions in the writing of official Soviet history abound and are in line with wild exaggerations on the part of their propaganda departments—and even wider differences are revealed by comparison of their claims of success with damage admitted by the Germans, who, after all, were best placed to count it. It is most revealing of all, therefore, when Soviet historians admit to failures—and there are many such admissions in connection with the rail-cutting program, most of which are put down to deficiencies in supply. But this was only part of the trouble. In January 1944 the Central Staff of the Partisan Movement was abolished and, in its place, closer control by military front commanders instituted. Political squabbles continued, but the soldiers were given more say. Clearly this was essential if the partisans were to be prevented from causing more damage to the Red Army than to the Germans.

The German "scorched earth" policy, which was infinitely more thorough than anything put into practice by retreating Russians in 1941 and 1942, had a compulsive impact upon the morale of the Ukrainians and White Russians. For the first time desertion from German organizations became wholesale. At last the mass of people was driven into a mood of intolerance and hatred against a specific belligerent. The number of ambushes increased even though they proved more costly to attackers than to Germans. Vengeance was rife. Yet to the very end of the German occupation of Russia, significant numbers of Soviet people remained loyal to the invaders—some because they were too far committed to retreat, others because they genuinely feared the oncoming Bolshevik tide and all that it portended. When the German Army retreated into Poland the émigré Russians went with them, some forty thousand belonging to the auxiliary police in the Central Front alone. Many of these were at once shifted to the West, and did good service on the German side in the fight against the Yugoslavians and the Western Allies.

The creation of a genuine Russian Army of Liberation (ROA) under Vlasov had, as we have seen, run into a series of objections by Hitler. It never functioned as a fully formed combat force, merely providing a corps of propagandists under German control. Through 1943, nevertheless, Vlasov contrived to gather the nucleus of a general staff, unknown to the Germans, a cadre upon which an army could well be based be it friendly or hostile to the Germans.

Indeed, secret armies became the vogue in 1943—notably those sponsored by the Russians. One was grouped around German ex-Communists who had escaped before the war or been captured by or had deserted to the Russians. An attempt was made to win over senior German officers as well as men who had fallen into Russian hands at the time of Stalingrad—but the response was poor. Militarily, therefore, this German "army" had little importance. But political personalities were much stronger, consisting of future East German leaders of whom Walter Ulbricht was one. For them it was simply a matter of waiting.

Though the Soviet westward advance virtually came to a halt due to exhaustion and tough German resistance in January 1944, preparations for its continuation into Poland, Rumania, Hungary, the Baltic and Balkan countries, besides Czechoslovakia and Germany itself, went ahead with undiminished vigor. The effort centered upon solving the logistic problems in terrain which had been devastated by the joint depredations of friend and foe. The Soviet leadership grasped at every straw, political and military. As they came within air range of non-Soviet countries they began to infiltrate agents to form resistance cells in addition to and often in competition with those already introduced by SOE from the West. Within Russia they trained the nucleus of national secret armies that were as political as they were military, ready to move in the wake of the Red Army as it invaded fresh ground.

Of these none was more important than the Polish People's Army, which came into being in the autumn of 1943, based upon the Communist element of the Polish partisans, who were already deadly rivals of the London-controlled Home Army, with its allegiance to the prewar regime. Rowecki, the Home Army's level-headed commander, had felt compelled, late in 1942, to recommence limited sabotage (later supported by the Western Allies), not because he saw any military or economic advantage in it, but simply because, like Moulin in France, he judged that a posture of aggressiveness on his part was the sole effective counter to calls by the Communists for direct action in support of the Russians in their plight. Already some of the younger hotheads had transferred from the Home Army to the Communist Workers' Party and had merged with the ghetto Jews. In the general atmosphere of mistrust of all things Russian, Rowecki rejected an offer by the Communist Gomulka to negotiate a pact of mutual assistance.

This he and the London Poles saw as the thin end of a Russian wedge for total Communist domination.

The Home Army now suffered two severe blows. On June 30, 1943, Rowecki was arrested in Warsaw and on July 4 Sikorski, the Premier and Commander-in-Chief of Polish Armed Forces, was killed in an air crash. To replace the latter in London, the Poles appointed Stanislaw Mikolajczyk as Premier and General Kazimierz Sosnokowski as Commander-in-Chief, both politically more extremist than Sikorski, neither with the latter's insight into the delicate problem of the Polish-Russian relationship. To replace Rowecki came his second-in-command, Bor-Komorowski, a leader of lower caliber and weaker composure than the one he succeeded. In January 1944 these three were set to grapple with the problems of an imminent Soviet presence in their homeland—the product of the summit conference at Teheran, at which the Allies had concluded an agreement with the Russians to permit Poland's postwar eastern frontier to be established on the old Curzon Line. This, in the eyes of the Poles, was a betrayal, even though they were to be compensated by parts of eastern Germany.

When the first Red Army troops entered eastern Poland on January 3, 1944, it was made plain by the Russians that, if an understanding with the Poles had been reached, combined operations between the Red Army and the Home Army might be acceptable. Coming as it did when the Poles were suspicious of Allied loyalty and when there was a belief that the People's Army had grown to some forty thousand members, the chances of a détente were at once remote. Nor did the initial actions by the Red Army inspire the Poles with confidence. Though Komorowski had instructed his men to avoid incidents with the Russians, Polish partisan leaders disappeared during visits to Russian units. At the same time Gomulka initiated the formation of a Communist government under Morawski in readiness to administer the territory taken by the Red Army.

The London Poles were in a dreadful dilemma. They recognized that armed resistance to the Red Army was futile. On the other hand they believed that surrender to the Russians would be a betrayal of those who had died and suffered in the cause. Tito was once asked in 1944 if he would permit Yugoslavia to fall under Russian suzerainty and had asked in return if that was likely after all his people had undergone. Soldiers like Sosnokowski and Komorowski would have given the same reply at that time, but they lacked Tito's political skill and strong geographical location. When, in March, the Home Army's 27th Division, six thousand strong and lacking heavy weapons, came out in open opposition to the Germans in Volhynia, it automatically found itself fighting side by side with the Red Army, whose officers "expressed their readiness to enter into cooperation" with the Poles providing this meant "operational subordination of the Polish forces to the Soviet Command locally and also beyond the River Bug." There was a concession too, for the division was to be free to maintain contact with the Polish authorities in Warsaw and London, so long as it formed itself into a Soviet-equipped regular division and did not partake in partisan activities behind the Soviet lines. But Komorowski refused point-blank. As a soldier, devoid of political adroitness, he could not recognize the advantages of bargaining for time. But, as Churchill sadly remarked at Teheran, "Nothing would satisfy the Poles." When, in April, the Germans counterattacked in Volhynia and drove the combined Russian-Polish force back, it was Komorowski who instructed the 27th Division to break out westward, thus symbolically breaking off relations with the Russians. From that moment there stemmed a refusal on the Russian part to treat with the Poles of the Home Army. It was announced that, once the Germans had been driven away, local Polish partisan forces were to be absorbed into the Red Army.

The Home Army had now settled on the fatal policy of military confrontation with the Germans and political resistance to the Russians. In late June came the crunch, when the Russians renewed their offensive, defeated the German Army Group Center and poured into Poland on a wide front. Polish policy was stated by Sosnokowski to Komorowski: "If owing to a happy conjunction of circumstances, in the last days of the German retreat and before the entry of Soviet troops, a chance should arise for us to occupy, even temporarily, Vilna, Lvov or any other important center, . . . we should do so, in order to appear as the rightful masters." This was Plan Storm. But at Vilna the Home Army got its timing wrong on July 6. Its attack with five thousand men against the Germans was beaten back with heavy losses and when at last it was able to occupy the city on the thirteenth, in the aftermath of the Red Army assault, it was at once to face a stiff rebuff. The local Polish commander was arrested at a conference with the Russians and the Home Army formation dispersed—some to eternity, others to Russian prisons, the majority into the Red Army and the remainder as fugitives seeking to rejoin the Home Army in the West.

At Lvov a parallel, dismal sequence of events was repeated. The Home Army fought like furies in the city and for its troubles was derided by the local Red Army commander as "untrained and badly armed, which, combined with great zeal, had been causing them great losses"—a fair assessment. And when at last the city fell, and the Poles celebrated, they were informed that there could be no question of their ruling. A Polish government was already in existence on Polish soil at Lublin and a Polish army, too, they were told on July 27. On the twenty-eighth they were given just two hours to lay down their arms. No practical alternative remained to the Poles of the old regime in the face of Russian superiority, just as, in France, no alternative was given to Communists confronted by Gaullist dominance. The London Poles appreciated the weakness of their position and on the twenty-seventh Mikolajczyk set out for Moscow to negotiate with Stalin—to save what he could. But in Warsaw Komorowski, in a mood of desperation, visualized nothing but disaster looming in a situation over which he was losing control.

Plan Storm, which postulated the seizing of vital centers concurrent with a German withdrawal, applied to Warsaw, though the taking of the city against opposition was never to the forefront in the original Polish considerations. Near the end of July, however, Polish emotions began to overwhelm common-sense circumspection. One must sympathize with their leaders, who operated under the most harrowing conditions. As fugitives from the Germans they had survived for months on end, at their wits' end while attempting to resolve matters of high policy the like of which would overtax diplomats working in the cool surroundings of a peacetime environment. Information was frequently suspect and invariably acquired through channels of communication which were constantly liable to disruption; at times the Home Army knew more about enemy intentions than those of its allies. Intelligence about the German condition, as July drew to its close, told of utter defeat in the approaches to Warsaw, their retreating columns pouring back in such confusion that but one conclusion could be drawn—correctly, as it happened, until July 21: the Germans intended to abandon the city. News of the bomb plot against Hitler on the twentieth strengthened the resolve of those among the Poles who believed that, since the Germans were on the verge of collapse, it might be possible to seize and hold the city well before the Russians arrived. Some thirty-eight thousand men of the Home Army were available, but with arms for only six thousand, of which a mere twenty-five were antitank weapons. They requested that the Polish Parachute Brigade, then stationed in England, should be flown in, but this was in the realms of fantasy. That the Poles should have contemplated an uprising, based upon such insufficient resources and on the partial assumption that outside help of impossibly large dimensions might be supplied, was in itself an exposure of their divorce from reality. Throughout the entire war the RAF had managed to deliver only 315 tons of supplies to Poland plus 313 people. The long flight from England or, as now was the case, Brindisi in southern Italy, was always among the most hazardous of night operations. To marry the parachute brigade in England to the handful of suitable aircraft in Italy was impracticable, and suicidal to try to transport it to Warsaw. Meanwhile any prospect of increasing the rate of arms and ammunition delivery could never be more than a gesture. Moreover, only the British were politically committed to help, and the RAF had neither the landing rights nor suitable facilities in Russian territory to institute a shuttle service. The Americans, who had such rights as part of a shuttle bombing scheme called Frantic, held back from involvement in the Polish imbroglio.

Help of any sort from the Russians for the Poles was most unlikely and not simply because of what had already transpired in Volhynia, Vilna and Lvov. By July 26 the Germans had removed the bulk of their stores from Warsaw and turned over local defense to the SS, as a sop to Himmler's ambition to claim all the credit for his organization. To accomplish this task Lieutenant-General Reiner Stahl could muster twelve thousand men of whom only ten thousand were rated reliable. They could call on antiaircraft artillery but few tanks. By then, however, the Germans had concentrated fresh forces on the flanks of the approaching Red Army, launching counterattacks which caught the Russians in the moment of overreach. The Russian advance began to slow down and in places went on the defensive. Nevertheless, on July 30 their spearheads were within ten miles of the River Vistula and still confident of victory. On the twenty-seventh Komorowski had no doubt that the Germans were capable of a protracted defense and therefore he postponed the date for the rising. But that day a proclamation from the German Governor instructed one hundred thousand young Polish men to report next day for work on the defenses—an instruction which impelled the Poles to issue mobilization orders to the Home Army, without Komorowski's actual permission, in order to protect its members.

Komorowski was being bullied by events and by the hotheads on his staff. News of Mikolajczyk's mission to Moscow made it seem all the more important to make a gesture of defiance to strengthen his bargaining hand. Calls from the Russians for a Polish uprising (shades of the FTP in Paris!) to join with "The Polish Army now entering Polish territory, trained in the USSR" could not be ignored since they preempted the Home Army's political initiative. Moreover, on the twenty-ninth the Russians seemed close to the outskirts of Praga, which lay on the other side of the Vistula. On the evening of the thirty-first a crucial meeting took place between Komorowski and his principal staff officers—all, that is, except the chief intelligence officer, who was absent gathering information. In the latter's absence a report was submitted to assure Komorowski that the Russian spearheads had entered Praga. Armed with this unconfirmed news, Komorowski recommended to the Deputy Prime Minister that the time for the rising had come—a complete reversal of the opinion he had held that morning. But this snap decision to begin the rising next day had hardly been taken before the chief of intelligence arrived to report that a massive German counterattack against the Russians was imminent—a report that was almost instantly corroborated by news that it had actually begun. The order for a rising had not yet been transmitted and might easily have been stopped. It would seem, however, that the strain upon Komorowski had been too much. Having at last screwed up enough resolution to strike he was drained of the strength to retract and go through it all again. The order was sent. Soon the streets were stealthily astir as the messengers went their ways and the ill-armed, ragged army got ready to move to its battle stations by 1700 hours. But movement demanded timely orders and in some cases these were not received until 1400 hours—too late for effectively coordinated implementation.

Of this partisan army Komorowski has written: "During the battles our commanders could hardly tell the soldiers from the civilians. Our people had no uniforms and we could not prevent the civilians from wearing white and red arm bands." The struggle of these untrained enthusiasts was all along to be for arms as much as position, in the same manner as the people of Paris fought. Their objectives were the German forces and their weapons, in equal priority with key points in the city—above all the radio station, communication centers, bridges over the Vistula and the airport. With these in their hands the Home Army hoped to form a perimeter (which included a bridgehead in Praga to the east), to fend off German counterattacks, proclaim their independence and await the arrival of the Russians.

Fighting began before 1700 hours because armed members of the Home Army bumped into German patrols at many places in the city. A coordinated uprising at once degenerated into a fiasco which cost the trained cadre precious lives for small returns. None of the vital communication centers were taken: the Vistula bridges remained firmly in German hands and the defenders of the airport cut down the Poles in swaths. The rising in Praga was an almost total failure quite unsupported by a Red Army presence. Sizable portions of the main city fell into Home Army hands but all too few enemy weapons so that, to all intents and purposes, the original plan had been baffled from the outset. The Home Army was, in fact, isolated, for the Russian advance in the neighborhood of the city had come to a full stop as the German counterstroke made itself felt. Although progress along the southern flank was to be maintained for the next few days, curling northward towards Warsaw along the course of the Vistula, it had lost its impetus. The Russian logistical difficulties were increasing at the end of supply lines which had been thrust forward 300 miles since June 23 into land which had been devastated first by guerrillas and then by the German demolition teams. German air power, too, was by no means quelled; their bombers attacked by day and night, blasting the Russian lines of communication.

No matter how misguided or unfortunate the Poles may have been in their raising of the national flag above Warsaw on August 1, their valor and total sense of self-sacrifice cannot be ignored. In the suburb of Mokotow on August 2 a strong German attack developed, described by one of the Poles.

> Their fire was definitely superior to ours. . . . They got through fences, jumped over walls and sprinted across streets, and one by one put our centers of resistance out of action. We saw that we were up against very good troops. . . . In places our units were beginning to retreat in disorder. . . . The tension among our reserve detachments was rising to a climax. The time was ripe for a counterattack. At a given sign the mass of men moved forward. The impetus and fury of this initial rush swept back the German line, while a second group cut them off from their starting base. . . . Now it was their turn to pull out in disorder. . . . This was our first major success and it resulted in the capture of large quantities of arms and ammunition. . . .

The capture of ammunition, vital though it was, merely initiated the natural cycle of events. It had to be used sparingly and with full effect. Komorowski has written: "They [the civilians] . . . used German weapons, which increased the problems of our scarce ammunition. For the civilians would waste a hail of bullets and hand grenades on a single German soldier." Not without justice could Stalin comment to Mikolajczyk during the dour negotiations in Moscow, "What is an army without artillery, tanks and an air force? They are even short of rifles. In modern warfare such an army is of little use. They are small partisan units, not a regular army"—a view he was also to pass to Churchill in London—one which may define Stalin's attitude towards partisans more honestly than any of his utterances.

218 · THE PARTISANS OF EUROPE

To the point though Stalin's opinion was, it rather begged the question. Partisan units necessarily depended upon regular forces for help. Given that the Poles had irked the Russians by omitting to give notice of their uprising—and for obvious political reasons in their unrealistic bid for recognition—they nevertheless offered the same kind of help to the Red Army as Russian partisans had offered under conditions no less difficult. Yet the gallantry of the Poles defending Warsaw and thus, initially, absorbing a division's equivalent of German troops, was meaningless in the shadow of the political and supply factors which overrode every other consideration. For if the supply of equipment—above all heavy equipment—and ammunition was to be satisfied, the diplomatic deadlock had to be broken. But Stalin, engaged in a bargaining session he knew he could not lose, saw no need to concede anything in his determination to win recognition for the Lublin government. Appeals by the London Poles to the British, Americans and Russians for aid would meet with sympathy in the West, but, in the East, a stony response. On the sixteenth after a solitary and unsuccessful attempt to drop an agent into Warsaw to act as liaison officer for supply dropping, Stalin cabled Churchill: "I am convinced that the Warsaw action represents a reckless and terrible adventure which is costing the population large sacrifices. . . . The Soviet command has come to the conclusion that it must disassociate itself from the Warsaw adventure."

There were in the West many who would have understood the Russian viewpoint had they known all the facts, but on the face of it there was a deep suspicion from the outset that the Russians were playing politics and could well have done more from the military aspect. They might easily have tried again to send in a liaison officer or even flown supplies "blind" to the Home Army, which, until the middle of August at least, was holding substantial areas of the city. They could have given immediate permission for U.S. aircraft to make use of the Frantic facilities for a shuttle supply service, but throughout August refused to do so. Roosevelt at this time was unwilling to press Stalin hard. On August 26 he had declined to support Churchill in a request to implement the shuttle service, unless Stalin directly forbade it, on the grounds that it might not "prove advantageous to the long-range general war prospect"—by which he probably meant the outcome of projected peacetime developments that seemed close to realization.

So the British were left to do what they could with their own meager resources, using RAF, South African and Polish-crewed bombers, having at once rejected the proposal to fly in the Polish

Parachute Brigade as totally impracticable. On August 4 Komorowski had "categorically demanded supplies," adding in a subsequent transmission, "Our ability to hold out in the struggle depends on receiving ammunition from you." Bad weather had already prevented flights by Halifaxes and Liberators from Brindisi the previous night, but on the night of August 4, against the better judgment of the air force commander, Air-Marshal Slessor, fifteen aircraft—seven of them manned by Polish crews—took off on the 900-mile journey. Two Polish aircraft got through and delivered their loads; of the remainder six (including five manned by the British) were lost and most of the others seriously damaged.

Slessor thereupon refused to send further missions until the moon had waned. Political pressure upon him was intensified, however, until he relented to allow Polish crews to fly if they wished. On the eighth three went, and safely returned, having delivered their loads to the correct place; on the ninth another four went, but these landed their cargo in Home Army hands outside the city. But on the thirteenth and fourteenth, when fifty-four aircraft were employed in a maximum effort with British and South African crews, the losses soared to eleven plus eleven damaged. The difficulties of flying through deep enemy defenses to find a pinpoint target that was surrounded by a ring of hostile guns and then swoop low to deliver the parachuted containers accurately were almost insuperable. Polish women had the task of displaying lanterns from the roofs of the old city to serve as an aiming point for the pilots, but these were extremely difficult to detect among gun flashes and the widespread fires that burned in the city throughout the battle. Crew fatigue—particularly among the Poles, who flew beyond the laid-down limits of endurance—linked to losses among the best trained of these expert crews began to take toll of the effort. On the thirteenth and fourteenth only seventeen loads reached Polish bands—fifteen in the city. Thereafter, until September 13, despite every effort with a declining number of aircraft available, not a single container fell within the Warsaw perimeter.

It is interesting to read the German side of the battle for Warsaw in its early days, and make comparison with Stalin's disparaging remarks about the Poles. Their pessimism on August 1, caused largely by fear of being severely outnumbered, was barely alleviated by August 5 despite the heavy losses they knew they had inflicted on the Poles. Up to then the Polish positions had been expanding, though they excluded the main points of strategic vantage. Penned in though they were, the Poles also laid partial siege to elements of the German garrison, which was as anxiously looking for external relief as the Poles. The German relief force was now assembled—tanks, artillery, aircraft and a strong infusion of the most desperate antiguerrilla fighters in the German pay, among them Kaminski's Russian brigade and a formation known as the Dirlewanger Regiment, whose ranks were filled by released criminals trying to win a pardon by acts of valor. There came, too, von dem Bach-Zelewski, detached from his job as Inspector of Antipartisan Forces at the instigation of Himmler, to take personal command. Later he described the situation as one of great confusion. Himmler had issued an order that prisoners were not to be taken. Kaminski's and Dirlewanger's men were trying to penetrate the Polish defenses while simultaneously executing prisoners. Bach-Zelewski had no doubt as to which of the two formations was the more useful. "The fighting value of these Cossacks," he stated, "was, as usual in such a collection of people without a fatherland, very poor. They had a great liking for alcohol and other excesses and they had no understanding of military discipline." They eventually got out of hand, shooting and looting with a terrible abandon until Bach-Zelewski was forced to impose a strict curb. For a start he had Kaminski shot and thus, as General Guderian, the German Chief of the General Staff, was to write, "disposed of a possibly dangerous witness."

Guderian wanted both the Kaminski and Dirlewanger formations withdrawn, but the latter, in the opinion of Bach-Zelewski, possessed the highest qualities. "They had nothing to lose and everything to win. . . . They gave no mercy in battle and did not expect any. As a result they suffered losses three times as great as those of any other German unit. . . . To remove them from the battle would have been nothing less than to give up any idea of an offensive." These few sentences go to the heart of the guerrilla struggle, describing as they do the essential motivations urging on every effective combatant in this savage form of conflict. Men such as Dirlewanger's would have been as good guerrillas as they were successful in combating guerrillas. The conventional reaction against guerrilla methods, in addition to a general sense of war-weariness, could be found in Colonel Schmidt's regiment, which supported the others. They were, in Bach-Zelewski's words, "well-trained troops dependable for any infantry job, but matter-of-fact, lacking any sort of joy in their trade or any real enthusiasm for fighting." Bach-Zelewski's opinions assume a double importance—in the manner in which they epitomize the partisan war in Warsaw and the extent to which they, inadvertently, gave a forecast of what might be the response if, later, the German populace were called upon to fight a clandestine war against invaders. Yet even the mildest German soldier could be maddened by guerrilla tactics—the use of women, the shot in the back. Mercy and quarter became scarce commodities.

The Polish high-water mark was reached on August 5. Gradually thereafter their perimeter on the surface was constricted by systematic house-by-house and street-by-street German clearance actions. Sniper fought sniper, ambush succeeded ambush in battles which frequently raged floor by floor in apartment buildings. In the first fortnight the struggle was predominantly on the surface, where the Poles, with a couple of captured tanks, were, locally, able to engage the enemy on something approaching level terms, and where the handful of short range PIAT antitank weapons, supplied by SOE, imposed a measure of respect on the German crews. But the fires lit by the Germans, which steadily consumed the buildings and drove the people out, forced the survivors to emulate the Jews who, in 1943, had gone underground. A well-organized system of subterranean passages existed, as a user describes:

> The cellars of adjoining houses were connected by openings knocked through the walls, and one could walk through them for hundreds of yards, emerging in the open air only to cross an inner yard and then ducking back. . . . Streets could be avoided altogether as tunnels had been dug under many of them. . . . The underground passages were usually adequately lit by candles or hurricane lamps. . . . There were many arrows to show the way. . . . The cellars were a hive of activity. Long lines of people, walking in single file, were strung along the passages; while in the cellars . . . whole families now lived.

The art of survival was precariously balanced. To be caught by the Germans amounted to sentence of death. The wounded could be offered no guarantee of proper treatment because medical supplies were initially short and soon running out. Food supplies too were low. Air deliveries having virtually ceased, and the Russians quite obviously being unable or unwilling to come to their assistance, the city's defenders could rely only on their own ingenuity to capture material from the enemy, or upon compatriots in the outlying woods to infiltrate help to them. But this the Russians forbade and, moreover, took steps to prevent by ambushing Home Army men and drafting them into the People's Army, which was held back.

Nevertheless German composure was disturbed even so late as August 9. That day the Governor of Warsaw was wounded and his deputy killed while they were being evacuated from their accommodation in the city. That day, too, the commander of the Ninth

Army, which had halted the Russians the other side of Praga, was complaining that the cutting of the railways which passed through Warsaw was imposing a severe logistic strain on his operations. Overall the Germans feared that the opposition was snowballing when, in fact, it was being checked—but that was in the nature of this kind of confused combat where the lines of resistance are indistinguishable. In essence the Germans concentrated most upon clearing the east-to-west communications in order to renew a rail service. Simultaneously, heavy artillery was brought up and began the systematic destruction of the Old Town, followed a few hours later by a request from Bach-Zelewski that the Poles surrender on condition that they should be given proper treatment as prisoners of war under the terms of the Geneva Convention. It is to his credit, too, that he countermanded Himmler's order to execute prisoners—no mean act of courage in itself despite being a sensible military solution in that it might give greater encouragement to the Poles to surrender. But the Poles rejected all overtures for peace. The executions continued.

This is not intended to be a blow-by-blow description of the battle for Warsaw. That would need a volume or more in itself. In any case its trend had been settled in the first few days—perhaps hours. Once the Poles lost the advantage of surprise and became contained, what was from the outset an unequal struggle was doomed to failure. Rebellions and revolutions, like partisans, thrive only on expansion and success; the reverse is inherently fatal. Attack though they continued to do until August 30, their gains were as nothing when each German assault almost invariably gained valuable ground. The ratio of losses in manpower was also inevitably against the Poles, whose steadily declining firepower could only be compensated for by an abortive expenditure in blood. The only thing which sustained the Poles was a vain hope that Red Army pressure would be renewed and that the Germans would withdraw. But far from seeing evidence of a Russian presence to the east of the river, the Poles witnessed the Germans strengthening their grip on Praga. Night by night a few aircraft, mostly manned by Poles, struggled through from Brindisi, but they were no help to the city's defenders, who spent most of their hours on the surface dodging German troops and persistent German air attacks, delivered with impunity. On September 8 there was a ceasefire to bury the dead and evacuate noncombatants. An offer to negotiate terms was rejected, however. Then, on September 10, when it was plain that the Poles resisted only for the sake of resistance, the Russians made a new move. They began an attack on Praga and forced their way to the river; their fighters drove off the German aircraft and they began free dropping of supplies to the defenders—some of which burst on impact, while many more were lost since Polish-controlled areas above ground were by then so constricted. Moreover, of the ammunition which arrived, much was useless since it was a Russian caliber and the Poles were using German- or British-type weapons.

On September 11 the Russians also gave the Americans permission to drop supplies. At midday on the eighteenth 107 Fortresses arrived, coming in high as if on a bombing mission, to drop twelve hundred containers which floated down, scattering almost everywhere except within the Home Army perimeter. It seems that only nineteen aircraft loads actually reached Polish hands—the rest went straight to the Germans. Thereafter the Russians refused further requests by the Americans to operate the daylight shuttle service—a refusal which brought to an end the entire Frantic operation amid rising Western suspicion of Russian political motives.

The end was now in sight as Russian attacks (spearheaded by troops of the Russian-controlled Polish Army) came to a halt in Praga. A few infiltrated to the west bank and joined hands with the Home Army, but they could not alter the situation. Home Army men were remorselessly driven from the last positions overlooking the Vistula. They could not be replaced. On October 2 a ceasefire was called and Komorowski met Bach-Zelewski to sign an instrument of surrender.

There are diverse estimates of the toll in life. Bach-Zelewski puts those of the Germans at twenty-six thousand killed, wounded and missing. The Home Army may have lost fifteen thousand but in addition anything between one hundred fifty thousand and two hundred thousand civilians may have become casualties—the difficulties of separating one from the other were quite insurmountable. Now came Hitler's order to dismember what remained of the city and to disarm and disperse the people. The Warsaw which the Russians were eventually to capture on January 17, 1945, was a shell, eighty-five per cent destroyed—the memorial to a struggle which had stood halfway between formal warfare and partisan combat. For it had been formal in that organized units had stood their ground without attempting to disperse, partisan because of the defenders' irregular spirit and the fact that they fought by improvised methods using whatever arms they could gather, and totally unsupported by heavy weapons.

The military achievements of the Warsaw uprising were practically nil since it had failed to prevent the Germans from successfully countering the Russian advance in the close approaches to the city but, on the contrary, had given the Germans an opportunity—albeit costly—to complete the elimination of the Home Army. The Russians, too, no longer needed to rate the Home Army as a military factor in the months to come. The political consequences were fundamental, however, since this was perhaps the turning point in Anglo-American evaluation of Soviet diplomatic integrity. Allowing that there was a failure on the Western part to appreciate the full significance of the German counterattack upon the Red Army at the beginning of August, there could be no mistaking the cynical intransigence of Stalin when he frustrated Allied attempts to intervene and prevented Russian assistance until it was too late.

The way for Soviet political infiltration of the Eastern European states now lay open. A power pattern had been established. Local secret armies which owed allegiance to previous regimes were shown to be ineffectual. But there would be more Warsaws yet. This, the first major urban guerrilla conflict, was one of many to come. The next, in fact, was already in course of preparation in the Balkans.

CHAPTER FOURTEEN

Backwash

Throughout Eastern Europe the broad-fronted advance of the Red Army had a far more sinister meaning for the populations than simply a spell of savage fighting. From the Baltic to the Balkans passing battles were but a noisy prelude to the horror to come, shock treatment in advance of a nightmare which nearly everybody dreaded.

For generations the inhabitants of the isolated Baltic States had been shuttlecocks in the German-Russian contest. Batted backward and forward during the First World War, subject to successive "cleansing" by revolutionary and counterrevolutionary forces in the midst of struggle towards their own independence in the early 1920s, they once more came into danger in 1940, when the Soviets occupied them as buffer states against the renewed German threat. The German invasion of 1941 was but another buffet, all the more painful because what was yearned for as a liberation resolved itself into a convulsion of repression and destruction as severe as the Soviet practice. Look east or west, the Baltic people found no reason for hope in 1944. And so, perhaps, it is understandable that they endured the war in a state of torpor, surviving by dint of acquiescence to their rulers.

There were partisans in the Baltic States who dwelt in the forests and villages. Occasionally, under duress from Red Army leaders specially flown in to "direct" them, they indulged in acts of local sabotage. But the effort was invariably halfhearted once the Soviet drive could no longer be sustained out of range, when a policy of circumspect neutrality was sought. Neutrality also predominated as the Red Army drew near in 1944, but this time as the product of panic. Refugees crowded the roads to the west, though a high proportion of the populace supinely awaited their fate—the massed deportation which they anticipated when the Russians arrived. Of the minority groups, some chose suicide as the quick way out and a handful resorted to guerrilla warfare in the hapless philosophy of "take one with

225

you"—German or Russian. For the guerrillas there could be no hope and, moreover, not the slightest comfort from the departing Germans, whose detestation of guerrillas nevertheless deterred them from engaging in guerrilla warfare themselves. Like nascent partisan movements everywhere, those of the Baltic States seem to have been filled with a naive enthusiasm which speedily withered under the implacable Russian counteraction. No doubt the staunch and dedicated two per cent thought it worthwhile, but their effect upon the Russians must have been practically nil. There are no reliable records of this pathetic struggle. The defenseless nations of northeastern Europe were again absorbed by the Soviet Union.

In southeastern Europe, because of the presence of strong foreign counterforces, the Russian takeover was more circumspect. While Warsaw suffered its martyrdom, Rumania bargained for a semblance of sovereignty. She more or less invited invasion, ingratiating herself with the Soviets after her new government ousted the pro-German dictator, General Antonescu, in a *coup d'état* on August 23. Of partisan warfare there was none, since the Rumanian Army merely changed sides to fight alongside the Red Army and shepherded the Germans out. Bulgaria's flank was turned. In August, however, Bulgaria was not actually at war with Russia, even though she was Germany's ally. This was easily rectified. Through discussions with Bulgarian consular staff the Russians arranged a well coordinated series of diplomatic moves, carefully phased to match military developments that made combat superfluous. On September 5 Russia formally declared war on Bulgaria. On the eighth they sent light forces into the country. At once the newly constituted Bulgarian government sued for peace, timing its diplomatic initiative to suit the convenience of the Communist minority members who had been given the key portfolios in the Ministry of Interior and in Justice. Behind the Red Army's advance the country fell under Communist domination, an unopposed takeover which was accompanied, it seems, by a massive purge of fifty thousand people—the removal of the old, pro-German gang, anybody who might appear to be a dissenter against the new regime, and the innocent who just happened to be standing in the wrong place at the wrong time when the police or troops arrived. In readiness was a prefabricated organization to replace the old—the so-called Secret Army which had been formed in Russia, and which now worked under the orders of an imported clique of politicians and officials who began slowly to absorb the indigenous Communist Party.

With Rumania and Bulgaria in Russian hands, the way into Hungary and Yugoslavia was wide open. In Hungary, however, there came a check to the south of Budapest, where the German Army consolidated as the Russians once more ran out of logistic energy. Furthermore Admiral Horthy, the head of state, had been successful in controlling dissident parties. Even so the growth of resistance movements, comprising left wingers dedicated to the overthrow of the Germans and center and right parties who were simply against the Horthy regime, had not gone unchecked. The abrasive elements of Hungarian society, particularly in the army, were involved to some extent, but of guerrilla activity there was practically none. Nevertheless constructive political moves were in the offing. Horthy himself came under heavy pressure from the Hungarian Front Party and, towards the end of September, began to bend in the direction of peace with the Russians, in an attempt to preserve the illusion of Hungarian autonomy in the Rumanian fashion.

News of Horthy's impending defection reached German intelligence early. To Budapest, in the early days of October, they sent the toughest antiguerrilla specialists—among them Bach-Zelewski, fresh from his suppression of Warsaw by main force, and eager to repeat the dose upon Budapest should an uprising take place. There was Skorzeny, too, briefed to exorcise the leading spirit of reaction by more subtle, less costly means. On October 11 Horthy reached agreement with the Russians on the substance of an armistice and made ready to announce it on the fifteenth. Once this became known to the Germans, Skorzeny executed a swift *coup de main* upon the Citadelle and abducted Horthy. At one clandestine stroke the armistice was made null and void, though local resistance simmered. Budapest would be spared the horror of partisan war, its fate, ironically, reserved for later at the mercy of regular warfare.

The appearance of the Russian Army on Yugoslavia's frontier on September 8, eager for a linkup with Tito's Partisans, posed a dangerous threat to the million-strong German force which remained in the Balkans. There was scarcely a garrison that in one way or another was not actively engaged in fighting guerrillas or lining the coast in the false expectation (as it happened) of an Allied invasion from the sea. Yet never once did the Germans relent. In August, for example, they cut loose against a misguided Cretan uprising, burned thirty villages and massacred one thousand victims—for the loss of only one hundred and fifty men. Despite recurrent alarms and the additional worry that, at any moment, the Allies might break through in Italy, debouch into the Po Valley and join hands with the Russians near Venice, Field-Marshal von Weichs, the German commander of the Balkan Theater of Operations, delayed withdrawal.

Not until September did he authorize the first thinning out from Crete and the Greek islands along with the removal of nonessential people and stores from the base areas. It was the end of the month, when the Red Army and Tito's Partisans at last closed in on Belgrade, before a final decision was taken to evacuate Greece, the southern half of Yugoslavia and Albania in their entirety and then it looked as if von Weichs had left it too late. Everywhere Allied aircraft bombed and strafed without hindrance and the Partisans grew bolder, a worse menace than ever with their better equipment and heavy weapons. Yet still the better-organized Partisans were unable to press home their attacks with irresistible strength against the better-armed German formations, despite the martial balance being closer.

It would be entirely misleading to suggest that the battle for the Balkans was primarily between Germans and Partisans. It was the Red Army and the Allied Air Forces which dominated. Every German move was designed to counter the maneuvers of the enemy regular formations. Even the eventual capture of Belgrade by a joint force of the Red Army and Partisans, which is sometimes claimed as a Partisan victory, is subject to evidence that the Red Army thrust was conceived as a symbol of political solidarity between Russians and Yugoslavs. The American historian Earl Ziemke gets at the truth when he describes a German counterattack on October 12 to relieve Russian pressure against Belgrade from the East: "Meeting only Partisans, the force from Belgrade had no trouble getting to the Morava." Reverses the Germans might regularly suffer against the Red Army, but they prevailed just so long as their main lines of communication leading out of Greece to the north were kept inviolate. Because they succeeded in maintaining a steady flow of traffic, they saved the bulk of their forces and, in due course, the German line stabilized in November, still with a foothold in Bosnia and Croatia. Neither the Red Army, the Allied Air Forces nor the partisans could prevent it.

As their winter offensives stalled in the approaches to Germany's frontiers, the Allies turned their attention to events in the liberated countries—notably in Greece. Here, throughout the summer, the feuds between parties and private partisan armies had simmered. The Russians took a hand, too, secretly employing one of their aircraft on a "training" flight from Italy to pick up a Soviet fact-finding mission from Tito's HQ in Yugoslavia and fly it to the ELAS HQ. The facts it found seem to have been disquieting. ELAS was a thing of tatters, more concerned with politics than fighting, ill-clad and poorly armed. There is little doubt that the mission reported in unfavorable terms to Moscow, to such effect that, when Churchill visited Stalin in Moscow on October 9 to settle, among other things, the future spheres of influence in the Balkans, he found a ready listener in the Russian leader, one prepared to agree instantly to a proposal running along Churchill's lines: "Your armies are in Rumania and Bulgaria. We have interests, missions and agents there. Don't let us get at cross-purposes in small ways. So far as Britain and Russia are concerned, how would it do for you to have ninety per cent predominance in Rumania, for us to have ninety per cent predominance of the say in Greece and go fifty-fifty about Yugoslavia?"

Though the Americans would later have misgivings about Churchill's Balkans policy, interpreting it as yet another example of British imperialism, Roosevelt was never averse to Allied forces contributing to Greek stability. When it became apparent that the Germans were at last set upon withdrawal, the Allied reaction was twofold; to expedite the Operation Noah's Ark sabotage scheme against the Axis communications, and to ensure stable government while the work of rehabilitating a population beset by famine was started. Concerning Noah's Ark, however, it must be recorded that the Greek guerrillas, above all EAM/ELAS, preferred to avoid the Germans, happy to see them depart as a prelude to the internecine struggle they sought. Such damage as was inflicted upon the old enemy was by Allied special forces: British commandos and the Special Boat Squadron, the American OGs and the Greek right-wing EDES under Zervas. They disrupted the railways, without completely stopping traffic, and ambushed convoys, but caused only a minute proportion of enemy losses. Rather more important, they seized landing grounds in readiness for the main Allied forces when they chose to arrive. But already, despite an agreement to withhold, the rival political parties were jostling to seize the reins of government in the aftermath of the German withdrawal. The guerrilla effort, therefore, was intermittent, only partially effectual and far from the "crowning mercy" they claimed it to be; the principal damage to the old enemy almost certainly fell to the credit of the air forces.

Nor did British land forces, arriving with perfect timing on the heels of the Germans, make a large contribution. Though it is obvious that the Allies possessed thorough intelligence of high-level German intentions (having, as they did, knowledge of German cipher), their tackling of the enemy was defective. Pursuit of a swiftly fleeing foe was hampered by lines of communication which the Germans, as usual, had desolated, completing the job begun by the partisans, and brought to an advanced state of disruption by the air forces. In any case the British were heavily committed to saving Greek lives, in a population at starvation point, and in preventing the slaughter of indigenous units which had helped keep order on behalf of the Germans. Already, however, disquieting Communist propaganda was souring relations. When, for example, ELAS partisans stood back while British troops, at loss to themselves, defeated a German column, it was not to be expected that the British would take kindly to a Communist newspaper report which gave all the credit to the ELAS and ignored the British contribution. Yet this was the realistic trend of Communist propaganda in its efforts to persuade the Greek people, and the world, that they alone were responsible for the liberation of the country. In due course ELAS's claims for Germans killed amounted to fifty thousand, whereas the Germans admit to only some seven thousand killed and wounded, many of whom probably fell to other agencies, few to ELAS.

An arrangement with Stalin that the prewar government should be restored to power after the Germans departed, provided EAM was represented, merely reproduced a situation similar to that in every other country where a Communist minority was in being. The essential difference, as Churchill has pointed out, was Russian abstention from Greek affairs in all respects. Therefore, when the new Greek Government returned to the country at the end of September and, in collaboration with the British, negotiated a settlement whereby all the partisan forces—both right and left—came under command of the British General Scobie, EAM/ELAS was placed in a dilemma like that of the London Poles but two months previously. If they were to observe the letter of the agreement and simply police their designated, outlying areas of responsibility, there would be no revolution, only disarmament once the new government settled into power. Instant action was therefore imperative before the British could react—if they were to react at all. Thus, as October passed, the ELAS began at last to indulge in strong, direct action, disguising their official role as peace-keepers in acts of coercion against their opponents; liquidating people who had taken the German part during the occupation and who, by implication, were anti-Communist. Within a matter of days the fiercest elements of ELAS and EDES were at each other's throats, particularly in Macedonia, where heavy fighting broke out as the German rearguard departed.

In Athens, which was under neither EDES nor ELAS control, an uneasy calm prevailed while the EAM mounted a propaganda campaign, taking the orthodox line that, since it alone deserved the credit for liberating the country, it alone should rule instead of a government which had absented itself. On November 7 Churchill was minuting:

"We should not hesitate to use British troops to support the Royal Hellenic Government under M. Papandreou," and, on the eighth, was warning his military commanders to prepare reinforcements for despatch to Athens. There Britons and Greeks were already at loggerheads after the British had forbidden ELAS to display one of its divisions in the Victory Parade. The crucial test came later in November, however, when Papandreou at last ordered the disbandment of all partisan forces. This was a deadly challenge, one which EAM could not ignore even though to disobey the order was to guarantee an armed struggle that was as little likely to succeed as the Warsaw uprising. For the nearest Russian troops, upon whose intervention the EAM might have placed some hope, were far to the north and moving westward instead of in a southerly direction. There is no evidence to suggest, in fact, that the EAM expected direct aid from the Russians, though little doubt that they counted on moral and diplomatic support particularly since, in days gone by, they had received Soviet encouragement. On December 2 EAM staged the first provocation—a general strike coincident with the abrupt departure of EAM from the capital to form a separate government and the calling in of ELAS bands, under General Sarafis, from the outlying countryside. To a barrage of charges that Scobie had exceeded his authority, rioting began in Athens, and the police came under ELAS fire and sustained heavy losses.

On December 5 Churchill made Scobie responsible "for maintaining order in Athens and for neutralizing or destroying all EAM/ELAS bands approaching the city." He added, "You may make any regulations you like for the strict control of the streets for the rounding up of any number of truculent persons. Naturally ELAS will try to put women and children in the van where shooting may occur. You must be clever about this and avoid mistakes. But do not hesitate to fire at any male in Athens who assails the British authority or Greek authority. . . . Do not, however, hesitate to act as if you were in a conquered city where a local rebellion is in progress. . . . We have to hold and dominate Athens. It would be a great thing for you to succeed in this without bloodshed if possible, but also with bloodshed if necessary." In the last sentence was the saving clause. Otherwise, we might reflect, the Churchillian rules for antipartisan warfare could well have been copied straight from Hitler's or Stalin's book. Guerrilla warfare is a great leveler.

The British were even more on the alert for trouble in Athens than the Germans had been in Warsaw at the end of July, for EAM depended on a steady political escalation of violence, whereas the

Home Army had relied upon sheer military surprise. Fighting broke out piecemeal over a period of days in all parts of the city as the two sides sought to contain the conflict, and yet to gain or keep possession of key installations and government offices. In the preliminary skirmishes the British retained the upper hand. They were well informed of EAM intentions and had placed guards on the vital points—points which ELAS was reluctant to attack since they preferred to exclude the British from the confrontation if they could. But it was the British who took the first major military initiative on December 6, launching an air and ground attack upon an ELAS concentration to the south of Athens—and suffering a severe repulse for their pains. By the twelfth the lines of battle were somewhat more clearly defined. ELAS, some thirty thousand strong, continued to close in and isolate the heavily outnumbered British, who, with loyalist Greeks, held a small enclave in the center of the city, a minute perimeter in the port of Piraeus, the Hassani airfield and a narrow beachhead on the Gulf of Phaleron.

ELAS exhibited the inherent strengths and frailties of a typical politically motivated guerrilla force. Although much better armed and trained than in July, it, on the one hand, dissipated its energy in acts of retribution against political opponents and in attacks on the prison in attempts to spring and lynch wartime collaborators, while, on the other, it misdirected its actual military effort by failing to coordinate resources and individual assaults against vital targets. Though they managed to capture the RAF HQ after nearly two days' fighting, they were repulsed in a series of piecemeal assaults on General Scobie's bastion in the city center. British tank and infantry teams hunted the wild partisans with efficient vigor, defeating enthusiasm with skilled coordination of firepower. By December 18 ELAS had attained its high-water mark. Then reinforcements from Italy reached the British in plenty, the port was secured and relief of their garrisons had begun. So too did the excesses.

Prior to the fighting in Greece, any member of the British forces would have condemned German cruelty in antiguerrilla fighting in Warsaw or anywhere else. They had been taught that their cause was against that very kind of behavior. Ask their views after but a few days' combat with ELAS in Athens and a different opinion emerged. By then the Britons had suffered from ELAS methods—sniping in the back from "cleared" areas by gunmen dressed in plain clothes, enticement by women into the line of fire. They would remember partisans who emerged from a house to surrender, and how they watched their comrades step forward to disarm them and then recall the burst of fire from a concealed enemy to kill their friends. Later they might ponder upon the reticence of people in areas freed from ELAS occupation —until they were shown a well, for example, containing the bodies of one hundred fifty slaughtered women and children—the women almost invariably with their breasts amputated. Small wonder that, within a matter of days, the British suffered from a sickened revulsion and, without compunction, shot down ELAS prisoners with the callousness of SS men. Small wonder, too, that, once the populace was assured of ELAS's permanent extinction, they celebrated with wild enthusiasm and resolved to resist Communism with measures as extreme as those of the Communists—always provided, that was, that the new National Guard (which included previous adherents of the Axis) could curb its more violent excesses when implementing security.

As the situation in Athens was brought rapidly under Allied control by a liberal use of firepower and uninhibited firmness, the EAM/ELAS reign of terror and lawlessness spread far and wide under the guise of retribution and political persuasion. Up country small British garrisons, which had been penned into isolated townships and were barely able to hold their own, lost valuable war material to the partisans. But largely ignoring these British pockets of resistance, Sarafis set his twelve thousand men against the eight thousand of EDES under Zervas in Epirus. Ironically, EDES was even weaker than its numbers suggest because Zervas had allowed personal integrity to override the essential ruthless ambivalence of a convincing guerrilla leader. Having attempted to fight the Germans and simultaneously carry out Papandreou's ill-starred peace-keeping program, he now tried to comply with Scobie's demobilization order, and also bowed to the wishes of followers who felt bound to return to their families as winter encroached. Armed by SOE (at the expense of the Communists) EDES retained its guerrilla outlook. With the British exclusively if temporarily engaged in a personal battle, Zervas suddenly found himself confronted in isolation by the sort of threat no good guerrilla can ignore—in this case the well-advertised approach of a superior force, reputedly of some three well-armed ELAS divisions. He reacted as if to the manner born and dispersed his force—evacuated by the Royal Navy and aided by his men's inherent skill in merging with the populace. By December 29 EDES in the Epirus was a thing of fragments.

Churchill came to Athens with the clear-cut aim of restoring order and supporting the monarchist constitution, though admitting that the Greeks must finally decide their future government by plebiscite. Churchill dominated, for the Americans, disturbed by his antiguerrilla directive of December 5 (which had been leaked to the press by their State Department), were ambivalent, while the Russian representative kept faith in silence. EAM/ELAS, because it was threatened by total elimination, engaged in time-wasting procrastination, striving to win breathing space for its partisans. But British regular organization and the rate of its reinforcement overwhelmed these isolated guerrillas. Once Churchill had persuaded the king to appoint Archbishop Damaskinos as regent, and he in turn had made General Plastiras Prime Minister in place of the discredited Papandreou, the outcome was assured. On December 27 the British began a preliminary assault in the vicinity of Athens. On January 4 it blossomed into a full-scale offensive employing the equivalent of three divisions, including the Greek Sacred Brigade, plus the National Guard and its cast of villains.

It was the turn of ELAS to recognize what the Polish Home Army had steadfastly refused to countenance—that they were abandoned by their allies and that survival lay in the long-term view. What they intended as an involuntary withdrawal from Athens, the preliminary stage to a classical dispersion, deteriorated into a rout. ELAS was capable only of ambushes; it proved as incapable then as it had throughout the war of effectively denying lines of communication to a strong opponent. The roads remained open for pursuit from Athens to Salonika. Instead ELAS implemented the philosophy of attack against weakness by acts of brutality against the unprotected populace. A British officer, who later surveyed the state of Greek villages on behalf of UNRRA, reckoned that half those destroyed, in a land of indescribable desolation, were the work of the Germans, the rest at the hands of ELAS. In the depths of a bitter winter the ten thousand hostages removed from Athens by ELAS trudged the roads, and were shot when they dropped from exhaustion.

On January 13 an armistice was arranged and talks towards a formal peace were bgun. At the end of a month's haggling the peace treaty was signed at Varkiza. The month had been well spent by ELAS. Though it contracted to hand in arms, its hard core dispersed to the mountains with the best of the modern weapons. To the British and Government forces was presented a collection of ancient and historic arms, fit for museums and as dangerous to whoever used them as to an enemy. For the victors, therefore, the war, perforce, continued in the hunt for the members of both EDES and ELAS who continued their depredations—searching for EDES men like Colonel Grivas (who was later to make a name for himself in the cause of Cypriot partisan warfare) and General Aris Veloukhiotis of ELAS, who was finally executed by his own followers and his head presented to the Greek authorities for public display in the hot weather.

For ELAS the price in dead is estimated at something like five thousand; for their countrymen, caught in the cross fire of civil war, the cost is unknown. In addition to victims of the fighting or those murdered in the pogrom were the hundreds who died of starvation because restocking of food supplies was delayed by the civil war. British casualties amounted to 110 killed and 1,190 wounded in this their first experience of antiguerrilla warfare in Europe since the 1920s.

The irony of the situation is apparent. Just three months previously it had been the Germans who patrolled Greece endeavoring to defeat the Communists with the aid of indigenous Greek Security Battalions. Now it was the British and EDES, helped by indigenous police and the hastily resurrected National Guard (many of whom had served in the German Security Battalions), who sought the same opponents in a far heavier outbreak of fighting than the Germans had ever permitted. Rarely had the Germans employed more than ten thousand troops; now the British doubled that number. It was just good fortune that they could spare them when operations in Italy had come to a halt in the winter mud-bath.

Unfortunately for ELAS in its desperate bid to seize power at the fleeting, opportune moment, it was compelled to make the same mistake as the Polish Home Army, forced to come into the open unsupported by allies against an enemy who, in the final analysis, was assured of victory by sheer weight of numbers and metal. Stalin kept faith with Churchill and raised not a finger to help EAM/ELAS. Indeed it was another ironic aspect of the situation that, whereas British and American newspapers (and the U.S. State Department) were strongly critical of British brute force, the Russian press remained obediently silent on the subject. The backlash of the Greek partisan war recoiled, therefore, most fiercely upon the Western Allies in both the military and political fields. There was worldwide disquiet at Churchill's forthright handling of the matter. Yet this was another foretaste of peacetime implications, a sign that short-term severe antiguerrilla measures have a doubtful value in a civilized setting when the rough demands of war are absent.

Each partisan collision in the war's closing days helped shape the coming peace. Repercussions were manifest and appeared first of all in Italy, where the Allied command anxiously watched the development of the partisan movement behind the German lines and, in particular, its vigorous Communist branch. Field-Marshal Alexander, who was now Supreme Allied Commander in the theater and thus involved in the Greek struggle, used as a pretext for his proposals to reduce the number of Italian partisans the excuse that logistics forbade the supply of more than a limited number. He asked the rest to disband. There was, of course, good tactical as well as political and logistic sense behind the request. The mass was untrained and a menace to itself; an élite was sure to be more effective. But the partisans bitterly resented any suggestion that they should disperse; neither political faction trusted the other to abide by any agreement; each was fearful that a march would be stolen as the end of the war approached; all realized that the war itself was something of a passing irrelevance. Nor was there a general welcome for suggestions that the partisans should abandon direct action in favor of concentrating upon guarding vital points against German demolition. The leadership needed to bolster their followers' martial spirit for the day when an insurrection might merge with the ultimate struggle for political power. Guerrilla attacks continued, and in the final days of the war, when the Allied armies broke what remained of the German armies, the Northern Italian plain, the mountains and the cities became infested with partisan bands on the rampage in the familiar orgy of retribution—in which Mussolini was a notable casualty when he was caught and executed by partisans.

Italy was a quicksand in which order was represented only by shifting rocks rising above the morass—those regular German divisions fighting their way towards a friendly frontier, and the Allied formations entering the partisan-liberated zones with feelings both of triumph and of trepidation. In the opening days of peace only the Allies could insist upon the surrender of weapons, and by firm handling enable the incoming Italian government to sustain power on the backs of a resurrected police force. But, as was customary in this situation, there occurred that inevitable, terrifying interlude when local partisan forces constituted the instrument of law and used their power to pursue vendettas and a rough justice that was aimed as much against potential political opponents as against collaborators and the old Fascist Guard. The cost of the partisan war in Italy is as difficult to compute as anywhere else. It is said that thirty-six thousand were killed; it is also reckoned that nearly ten thousand civilians were executed in the reprisals. The immediate postwar victory parades of partisans, whose hands were red with the blood of their own countrymen and whose advertised allegiances changed as frequently as the political climate, disgusted the men who had fought for ideals. But partisans and ideals are uneasy bedfellows.

CHAPTER FIFTEEN

A Crashing Anticlimax

On the eve of his suicide, as Hitler contemplated the dying contortions of his Thousand Year Reich from his stronghold in Berlin, the German leader might have echoed Max Hoffmann when the latter, with regard to Revolutionary Russia, had written of "a huge swarm of maggots, a squalid swarming mass." The Europe which Hitler had endeavored to bend to his will was, at the end of April 1945, in ruins. His most cherished allies had deserted him and the battle for the last grains of soil was an imbroglio as chaotic as any of the partisan campaigns which had infected the latter years of the war. To the bitter end, however, he called for unremitting resistance and uninhibited destruction within Germany's frontiers.

Until the summer of 1944 very little attention had been paid in Germany to the problem of engaging in partisan warfare either within the occupied countries, after they were abandoned, or inside the nation as the threat to her frontiers drew nigh. The first halfhearted attempt came in the north, when Finland sought terms from the Russians in the summer of 1944. Here the Germans failed to pursue the matter seriously because they could not envisage the Finns being offered a settlement that was acceptable. Such studies as were made thus hung fire in the exploratory stages. After a decade's authority, at the head of conventional forces, Hitler recoiled from the methods which had brought him to power. He spoke of recruiting as many Finns as possible into German Army formations and thus freeing them from Finnish jurisdiction. Only General Rendulic, the commander of the German corps in Finland, upon whom experience against Yugoslavian Partisans had left its mark, proposed a concrete partisan scheme. He suggested that the Finnish General Talvela should form a resistance organization based upon a German division and an assault gun brigade to act in independence. Even this, though, merely illustrated the rigid state of the Wehrmacht mind, the way it was shackled to formality and

237

incapable of producing the hyper-free-thinking instinctive to the genuine irregular fighter. Therefore, as it was in the Baltic States, so it became in Finland: there was no clandestine warfare of any importance. The Finns were allowed to bow quietly out of the arena in September.

Quite naturally the institution of clandestine warfare inside Germany took low priority—in the aftermath of the July bomb plot and in face of the sudden demand to strengthen the frontiers of the Reich. Though the bomb plot was an act of purest resistance it stopped well short of an attempt at internecine warfare, being, in effect, a unilateral political putsch of the 1920 variety. The Allies had no part in it, even though the plotters had made contact with Allen Dulles of OSS in Switzerland. Dulles, whose main task it was to discover what went on in Germany, declined to bargain with the anti-Hitler elements, refusing their request for guarantees in the event of the Germans pulling out of the war against the West. The Western Allies were not prepared to desert the Russians and instead were set upon the absolute military overthrow of Germany within the full meaning of the policy of unconditional surrender announced during the Casablanca Conference in January 1943. The plot, therefore, was guaranteed to fail, assured of creating a violent outburst of anti rebellion measures and reassertion of authority by every antipartisan force within the Nazi Party. Once Himmler and his minions were given an absolutely free rein, no single mind or organization could expect to express itself and survive. Attitudes which were the antithesis of any aspiring partisan movement were inculcated with fervor. The SS was elevated to the pinnacle of power and overrode the judiciary, civil administration, industry, the Wehrmacht—everything that mattered in German life. Nobody dared speak out of turn as the Nazi Party, in its most bigoted mood, completed the formal mobilization of the nation.

In September 1944 a searching comb-out of civil life, with a lowering and raising of the ages for conscription, swelled the ranks of the Wehrmacht to the detriment of civil industry. Himmler had been placed in command of the Home Army and was raising fifty new, conventional divisions at reduced establishment, under the evocative name of *Volksgrenadiers*. Sent to fill holes in the static defenses of the Reich, they left behind wide gaps in society. After September the only males of sound health to be seen in the German streets were servicemen home on leave; the rest were the aged, the crippled and children below the age of sixteen. At one swoop Himmler had extracted the vital elements of an indigenous partisan force, put them into uniform and merged them into conventional armed forces. Moreover, the best special raiding force of all, the Brandenburgers, had been converted into a panzer grenadier division and would finally become a part of Panzer Corps Gross Deutschland in Army Group Center.

There was nothing original in German plans for the defense of the Fatherland. As winter approached the main effort was directed towards re-creating a mobile strategic reserve of conventional forces. And when these were employed in the Ardennes offensive, in December, the technique was one of onrush by heavy, armored columns.

Not that the Germans entirely overlooked the value of special raiding in this offensive. While the Brandenburg Division was lost for the purpose on the East Front, there was, for use in the West, a special SS raiding brigade equipped with captured American vehicles under Otto Skorzeny, whose task it was both to precede the advance and to inject *coup de main* parties into the enemy rear. Some would drop by parachute and some, copying Company 800 in 1940, would attempt to seize bridges over the River Meuse. More were to infiltrate in jeeps deep among the Allied rear, there, like SAS, to spread alarm and confusion, though it was only a rumor that General Eisenhower was to be their main target. It is significant that only the latter plan achieved success. The principal *coup de main* was far too obvious and drew attention to itself; it required twenty American-type tanks and could be given only two; it was tackled and stopped in the manner of a conventional force, by conventional forces. But the jeep parties achieved an effect out of all proportion to their size. From every minor ambush they laid grew a crop of rumors expanding into a widespread panic stretching back through Belgium and France. For every inter-ruption of lines of communication they achieved—by the waylaying of couriers, the cutting of telephone lines or the destruction of radio stations close to the battle zone—there were a hundred and one delays caused by the Americans' extrazealous security measures. Repeated halts at a myriad of road check blocks created quite as much hindrance to the passage of information and traffic, and the fraying of tempers (including Eisenhower's at his being overprotected), as scattered bul-lets from the forests and bangs in the night. Gradually the alarm declined as the commando parties were forced to return home—but of the nine teams dispatched only two were lost. Into their places stepped a reactivated Belgian resistance, combing the forests for German stragglers as German attacks died in their tracks.

The failure of the Ardennes offensive was, of course, but an incident in a resolved situation. Germany was finished, her frontiers crumbling. When Finland left her side, the entire German northern flank was thrown into jeopardy. Henceforward Sweden had less need for caution and could safely bend her neutrality towards the winning side, acting quite openly as a refuge and base for Norwegian and Danish underground organizations while putting additional political difficulties in the German way. Nevertheless resistance and sabotage in Norway quietly followed its routine course—a tiny thorn in the German side, while Milorg braced itself for the day of liberation, hoping to keep the level of violence low. The Danes did rather more even though they had technically never been at war with Germany. At first only embryo cells had begun to form since the early liberal German administration did little to provoke serious concern or countermeasures. The first resisters, backed by SOE from London and a "cell" in Stockholm, came from the army and regarded themselves as a security force that would take over as the Germans departed. But once civilian resistance, partly at Communist instigation and largely supplied by British air drops, sprang up in 1943, there was a dangerous increase in tension to match the population's rising discontent with German repression, and their desire to demonstrate sympathy for the Allied cause to make sure of recognition for a popular postwar government.

In September 1943 a Danish Freedom Council was formed to make contact with the two principal providers of external aid—SOE and the Russians—to supervise the general activities of the small secret army and, in due course, play a significant political role as an unofficial government for those who rejected Danish neutrality. But Denmark is just about the worst European country for guerrilla warfare. Small, devoid of mountains or forests, yet well provided with land communications, it offered the Germans every facility for economic counteraction. The Danes had scope for nothing more deadly than rail sabotage, which went on intermittently throughout 1944 and 1945. Highly organized, the Freedom Council did what it could to satisfy the demands of those who called for action—and assured Denmark its roll of martyrs. But always the aim was to sustain the monarchy and prewar style of government, preserving the political fabric in its original state. The Russians took an eager interest in the resolution of Denmark's neutrality and the Communist threat was redoubled when it seemed possible that the race between the converging spearheads of the Red Army from the east and the British Army from the south in April 1945 might allow the Russians to win. The Danes, striving desperately to save their country from becoming a battleground, realized that, like the Poles, they might be compelled to call out the Secret Army to seize control from the Germans before the Russians arrived—or stay safely passive in the hope that the British would get there first. In the event,

British conventional forces arrived well ahead of the Russians on the day the Germans formally surrendered. There was thus sufficient time for the brigade of Danish troops, which had been secretly formed in Sweden, to cross to the homeland and occupy strategic points, even as the leading British troops drove up. Only on the Island of Bornholm did the Russians put in an appearance and then on the unobjectionable pretext that the German garrison had refused to surrender on May 7 when the rest of their armies laid down arms. The Russian occupation was to last until the spring of 1946—a reminder of what might have happened had they been given room elsewhere.

In Norway there was not the slightest trouble. The large German garrison capitulated to Milorg when General Jodl signed the act of surrender at Reims on May 7. If the Germans had intended to form a northern redoubt the notion had been discounted when, in November 1944, the 6th SS Mountain Division was withdrawn to Germany, leaving only Wehrmacht troops, now under Rendulic, in occupation. Though the Allies might worry about a German stand in the mountains, they need not have feared. Even had a belligerent will been present, it would soon have died from lack of support and with the onset of hard winter.

Resistance within Germany, if it were to be found at all, was likely only where the most dedicated Nazis—the SS organizations—migrated. By the end of 1944 the SS represented absolute power in the land and drew on the nation's best manpower sources. Rumors of a national redoubt in the south abounded. Switzerland, from whence OSS, under Allen Dulles, probed high and low into Germany and Italy for clues, was the clearinghouse for tittle-tattle. A rich crop of rumors stimulated the interest of the directors of Allied intelligence. Their agents were ordered to look closer for specific information. Diplomatic contacts and spies searched far and wide. To augment their number, eighty-two agents were dropped by parachute across the breadth of Germany between January 21 and April 26, 1945, and soon their short-range radios were transmitting signals to Mosquito aircraft which flew high and fast above secret locations, gathering a mass of information. The story which emerged was of an antheap in convulsion, an offering of so much conflicting evidence that SHAEF could no longer ignore the possibility that serious resistance was planned in certain key parts of Germany—the most likely place of all being in the south.

To this day, there is uncertainty in the minds of many Germans whether a southern national redoubt—Festung Alpenland as it is sometimes called—was ever intended or whether it was a chimera. Before the war a scheme existed to bring industry to the Alpenland, to alleviate poverty in the region, especially after Austria was annexed, and to locate factories where they would be safe from aerial bombardment. Very little was in fact done—the vast majority of underground factories constructed during the war in central Germany were in the Harz and Thuringian mountains. As for defense works, there was a halfhearted project to build a fortress line as insurance against the day of the collapse of the Italian front, for which purpose Slovak workers were drafted into Austria. But nothing of importance was built and hardly anything of logistic significance transported to the area. Nevertheless the southern Reich was crawling with maggots of all kinds, though mostly to the eastward, where the defenses creaked under strain of the culminating Russian offensives.

In January 1945 the 6th SS Panzer Army had been transferred to Hungary in one last effort to save the Hungarian oilfields. It failed, but to the bitter end remained imbedded on this front. Echeloned back into Bohemia was to be found every possible variety of outlawed army, including SS formations, recruited from Soviet races, and the two divisions of Vlasov's unhappy and ill-loved army—all crowding westward rather than fall prey to the Russians. They infested territory which, traditionally, was a zone of resistance. But the Germans and their pathetic adherents were no longer the absolute masters. Czech resistance was joining hands with the advancing Russians. Recovered, to some extent, from the ravages of post-Heydrich decimation, they were ready to support both Russians and Americans at the old frontiers. The fundamental split between Russian-sponsored Communist partisan groups and the Western-orientated groups, which owed allegiance to the London Czechs, remained, of course, unhealed by the National Council, which had been set up in Prague. As a result there was no consolidated plan of action apart from a tacit understanding that, as the Allied Armies drew close, some sort of national rising should occur—"when the time was ripe." In practice a series of improvised, local rebellions on the eve of liberation took place at random in individual towns and cities.

Helplessly the Germans watched the erosion of their position within Bohemia. In one last desperate gamble they tried to recapture the loyalty of the Vlasov army, whose two divisions, located within thirty miles of Prague at the end of April, were expected at any moment to change sides and take their chance alongside their countrymen. They had refused to fight in the line with the German Army facing the Russians, they had stripped off their German Army badges, and they were not in the least placated by a belated German offer of full support divested of political strings. They stood inert—in a dilemma. The Germans, meanwhile, shifted westward, seeing in the Vlasov divisions, so it seems, the chosen, sacrificial rearguard for their élite formations as they withdrew into the national redoubt or into Western captivity. Then, on May 4, Czech partisans seized Radio Prague and broadcast appeals for help from all quarters, including the Vlasov formations.

There ensued a period of indescribable chaos. The Germans within Prague managed to reach a temporary moratorium with the pro-Western guerrillas on threat of razing the city. At the same time they injected the best of their available SS divisions to quell the rising as it grew in intensity. Simultaneously Vlasov's army degenerated into anarchy, a condition not so very dissimilar to that which had once characterized Makhno's partisans of Revolutionary days. Proclaiming they would fight both Russians and Germans, they moved to the aid of the Czechs, attacking the Germans en route. On May 7, however, the instrument of surrender had been signed at Reims and therefore, though some American units drew close to Prague, their main body stopped at Pilsen and took no part in the struggle for the capital. Thus the Germans and Vlasov's men were faced with unavoidable capitulation to the Russians—the last thing they wanted. The Vlasov army, torn by internal dissent, at once became a thorn in everybody's flesh—a typical, itinerant partisan group of embarrassing political significance. Having stiffened the Czech uprising in its weakest initial phase, it now threatened the Czech Communists of the National Council as they introduced measures to assume power with Russian assistance. It thus gave breathing space to the National Council besides pinning German troops to antiguerrilla fighting when their overwhelming desire was escape to the westward. They also embarrassed the Americans by moving west themselves to surrender—a scheme to which the Russians violently objected. Eventually the majority found their way to the Americans, to swell the crowd of displaced persons thronging the countryside, though Vlasov himself was less fortunate. He was removed from American custody by a Russian patrol, eventually tried for treason and finally executed. One thing was assured. German schemes were baffled in Czechoslovakia; their forces could escape neither south nor westward and thus contribute resistance in Festung Alpenland. On May 8 they sued for terms, although scattered fighting was to continue against itinerant German groups for another week.

Overall German resistance against the final Allied offensives bore a strong resemblance to guerrilla warfare. Nationwide their isolated bastions held out until overwhelmed by a hostile onrush. Knots of resistance were formed and fought—but when broken the defeated went, uncomplainingly, straight to the prison camps never to fight again. The population—the women, the aged, the children and the lame—kept calm and stayed home to display white flags when the enemy drew near. Columns of German prisoners were herded behind the very barbed wire which, till a few days previously, had imprisoned the hundreds of thousands of Allied prisoners of war and the conscripted European labor corps which had been imported for purposes of the German economy. Rarely before can so diverse a racial agglomeration have been gathered into one country, its truly remarkable feature being a placidity of behavior under the most appalling administrative chaos at a time when the cry for vengeance upon the Germans was a watchword. Atrocities there were—the full gamut of murder, rape, robbery and arson—yet never on a cataclysmic scale. The presence of large, disciplined armies working to a preconceived plan of occupation stabilized the situation more thoroughly than when irregular, partisan forces were employed in other countries.

It seems remarkable that this polyglot collection of displaced people should have dwelt among the Germans and caused so little trouble. Foreign workers might easily have sabotaged the factories in Germany —and evidence is available that they did so, but only on the smallest scale; [1] strikes and go-slows, too, might have been instituted. But they were pinned firmly to their work—mostly in fear of well-advertised fatal brutality; occasionally, as in the case of Polish women, by pitiless flogging. There are, indeed, recorded instances of conscripted French workers who look back benignly on their days in Germany, claiming they would have been ecstatically happy if only their families had been with them.[2]

Both foreigners and Germans went on manufacturing an ever-increasing volume of material and stopped only when the bomber offensive caused a total breakdown in the transport system and fuel supplies. The rising level of war production was itself the index of failure to disrupt by both the bomber offensive and German dissidents. Communists were present but chose to remain silent, lying in wait for the day when overt action would be unresisted. In reality the ultimate breakdown in industry reflected the ineptitude of an administration that daily fell closer under the control of Himmler and his henchmen

[1] For example, a few French women, in a small-arms ammunition factory, excluded the propellant from a percentage of cartridge cases. When discovered they were executed.
[2] A German officer is on record as complaining that, whereas he was allowed to flog Polish women, he was not allowed to do the same to French women. Not only is this quoted as an example of typical German race discrimination, but also to show a cause of bitterness between the Poles and the French—deviously interpreted, by some, as a deliberate German attempt to stir up racial strife.

in the aftermath of the bomb plot. In this respect therefore, the generals' resistance had an unexpected, indirect effect. The German people became afflicted by what became known as "cadaver obedience."

On March 15, 1945, the Reich Minister for Armaments and War Production, Albert Speer, told Hitler that Germany's case was hopeless. Hitler's response was typical in its savagery—he ordered a scorched earth policy on the grounds that "if Germany lost the war its people would have no right to live; the eastern race was too powerful and would destroy Germany in any case." It had been Speer's intention to save power plants and factories in order to protect the future livelihood of German workers—a kind of resistance that had been, after all, among the most profitable when implemented by other European resistance organizations, particularly those in the West. It was simply ironic that he accidently germinated an idea that was quite contrary to his aim and it took the next fortnight deviously to persuade Hitler to reverse the order. Speer's efforts, in effect, were puny. In the latter days of April he seems to have mitigated some of the more damaging effects of orders that were given for wholesale demolition of bridges, regardless of whether for military purposes or simply as an act of self-immolation, but, by and large, events took their course. In April the German state was breaking into fragments over which central government had no coherent control.

Therefore, in the climactic chaos of Hitler's last days in power, contradictions and anomalies abounded. Normally the defense of German soil rested upon corps' areas—the Wehrkreis—each commanded by an army officer. The one which chiefly concerned Festung Alpenland was Wehrkreis VII, which, since March 1943, had ben the responsibility of General Karl Kribbel. In September 1944 he was informed that the Berchtesgarten area was to come under direct army command of Hitler's headquarters, but apart from that seems to have heard nothing except rumors of what was intended for the area. This was understandable since, by then, the Higher SS were virtually in charge, guarding their secrets closely. Although the army was allowed to retain its nominal place in the chain of command, each Wehrkreis was divided into security zones under an officer of the Security Police. Every other organization from every kind of force—the SA, Hitler Youth, police, fire services, labor organizations, communications, Red Cross, Volksturm and Werewolves—came under direct SS command. Of these the Volksturm—a collection of old men and schoolboys gathered into the equivalent of the British Home Guard, armed with any available weapon—can be dismissed as a factor in partisan warfare except insofar as it attracted the last dregs of manpower into the uniformed forces.

The Werewolves were far more threatening since their cadre was formed of the most virulent SS and raiding groups. Taking their evocative name from the old definition applied to the voluntary Landsturm of 1813, they were officially raised in November by order of Himmler and referred to by him as "W." It was ironic that the German radio station called Radio Werewolf, opened on April 1, was to call Werewolves "freedom fighters."

Though the Germans failed to transfer the 6th SS Panzer Army and the SS Mountain Division to Festung Alpenland,[3] they did bring in scattered units of the Brandenburg Regiment and Skorzeny's commandos. These were the last parts of the German Armed Forces with the slightest capability of adapting themselves instantly to partisan warfare. Speed of improvisation was, of course, mandatory if anything at all was to be achieved, for there is little doubt, for all the "discoveries" of Allied intelligence, that no worthwhile plans for Festung Alpenland or Werewolves were in existence until March 1945. Too late, with invasion actually in progress, the Germans endeavored to initiate internal resistance—something the British had found extremely difficult to organize in 1940 even when under the mere threat of invasion. In response to Goebbels's propaganda, men and women volunteered to join the Werewolves.

At a glance sections of German terrain appear ideal for partisan warfare—the Harz Mountains and Thuringian hills, for example, with their deep gullies and thick forests seem to provide boundless hiding places. But partisan bands survive at the whim of the population and prosper when antipartisan forces are lax. Antipartisan forces, however, thrive on good road communications, along which they can rapidly concentrate against guerrilla bands, and Germany has a highly developed road system; even the forests are intersected by a maze of well-founded rides, which cancel out any advantage of shelter that belts of conifer and beech trees provide. Although Melita Maschmann writes "we adjusted ourselves to the idea of fighting on," the apathy of the majority and the positive hostility of a minority in the populace made partisan survival tenuous in the extreme. Anti-Nazi elements which had lain dormant since 1933 now began to reappear. Among the first acts of Allied military government would be the replacement of every pro-Nazi burgomaster by a non-Nazi aspirant, one who could be

[3] According to the SS General Gottlob Berger, who was in charge of Volksturm training, it was never intended to leave Sixth SS Panzer Army in the Alps, since it was always regarded as the central mobile strategic reserve.

of almost any alternative political persuasion. In the town of Waldstadt [4] in Thuringia the new incumbent appointed by the Americans was one of those prewar Communists who had turned Nazi—likened by the townspeople to a rare steak: "brown outside and red within." Complete with Russian-born wife he was to survive in office when, a few months later, that part of Germany was relinquished by the Americans to Russian occupation.

Thuringia, though at first designated as a suitable locality for the German Army Headquarters, found little favor as a military zone. The German defenders melted away, the Americans flowed through, there was hardly a Werewolf's whimper let alone a prolonged defense. When American soldiers carelessly forgot a rifle and pistol in Waldstadt the Kramer family buried them in the garden, hoping never to see the weapons again.

But the SS were in the Alps brewing something more sinister. Melita Maschmann was sent to join the Werewolves and found herself attached to the Tyrolean Hitler Youth under instruction in sabotage by SS officers—one of five thousand candidates. The day before the Americans arrived in Innsbruck, she and three colleagues joined part of Skorzeny's band on the upper slopes of a valley, in a drafty hut which was intended as their future base. They lived in a world of Nazi make-believe, deluding themselves that the old philosophy might survive and then revive. Yet there was no urgency about their preparations. In Maschmann's opinion "the men were really only concerned to be in safety during the first dangerous weeks after the war." What hope was there in any case? Every other European resistance movement had drawn strength from friendly nations. Germany had forfeited all friendship.

Gradually ill health and boredom forced them down to the populated floor of the valley, where, almost at once, they were noticed by the inhabitants and reported to the Americans, who arrested them. Joining in the hunt was an Austrian resistance which came to light in the closing stages of the war. Skorzeny contemplated escape or suicide but, instead, opted to surrender on May 15. He wrote, in 1957, "We felt that the European idea must grow out of the existing chaos and it could well be that those most qualified to foster it were the soldiers who had really been inspired by glowing love of their country." In due course Skorzeny would be tried for war crimes. At his trial a most telling witness in the defense would be one of the most celebrated of British special agents—Yeo-Thomas. Yeo-Thomas's evidence made

---

[4] Waldstadt is a made-up name in order to preserve the anonymity of my informants.

plain the utter ruthlessness which guerrilla warfare forced upon its participants, indicating that every nation's partisans had felt compelled to adopt subterfuge and that, to protect themselves from discovery, enemies sometimes had to be killed out of hand. Skorzeny was acquitted.

The Werewolves gained little experience. Hostile acts they mostly shunned, since that would merely have drawn unwanted attention to themselves. Here and there in Germany there was a political assassination, sometimes an enthusiastic fanatic might stretch a wire across the road at night, hoping to decapitate the unwary driver of a jeep speeding through the dark, but events such as these were rare. A plan to shoot all Allied-appointed burgomasters collapsed. With scarcely a sound, the militant Nazi sect died amid an occupation which, in the West at least, was more benign than the majority of Germany's enemies liked. Nevertheless this magnanimity, which gave the Germans hope for the future, may well have quelled the last stirrings of belligerence within them.

At the end of the war, the Americans took prisoner General Kurt Dittmar of the Wehrmacht. Asked about the authenticity of Festung Alpenland he is reputed to have replied, "It's a myth." Commenting upon SS General Berger's account of the growth of some form of redoubt, General von Henzl repeated, with customary Wehrmacht skepticism, that it was "too uncertain to be used for an objective military evaluation." Yet Major-General Kenneth Strong, who was chief intelligence officer at SHAEF, has this to say: "The capture of a Werewolf headquarters convinced me that only the rapid advance of the United States troops had prevented the creation of a widespread network of Resistance posts which might well have interfered with our operations."

In partisan warfare, personal attitudes are, perhaps, more formative of the mode of combat than in any other type of battle. In an essay written shortly after the war, a scholarly German general, Günther Blumentritt, wrote,

Adolf Hitler ordered the call to the colors and the organization of the Werewolf in 1945, an order that was absolutely insane and which would have brought much more mishap to Germany if it had been actually put into action. Except for some single operations of mostly irresponsible youth the common sense of the German people never permitted such a "patriotic rise." On the whole, illegal warfare or passionate rebellion does not appeal to the German and also not to other Germanic nations. The illegal movements are much more popular with Slavic and Roman people who are also much more passionate than the Germans.

This rather poignant cry is part and parcel, of course, of the typical German Army officer's apologia and confusion of thoughts in the aftermath of failure. Since Blumentritt himself had earlier in his essay extolled nineteenth-century uprisings by German partisans (omitting those in 1848 and forgetting the Freikorps), whose rebellions "can be considered as patriotic . . . they live on in songs, poems, even in the theater which glorify them as heroes and martyrs," his conclusions hardly bear examination—even if we disregard the work of German neoclandestine organizations in the twentieth century. But his reflections upon the racial aspects of partisan warfare are appropriate and worthy of further study on grounds of comparison between the attitudes of partisans whose roots were set in the various European regions. It was Germany's fate and misfortune that she was to provide material for this study in the collision between Eastern and Western methods upon her soil in 1945.

CHAPTER SIXTEEN

A Horrible Reality

When Waldstadt fell to the Third U.S. Army in April 1945 the inhabitants endured the experience with an instinctive stolidity of behavior that reached far back into German history—with the knowledge that conquest and reconquest throughout the centuries implied an indisputable subjugation by hostile forces whose ways had to be learned and obeyed. To the old, solid core of prewar Communists the occasion might even have appeared a happy one—if only the conquerors had been the Red Army. But, apart from light skirmishing, the town fell unresistingly into American hands and the processes of establishing military government, to protect the lines of communication and eradicate the most virulent Nazi elements, went ahead in a routine way. The lieutenant whose task it was to run the administration was fortunate in his interpreter. Frau Kramer was English, though she did not receive preferential treatment. She was present when the burgomaster was interrogated, found pro-Nazi and deposed. Each day she was made to stand when performing her duties until at last she collapsed out of sheer exhaustion. With her family she had been evicted from her home to make room for Americans. Nevertheless she considers that the Americans "were relatively kind to the inhabitants." She has good grounds for making that comparison.

For Waldstadt was located in country destined, in July, to become part of the Russian zone of occupation. Frau Kramer recalls that, as the day for change drew near and restrictions upon travel were tightened, she knew fear such as she had never known during her domicile in Germany. Throughout the turbulent 1930s and war years, despite her English origins, she had felt secure and never once spied upon. Now the future threatened and induced feelings of hopelessness and resignation. She writes:

When the Russians took over they searched every house for incriminating evidence [the Kramers suffering a bad moment when the search seemed about to reveal the hidden American guns] and many men were arrested. This was followed by a further search by so-called police drawn from the local Communists. The Russians took people away wholesale, even those who played only very minor roles in the NSDAP. Many innocent people were arrested if their names happened to coincide with those of men on their "wanted" lists (which, incidentally, had been supplied by the local Communists) while most of the really guilty had already escaped across the border. The owners of local factories were dispossessed and replaced by Russians. Heads of departments and foremen who kept their jobs were given so-called Stalin food parcels each month to supplement the rations—which were close upon starvation level.

Because the Germans had waged war with scant humanitarian political foresight and prosecuted it without mercy against partisans and civilians alike, they had heightened the worst excesses of the anti-Bolshevik struggle of the 1920s and projected them into the 1930s and 1940s. Contrary to their claims for recognition as noble cultural leaders, they matched, and sometimes outdid, the bestiality of their Communist adversaries throughout Europe. At Nuremberg Jodl remarked:

> The fight against partisans was a horrible reality. . . . In connection with a book by Ponamarenko, an American paper said that 500,000 Germans were supposed to have been killed by the partisans. If a nought is crossed off from that figure, it is still quite a considerable achievement for a peaceful Soviet population. But this book is also said to state that the population became increasingly hostile, that murder and terror became more frequent and that the peaceful Quisling mayors were being killed. At any rate, it was a tremendous fight which was taking place in the East.

Compared with the East, fewer resources had to be committed by the Germans to the antipartisan struggle in the West, because there the enemy challenge was less threatening except in the months of June to August 1944. Wherever this kind of conflict arose the German response was consistently ruthless, yet applied as secondary to conventional operations at the front. Except in the case of the major uprising in Warsaw, resources applied to the antipartisan struggle were made available only when they could be spared from the main battle. Usually the Germans managed to neutralize, if not eliminate, partisan guerrillas until those last eighteen months of the war, by which time they were totally overwhelmed by a military situation which had got out of control. They were never able to prevent resistance, the escape organizations and espionage. The existence of a permissive, total war environment, that encouraged battle without political restraint, was in itself symptomatic of the German miscalculation of the political and economic facts of life. Apart from their fundamental folly of endeavoring to subdue Europe with inadequate resources, there prevailed their misconception of the underlying purpose of partisan war-making, their failure to understand that the partisan effort, though possibly militarily insignificant, was of cardinal importance in the vital struggle for postwar domination. It is true that Hitler, believing in his invincibility and remaining faithful to the methods which had brought him to power, could confidently dismiss proposals for postwar political settlements which ran contrary to his own theories. The initial success of totalitarian methods convinced him of their validity in trying to perpetuate the Third Reich for a thousand years. But once his grip upon the situation began to loosen, in consequence of the failure to conquer Britain or eliminate Soviet power, the inevitability of defeat automatically threw a system of enforced European unity into the melting pot of confusion. The swarming partisan movements came to represent the traditional competitive elements of Europe's evolving political structure. Suppress these though they would, the Germans could only delay, not prevent, a natural process deeply steeped in past experience.

When partisan movements began to run riot after 1942, their backlash against the Germans became as politically constructive as the initial German invasions had been militarily provocative. The struggle became oppressively ferocious, however, only when the essential two per cent of genuine rebels were to be found close to the pinnacle of political power. The Russian partisans were persistent because they were directed by men wedded to the idea of partisan warfare as a political instrument, and the same can be said about Tito and the Yugoslavians. On the other hand the French were lukewarm because their leadership was split and even the Gaullist element, which eventually lent support to the need for clandestine warfare, was a long time coming round to its all-out implementation. Though partisans on their own never conquered and permanently held territory (and were invariably liable to instigate civil war), they nevertheless produced the leaders who would shape the political parties which, eventually, would subdue nations. Thus, when the Germans tried to eliminate Tito and those of his kind in 1944 they were striking at the heart and brain of both partisan and political power. We may ask, in fact, why they failed to attack the leaders with greater vigor since, by 1942, through their violent stupidity, they had passed the boundaries of placation and had nothing further to lose by oppression. There is no definite answer to this: perhaps projects were in the pipeline to assassinate Roosevelt, Churchill and Stalin, perhaps they were not. The threat was ever present in the minds of the security authorities. It is as likely that the revulsion caused in Nazi minds by the Heydrich killing and the attempt upon Hitler led to sincere misgivings about hierarchical slaughter. Dog drew back from eating dog. But underlings and the people were of less account.

Yet the people, too, once they had measured German arrogance at first hand, came to understand the falsity of German propaganda and swung hard against it, rejecting everything German—even when it happened to represent the truth. Thus it became relatively easy for politicians to raise enthusiasm on the wings of evocative slogans that called for "People's Patriotic War"—an invitation to the equivalent of a beguiling religious contest such as, throughout history, had led to the most hideous, bigoted violence.

European partisan warfare, with all its moral and social degradation, was elevated by a torrent of words and pictures into a crusade. Savageries were twisted to give an impression of civilian-based partisans making a major contribution to the defeat of the Germans. For while it is indisputable that specially trained, uniformed guerrilla-type units, such as the Brandenburg Regiment and SAS, achieved results out of all proportion to their size, it is equally doubtful whether civilian-based guerrillas made, in military terms, anything like the equivalent contribution. Partisans won increasing popular acclaim as the war progressed because, for devious purposes, the value of their political appeal was recognized. After the war a stream of books recounted their story in the guise of heroic adventures interrelated with the ever popular international spy-tale genre. The glamorization of resistance celebrities became big business, the promotion of sensation profitable. Regularly presentations of patrial truth passed muster as history: the film *Odette* provides a classic example of this treatment. Emphasis was placed on the courage, the horror and the pity, but so mingled as to obscure the socially destructive significance of the partisan war, with its fundamental undermining of civilization. Apart from some notable memoirs by the most distinguished participants, such as Fitzroy Maclean, Woodhouse and Skorzeny, it was late in the 1950s before authentic and reasonably balanced histories began to appear—works such as those by Aron, Michel, Deakin and Foot beginning, at last, to evaluate rather than romanticize.

By then it was too late to correct the damage that had been done. As a supplement to memoirs and popular stories had come the products of erudite analysis—lectures on the art of insurgency by academics and political military philosophers, dissertations on the development of Communist partisan warfare—a minute sifting of guerrilla war experience between 1939 and 1945 towards the evolution of a standard doctrine that became available for instant study and application by anybody with rebellious inclinations in search of a shortcut for resolving intractable political problems. Publications by students of the subject, such as Otto Heilbrunn and F.O. Miksche, could be integrated with lectures by soldiers with recent experience of the evolving postwar partisan conflict. There was no shortage of references such as there had been prior to 1939. Partisan warfare had been etched indelibly into an image of respectability which transcended the environment of degradation in which the guerrilla frequently existed. Though international law was more closely drawn after the Nuremberg Trials, giving clearer definition, for example, to the conditions appertaining to the taking and treatment of hostages, the philosophy that anything in irregular warfare was justified by the political ends, held sway. Today the guerrilla, the partisan, the rebel, the *franc-tireur,* the terrorist, the bandit—call him what you will—is part—almost an established part—of life, a sinister figure lurking behind inflammatory political issues. He has achieved stature as arbiter in the solution of intransigent problems and enjoys a prestige of good or evil (depending on whose side he is) that was unimaginable prior to 1939 and unthinkable even during the days of primary major success in Ireland in 1922.

In the context of the Second World War, with its thunderous background of complementary bomber attacks against centers of population, it is, perhaps, a trifle academic to study what might have happened had there been no guerrillas—if statesmen and commanders, while aware of this technique's feasibility, had rejected this method as the morally destructive force among populations that it is. But because a lowering of the temperature in warfare, a de-escalation from "totality," is so anxiously sought, every contribution to this cause is worthwhile—the more so since bomber attacks against civilians have demonstrated their fallibility while guerrillas still enjoy a vogue.

As a preliminary to the softening of war's tone, the elimination of provocative hate propaganda is, of course, essential. Total war and, therefore, partisan struggle thrive upon it. If this reduction had been practiced universally in the first instance of both world wars, the effect would have been exceptional, although probably of greatest advantage to the Germans: they would have profited most since, in the long run, they managed to attract more hatred than any other combatant. Where they acquired the greater hatred, in the East, the partisan war was the more virulent. Conversely, had there been no guerrillas, either in the East or in the West, there would undoubtedly have been fewer incidents of violence as fuel for the hate-propaganda machine. Warfare might then have reverted to the more limited kind, in the hands of professionals whose normal desires are to achieve an economical victory. Disciplined, uniformed armies once fostered a sensible tradition of live and let live, reaching tenuously back to the age of chivalry and the times when the losing side resigned at the call of regularized military common sense.

Looked at purely from the military viewpoint the elimination of the partisan fighter from the scales of war might well have allowed both sides to place a greater number of orthodox soldiers in the front line. The Germans might have got slightly the better of that deal since their guerrilla units exerted a smaller direct influence against the enemy rearward areas than anybody else. It is demonstrable, of course, that the partisan effort distracted significant numbers of German troops only in the East and in the Balkans, and that, by the time the Western clandestine movements were erupting into open, guerrilla combat the strains upon German resources were such that conventional forces would, in any case, have won on their own. It can further be argued that the Russians, who committed the largest proportional effort to raising partisan bands, might have got far better value for money had they chosen to recruit such people into their regular forces and applied that effort with greater coordinated skill. Lack of coordination was always the fundamental cause of breakdown among partisan forces; restrictive circumstances and poor communications usually militated hard against their efficiency. On the other hand, the Russians could claim that, at the slightest hint of danger, the German rearward zones became unsettled and suffered from diversion of effort through the need to guard every installation—and that, since it would have been impossible to recruit their entire teeming population into conventional forces, it was justifiable to use the residue for partisan warfare, no matter how inefficient it might be.

The crucial argument against the value of partisans, in the context of the total Second World War, was their inability to hamper the Germans when the Germans were winning. In other words, subtract what few partisans there were in operation before Stalingrad and little difference would have been made to the outcome. The Germans would have penetrated as fast and as far as they did regardless of the partisans. It was a technical, logistic breakdown, exhaustion and—above all—a faulty strategic plan which told fundamentally against them. Partisans only came into their own in Russia after the issue had been decided. Therefore, in material military terms, their merits must be judged simply by evaluating them in connection with their assistance to the winning side—as helpmates in hastening operations, in harrying the Germans and by minimizing loss of life or damage to their own people within their own terrain.

There can be no doubt that partisans frequently smoothed the way for advancing conventional forces. Prevention of bridge demolition, the saving of vital communications facilities and the disruption of German columns in retreat were beneficial to the main armies. That partisans did little to hamstring German counteroffensives is equally true, adding point to the contention that the partisan is better value as an instrument of tactical and strategic aggression than of defensive retraction. But in practice, as saviors of life and property, partisans earned themselves a ghastly record. At their door, among land forces, the worst examples of excessive damage and massacre are laid. Partisans were too frequently forces of moral destruction, their style of operation provoking aberrations that were the negation of humanity. Thus one reverts to the accusation that partisans engender bestiality and that, had they been excluded from the Second World War, there would have been far less hatred in its implementation and in its aftermath. Only the genuine secret armies under the discipline of an original military hierarchy performed in moderation, even though these recorded excesses.

If there had been no partisans, what then would have been the political outcome in the reconquest of Europe? This, of course, is impossible to answer because, in the absence of partisans and hatred, political factions would have continued to pursue their aims. The Red Army would have accomplished results comparable to their achievements in the East, for partisans played but a small part in aid of its advance through what are now the satellite states. The misconceived partisan rising in Poland merely cleared from the board what might have been an aggravating counter-Communist piece. In the West, too, a similar projection of power by political parties, supported only by conventional armies, would probably have produced the same result. The political partisans of Western Europe and Italy were nicely balanced, almost self-canceling, and reduced to their true perspective by the speed with which they were neutralized and absorbed within the regular forces as soon as the dust of battle had subsided. It was in Southeast Europe that the issue was most obscure—as had usually been the case in Balkan politics. There the partisan war tended to follow the ancient pattern, with the one vital exception that, in Yugoslavia, a Communist government arose which was stronger than any central direction previously known in that ethnically fragmented country. Had Tito's Partisans failed to prosper, as part of a complete state, anarchy might have reigned supreme and prepared the vacuum into which the Red Army could have moved to impose permanent Russian domination, as in the rest of Eastern Europe. It was a national regime, founded upon a partisan army that was rapidly converted to regular status, which consolidated Yugoslavian nationalism and enabled Tito to assert his independence from Russia at the right moment in the postwar years.

Essentially, partisan warfare represented a defensive mode in the strategic sense even if, in the tactical scheme, it was compelled to be offensive in order to create an impression. Militarily the partisans were pawns—extraordinarily brave, whether as combatants or innocent bystanders injured in the action, but with only marginal impact on the main armies which settled the important military issues by coordinated conflict. It is even debatable if their roles as morale boosters or postwar police forces were fully justifiable. What comfort is to be drawn from postwar suffering and hatreds, the byproducts which remain to poison the atmosphere, nationally and in local communities? Feuds and rivalries persist to this day, recalled by the participants and kept alive by their descendants. An analysis of party political alignments throughout the non-Communist states of Europe delineates the old wartime loyalties. The occasional disturbances and migrations in the Communist bloc countries exhibit motivations such as activated the right-wing parties throughout the war. Passion is rearoused when deadly memories are revived. In France, a film called *Le Chagrin et la Pitié* (with its painful story of French collaboration and postwar retribution) caused a national outcry. There was cogent justification in the attempts to restrict its showing.

It can be argued that the nations which avoided intensive, overt partisan warfare profited from their abstention—though in terms of actual destruction the account becomes distorted by the cost of damage which almost invariably occurred in the course of "liberation" by Allied regular forces. The governments and people of those territories occupied by the Germans found themselves on the horns of a dilemma: they dreaded the price of liberation but, as time went by, they found enemy occupation unbearable in conditions of dangerous political confusion. To this day, there are survivors who decry the methods—both conventional and unconventional—that were employed to resolve the dilemma, without offering alternative solutions to the problem. History teaches that nations which advertise their incapacity for determined self-preservation have been the first to fall victim to predators. The durability of the modern police state must surely make independent governments ponder upon the fatal consequences of permitting themselves to fall, by default, under the control of practitioners of repressive methods, to enter a dark tunnel of indefinable length.

If the current indications of a European détente owe anything to the partisans—to the men who were strong in resistance and are now strong in senior government officialdom—that is something to be treasured. It is indicative that, while a proficient antiguerrilla is often an efficient guerrilla, superannuated guerrillas are among the first to condemn the practice. One must hope that the vogue for guerrilla warfare, which permeates the thoughts of impatient and inexperienced men and women, will wither away, and that an understanding of cold history and the *raison d'être* of partisans will hasten the process. It is the tragedy of our time that the organized lawlessness which eats into the freer societies bears close resemblance to partisan activity such as was propagated during the Second World War and exploited in the succeeding quarter century. We owe no gratitude to the partisans of Europe for this.

SELECTED BIBLIOGRAPHY

This is by no means an exhaustive list of books on partisan warfare, but it does include those which seem to me of considerable importance and which have been of most help in the preparation of this book. They are supplemental, of course, to material I have consulted in the archives and acquired by reading numerous official histories, not all of which are listed here.

Allen, William S. *The Nazi Seizure of Power: The Experience of a Single German Town, 1930–1935.* New York: New Viewpoints, 1965.

Aron, Robert. *Histoire de la Libération de la France.* Paris: Librairie Artheme Fayard, 1959.

Bennett, Richard L. *The Black and Tans.* Boston: Houghton Mifflin, 1960.

Blair, C.N.M. *Guerilla Warfare.* Great Britain, Ministry of Defence, 1957.

Braddon, Russell. *White Mouse.* New York: W.W. Norton & Co., 1957.

Camus, Albert. *The Rebel.* New York: Alfred A. Knopf, 1954.

Churchill, Winston S. *The World Crisis 1911–1918.* New York: The Macmillan Co., 1942.

———. *The Second World War.* 6 vols. Boston: Houghton Mifflin, 1948–1953.

Clarke, I.F. *Voices Prophesying War, 1763–1984.* New York: Oxford University Press, 1966.

Cowburn, B. *No Cloak, No Dagger.* Toronto: Nelson, Foster & Scott, 1960.

Craven, Wesley F., and Cate, James L., eds. *Army Air Forces in World War Two.* Vol. 3. Chicago: University of Chicago Press, 1951.

Crowe, J. *General Smuts' Campaign in East Africa.* London: John Murray, 1918.

Crozier, Brian. *Franco.* Boston: Little, Brown and Co., 1968.

Dalton, Hugh. *The Fateful Years: Memoirs, 1931–1945.* London: Frederick Muller, 1957.

Deakin, F.W.D. *The Embattled Mountain.* New York: Oxford University Press, 1971.

Dedijer, Vladimir. *With Tito through the War: Partisan Diary, 1941–1944.* London: Alexander Hamilton, 1951.

de Gaulle, Charles. *War Memoirs.* New York: Simon and Schuster, 1955–1960.

De Launay, J., ed. *European Resistance Movements.* Oxford: Pergamon Press, 1960.

Dreyfus, P. *Vercors, Citadelle de Liberté.* Paris: Editions B. Arthaud, 1969.

Drum, Karl. *Airpower and Russian Partisan Warfare.* New York: Arno Press, 1962.

Ehrman, J. *Grand Strategy.* Vol. 5. London: HM Stationery Office, 1956.

Foot, M.R.D. *SOE in France.* London: HM Stationery Office, 1966.

Footman, David. *Civil War in Russia.* New York: Frederick A. Praeger, 1962.

Frankland, N., and Webster, J. *The Strategic Air Offensive against Germany, 1939–1945.* London: HM Stationery Office.

Garlinski, J. *Poland, SOE and the Allies.* London: Allen & Unwin, 1969.

Giskes, H.J. *London Calling North Pole.* London: William Kimber & Co., 1953.

Hahlweg, W. *Guerrilla, Krieg ohne Fronten.* Stuttgart, 1968.

Hanser, Richard. *Prelude to Terror.* London: Rupert Hart-Davis, 1971.

Haukelid, Knut. *Skis against the Atom.* Translated by F.H. Lyon. London: William Kimber & Co., 1954.

Heilbrunn, Otto. *Partisan Warfare.* New York: Frederick A. Praeger, 1962.

Hitler, Adolf. *Mein Kampf.* London: Victor Gollancz, 1939.

Hoffmann, M. *Die Aufzeichnungen.* Nowak, 1930.

Holt, Edgar. *Protest in Arms: The Irish Troubles, 1916–1923.* New York: G.P. Putnam's Sons, 1960.

Iranek-Osmecki, George, trans. *The Unseen and Silent: Adventures from the Underground Movement Narrated by Paratroops of the Polish Home Army.* New York: Sheed & Ward, 1954.

Komorowski, Tadeusz. *The Secret Army.* New York: The Macmillan Co., 1951.

Kovpak, Sidor Artemovich. *Our Partisan Course.* Translated by Ernst and Mira Lesser. London: Hutchinson & Co., 1947.

L'Amicale Action. *Livre d'or de l'Amicale Action.* 1953.

Lawrence, T.E. *Seven Pillars of Wisdom.* Garden City, N.Y.: Garden City Publishing Co., 1938.

Lett, Gordon. *Rossano.* London: Hodder & Stoughton, 1955.

Lettow Vorbeck, P. von. *My Reminiscences of East Africa.* London: Hurst & Blackett.

Leverkuehn, Paul. *German Military Intelligence.* Translated by R.H. Stevens and Constantine FitzGibbon. New York: Frederick A. Praeger, 1954.

Liddell Hart, B.H. *T.E. Lawrence in Arabia and After.* London: Jonathan Cape, 1935.

———. *Thoughts on War.* London: Faber & Faber, 1944.

MacDonald, Charles B. *The Mighty Endeavor: American Armed Forces in the European Theater in World War Two.* New York: Oxford University Press, 1969.

Maclean, F. *Eastern Approaches.* London: Jonathan Cape.

Marlowe, John [pseud.]. *Rebellion in Palestine.* New York: William S. Heinman, 1946.

Maschmann, M. *Account Rendered.* New York: Abelard-Schuman, 1964.

Neeson, Eoin. *The Civil War in Ireland, 1922–1923.* Cork: Mercier, 1966.

Nirenstein, Albert. *A Tower from the Enemy: Contribution to a History of Jewish Resistance in Poland.* Translated by David Neiman and Mervyn Savill. New York: Orion Press, 1959.

Orwell, George. *Homage to Catalonia.* London: Secker & Warburg, 1938.

Piquet-Wicks, Eric. *Four in the Shadows: A True Story of Espionage in Occupied France.* London: Jarrolds, 1957.

Ponomarenko, P.K., and others. *Behind the Front Line.* London: Hutchinson & Co., 1945.

Purnell. *History of the First World War.* Edited by B. Pitt. Purnell, 1969.

———. *History of the Second World War.* Edited by B. Pitt. Purnell, 1966.

Ristic, Dragisa N. *Yugoslavia's Revolution of 1941.* University Park: Pennsylvania State University Press, 1966.

Seaton, Albert. *The Russo-German War 1941–1945.* New York: Frederick A. Praeger, 1971.

Skorzeny, Otto. *Skorzeny's Special Missions.* New York: McGraw-Hill Book Co., 1957.

Starke, J.G. *An Introduction to International Law.* London: Butterworth & Co., 1963.

Strong, Sir Kenneth W.D. *Intelligence at the Top: The Recollections of an Intelligence Officer.* New York: Doubleday, 1969.

Sweet-Escott, B. *Baker Street Irregular.* London: Methuen & Co., 1965.

Thomas, Hugh. *The Spanish Civil War.* New York: Harper & Row, 1961.

Trial of the Nazi War Criminals at Nuremberg. London: HM Stationery Office, 1946.

Trotsky, Leon. *My Life.* London: Butterworth & Co., 1930.

U.S., Department of the Army, *German Anti-Guerilla Operations in the Balkans, 1941–1944.* R.M. Kennedy, 1954.

———. *The German Northern Theater of Operations 1940–1945.* E. Ziemke, 1959.

———. *Guerilla and Counter-Guerilla Warfare in Greece.* K. Gardner, 1962.

———. *The Supreme Command.* Forrest C. Pogue, 1954.

Warlimont, Walter. *Inside Hitler's Headquarters, 1939–45.* Translated by R.H. Barry. New York: Frederick A. Praeger, 1966.

Warmbrunn, Werner. *The Dutch under German Occupation, 1941–45.* Palo Alto: Stanford University Press, 1963.

Warner, P. *The Special Air Service.* London: William Kimber & Co., 1971.

Wheeler-Bennett, John W. *Nemesis of Power.* New York: The Macmillan Co., 1953.

Whiting, Charles. *Hitler's Werewolves.* New York: Stein and Day, 1972.

Woodhouse, C.M. *Apple of Discord: A Survey of Recent Greek Politics.* London: Hutchinson & Co., 1948.

INDEX

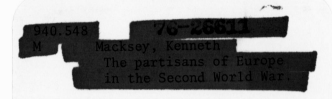